Fractal Design Painter®

CREATIVE TECHNIQUES

by Jeremy Sutton

Hayden
Books

Fractal Design Painter ® Creative Techniques

Library of Congress Catalog Number: 96-75900
ISBN: 1-56830-283-5

Printed in the United States of America 1 2 3 4 5 6 7 8 9 0

This book was produced digitally by Macmillan Computer Publishing and manufactured using 100% computer-to-plate technology (filmless process), by Shepard Poorman Communications Corporation, Indianapolis, Indiana.

Warning and Disclaimer

Credits

Publisher
Lyn Blake

Publishing Manager
Melanie Rigney

Managing Editor
Lisa Wilson

Marketing Manager
Nancy Price

Acquisitions Editor
Marta Partington

Development Editor
Marta Partington

Copy/Production Editor
Marta Partington

Technical Editor
Michael J. Partington

Publishing Coordinator
Rosemary Lewis

Cover Designer
Karen Ruggles

Book Designers
Barbara Kordesh, Gary Adair

Manufacturing Coordinator
Brook Farling

Production Team Supervisor
Laurie Casey

Proofreaders
Kim Cofer, Christine Tyner, Pamela Volk

Page Layout
Daniel Caparo, Terrie Deemer, Dave Eason, Joe Millay

About the Author

Jeremy Sutton was born in London, England, in 1961. He lived in the Netherlands for several years prior to moving to California in 1988. Jeremy read Physics at Oxford University, England. While studying and then working in Physics, Jeremy explored traditional fine art media, particularly drawing and painting portraits. He was introduced to using the computer as an art tool in 1991.

Jeremy is currently a faculty member of San Francisco State University where he teaches digital painting. He performs live digital portraits at special events, and demonstrates and teaches Painter at workshops and conferences throughout the world. Jeremy's artwork has been exhibited and published internationally. His live portrait subjects range from politicians and business leaders to musicians and artists. Jeremy's art has won awards in a number of art contests including those organized by Online Design, Computer Pictures and Campbell's.

Trademark Acknowledgments

All terms mentioned in this book that are known to be trademarks or services marks have been appropriately capitalized. Hayden Books cannot attest to the accuracy of this information. Use of a term in this book should not be regarded as affecting the validity of any trademark or service mark. Painter is a trademark of Fractal Design Painter®.

Acknowledgments

First and foremost, I wish to express my deep gratitude and appreciation to the artists who have contributed their wonderful artwork to this book. In addition, they have also contributed considerable time and effort sending digital files across the world and explaining their techniques to me.

A big thanks to all the folks at Fractal Design Corporation who have been invaluable in their support and encouragement. Daryl Wise has been instrumental in putting me in touch with many of the artists whose work appears in this book.

Thanks to my editor, Marta Partington, whose enthusiasm, belief in the project, and excellent feedback enabled this book to emerge from concept to fruition.

Thanks to Michael Partington for his diligence and hard work in technical editing.

Thanks to all the many other people who have assisted and encouraged me along the way. These include Sha'ron Amit, Danielle Gaines, Ivan Gill, Andi and Gary Kaye, Peter Lakos, Lawrence Langs, Sylvia Larangeira, Sarit Sexton, John and Maria Stanley-Clamp, Simon Stanley-Clamp, Debbi Sutton, Margaret Sutton, Ros Sutton, Claude Szwimer (the French connection), and Frank Quilty.

Hayden Books

The staff of Hayden Books is committed to bringing you the best computer books. What our readers think of Hayden is important to our ability to serve our customers. If you have any comments, no matter how great or how small, we'd appreciate your taking the time to send us a note.

You can reach Hayden Books at the following:

Hayden Books
201 West 103rd Street
Indianapolis, IN 46290
(317) 581-3833

Email addresses:

| America Online: | Hayden Bks |
| Internet: | hayden@hayden.com |

Visit the Hayden Books Web site at `http://www.hayden.com`

Dedication

In loving memory of my father, Maurice Sutton.

Contents

Frames and Borders

Transforming Photographs

Collage and Montage

Variations on a Theme

Fabrics and Wallpaper

Typography and Caligraphy

Media Graphics

Cartoons and Comics

Video and Animation

Web Page Design

Introduction

This book has two central goals:

1. To be an inspiring and diverse showcase of what has been achieved by a wide variety of artists who were using Fractal Design Painter.

2. To be a practical guide to learning and applying the techniques utilized by these experienced artists.

The book has been divided up by general topic area to help you find your way around and locate, as efficiently as possible, the area of most interest to you. It has not always been an easy task to pigeonhole a technique in one category or another. There are, in truth, no clear boundaries. Thus, I have just judged which category is the best fit for each technique.

All the techniques are applicable on both Macintosh and IBM-compatible PC platforms. The Macintosh terminology precedes the PC terminology. Where appropriate, the Macintosh commands are placed in plain brackets () and the PC commands in curly brackets {}. There are slight differences between Macintosh and PC platforms in the situations where you can click and drag. In these cases I have used commands that work for both platforms.

The terminology used is generally the same as the terminology used by Fractal Design within the *Painter 4 User Guide*. There are a few exceptions where, for the purpose of clarity, I have adopted a slightly different naming convention. One example is my use of the term "Brush family" for the groupings of related brush variants (2B Pencil is a variant in the Pencils Brush family).

Each technique includes a reproduction of artwork that uses the technique. The artwork is accompanied by four subsections: Comments, Studio Usage, Related Techniques, and Step-by-Step illustrated instructions.

One of the most fascinating aspects of writing this book has been the insights I've gained in discussions with the artists into their personal approach to creating art and using Painter in that process. I have tried to share some of their approach and their process in the Comments section of each technique. I believe this is important in order to fully appreciate the context in which a particular technique is used. Most of the artwork embodies many interesting techniques, so I have also tried to provide some indication of other notable techniques used in the artwork.

The **Studio Usage** section within each technique provides a brief summary of the technique and an explanation of how you actually apply it.

Many techniques draw upon common skills, sets of actions, or themes. The purpose of the **Related Techniques** section in each technique is to enable you to rapidly locate related techniques and necessary information.

The **Step-by-Step** descriptions are as concise as possible so that you can quickly and simply follow the steps. They assume a level of familiarity with Painter—how to interact with the interface and locate the main floating palettes. The accompanying screen captures are designed to assist you in following every step.

At the back of this book you will find a **Glossary** and a **Listing of Artists**. The **Glossary** provides brief explanations of some of the terminology used in the book. Where relevant, there are suggestions of specific techniques to refer to. The **Listing of Artists** includes contact details and, in most cases, biographical information on each artist whose work is featured in this book. These listings include references that allow you to locate the specific techniques in which each artist's works appear.

I hope that you find this book both enjoyable and productive.

Jeremy Sutton
June 4, 1996

jeremy@portrayals.com
Web Site: http://www.portrayals.com/portrayals

Quick Tips

In this section, I have drawn together useful, practical tips employed by the artists who contributed artwork to this book.

Final Resolution

The general rule is to create your canvas at the maximum resolution you want to end up with (since quality is sacrificed every time you resize from a lower resolution to a higher one). If your artwork may be used for print media, it is safest to create it at 300 dpi (although this will also result in relatively large file sizes). If it is for CD-ROM or online use, then a screen resolution of 72 dpi is usually sufficient.

Maximize Source Image Quality

If you are beginning with existing images, such as photographs, then it is advisable to clean these images up, correct the contrast and distribution of tonal values (equalize), and apply color corrections before proceeding to use them in your artwork. In other words, start with the maximum quality possible.

Work on a Clone Image

When starting from an existing image, it is advisable to open that image in Painter and then make a clone of it and work with that clone, rather than the original image. This way has the dual benefit of preserving your original image in case you make an error, while giving you the versatility and power of working with a clone source.

Tear Off Palettes

Wherever possible, you should minimize the area of your desktop that is taken up by palettes. A good way to do this is to tear off frequently used palettes, such as the Art Materials: Color. Do this by selecting any icon other than the one you want to tear off. Then click and drag off the unselected icon in a single motion.

Use Keyboard Shortcuts

All six main floating palettes have convenient keyboard shortcuts that allow you to open and close them very easily. These have not been included in the text in this book. The shortcuts are the following:

Toolbox	(⌘-1) {Ctrl-1}
Brushes	(⌘-2) {Ctrl-2}
Art Materials	(⌘-3) {Ctrl-3}
Objects	(⌘-4) {Ctrl-4}
Controls	(⌘-5) {Ctrl-5}
Color Sets	(⌘-6) {Ctrl-6}

Naming Conventions

Before you embark on a project, it is well worth deciding on a consistent, useful, naming convention for all your files, so you can easily archive them and identify them. It can be useful to begin the file names with the reverse date, that is, 96.05.23 for May 23, 1996, so they are automatically listed chronologically by name. The final file name may consist of "reverse date.project name.version number.file format" (PC users are limited to "8 characters.3 characters" and will have to be inventive accordingly).

File Formats

A typical guide is to keep your working files saved as RIFFs, so they retain wet layer and object information. The final versions can then be saved as TIFF for print media, PICT (Macintosh users) for CD-ROM, Photoshop 3.0 for further work in Photoshop, JPEG for large high quality online images, and GIF for small online images and icons.

Memory

I recommend that you look at the note on memory contained within the Painter 4 CD-ROM in the REFERNZ folder.

Special note for Macintosh users: look at the Memory Control Panel (accessed from the Apple menu) and make sure that Virtual Memory is turned off.

Further Resources

The Painter 4 CD-ROM contains extensive Technical Notes in the REFERNZ folder (file names are Painter Tech Notes.pdf on Mac and technotes.pdf on PC). These are well worth a look. They explore areas not covered in the User Guide, such as editing scripts and making multirank image hose nozzles. Also in the REFERNZ folder are Painter Tips and Hints (file names are Painter Tips and Hints.pdf on Mac and tips.pdf on PC), which provide valuable advice on memory management and cloning.

The Fractal Design Web Site (http://www.fractal.com) is also a very valuable resource. I highly recommend visiting it if you have not already done so. You may also find it useful to visit my own Web site from time to time where I feature a new Painter tip every other month, as well as a gallery of 2-D animated Painter artwork.

Hiroshi Yoshii

Hole

Comments

This sketch began as a simple pencil sketch on non-digital paper, which was subsequently scanned and opened in Painter. Pencil, Chalk, and Charcoal brushes were then used with black to complete the sketch. When satisfied with the composition, Yoshii created a clone of the sketch. He used the tracing paper image of the sketch, showing through the clone paper at 50% opacity, as a visual guide in creating the components of the final painted image.

Studio Usage

It can be useful to utilize a quick, preparative sketch as a guideline for building a complex, painted composition. This technique explains how to do just that by using the Tracing Paper feature of Painter. By using this feature, you'll be able to see your painting superimposed over the entire original sketch at any stage.

Related Techniques

Thick Powdery Look 7

Sepia Pencil Drawing 54

Transition from Drawing
to Photograph 119

1 Clone Sketch

With the preparative sketch open on the desktop, select File→Clone. You'll create an identical copy of the original sketch image.

Note: *The two images are linked so that the original sketch is assigned to be the "clone source." You can see this if you select File→Clone Source. The original sketch name has a check by it.*

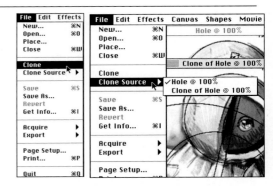

2 Clear Clone

Select Edit→Select All (⌘-A) {Ctrl-A}, followed by the Delete key.

3 Turn on Tracing Paper

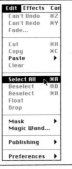

Select Canvas→Tracing Paper (⌘-T) {Ctrl-T} or click on the small Tracing Paper icon that depicts overlapping black-and-white rectangles in the upper right side of the document frame. You'll activate the tracing paper function, which shows the clone source image at 50% opacity together with the clone image, also at 50% opacity. The tracing paper can be deactivated by simply going back to Canvas→Tracing Paper (or clicking on the Tracing Paper icon again).

4 Paint on Clone Image

With the brushes you want to use, paint on the cleared, clone image with tracing paper turned on, so that you'll get your visual guide from the original sketch clone source. Turn the tracing paper off to see the look of your brush strokes at 100% opacity.

Note: *You can see in this example the way Yoshii used the original sketch to help him plan out and paint all the components of the composition.*

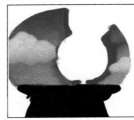

Quick Sketches *Watercolor and Pastel*

Dennis Orlando

Hibiscus

Comments

This flower was based on a photograph that was placed under the acetate flap on the graphics tablet and used as a visual guide for the initial sketch. Orlando starts off painting at low resolution with a variety of customized brushes that are described here. He builds up the painting in layers, periodically increasing resolution and working in finer and finer levels of detail.

Studio Usage

By mixing a number of the Painter Natural Media tools, such as Pencil, Water Color, and Pastel Chalk, a quick foundation for a painting can be built. Each of the tools enables underlying color and tone to show through. Each tool offers its own unique qualities for creating the basic lines and forms of the composition, which is useful when you want to create a foundation of loose, fluid strokes that can be built onto in order to form the final painting.

Related Techniques

Increasing Resolution
during Painting Process   6

Digital Wet-on-Wet   8

Watery Chalk   16

Watercolor Cloning   18

Versatile Chalk   30

1 | Create Pencil Lines

Select the 2B Pencil variant of the Pencil brush family in the Brushes palette. Move the Opacity slider in the Controls palette to 100%. Draw in the rough outlines of the composition.

Note: *The 2B Pencil gives a thin grainy line that will show through the subsequent light Water Color and low opacity Pastel Chalk.*

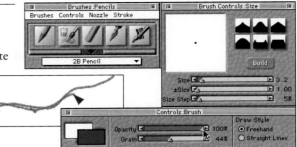

2 | Apply Water Color

Select the Simple Water variant of the Water Color brush family. Select the Controls→Size palette from the Brushes palette. Adjust the brush Size slider to suit the scale of your canvas. Open the Papers library in the Art Materials palette. Click on the horizontal bar to open the library drawer. Click on the library button. Select the More Paper Textures library. Select the Small Canvas paper. Close the drawer by clicking on the bar again. Adjust the grain Scale slider. Apply the Water Color brush to fill in areas of color. When finished, select Canvas→Dry from the top menu. This dries the Water Color paint into the background canvas so that it can be painted over by the Pastel Chalk.

Note: *The Water Color brushes paint into the Wet Layer above the canvas. If you do not dry the Water Color, then that paint will remain as an independent layer above any other paint added to the canvas.*

3 | Apply Artist Pastel Chalk

Select the Artist Pastel Chalk variant of the Chalk brush family. Expand the Brushes palette so the Method Category and Method Subcategory menus are visible below the Variant menu. Change the Method Subcategory from Grainy Hard Cover to Grainy Soft Cover. Using stylus pressure to control opacity, build up shading in the composition over the Pencil and Water Color.

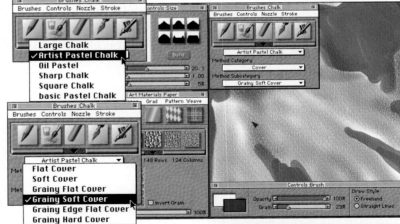

4 | Add Color Variability and Apply Just Add Water

Open the Color Selector in the Art Materials palette. Expand the Color Selector so that you can see the Color Variability sliders. Move the Hue Variability slider to the right. Make some test strokes and adjust the variability slider. Try mixing colors by applying different colors over each other with low opacity. Select the Just Add Water variant of the Water brushes to blend the colors.

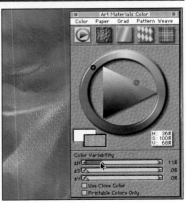

Angels from Harrington Street

Comments

This picture was one of several variations that Garcia derived from an original scanned pencil sketch. It was one of the paintings reproduced in the book *Harrington Street*. All of the variations involved applying various brushes and effects in Painter. In this case, Garcia created an image in which he emphasized the outline of the figures and just added a few subtle changes to the drawing, keeping intact and visible the delicate, original pencil line work.

Studio Usage

One of the benefits of working on the scanned sketch, rather than on the original, is the freedom that it gives you to try out different ideas without permanently altering the original. For example, you may want to emphasize some aspect of the sketch, the lines, the form, or the colors. In this case, you can see a simple approach for using Painter's Eraser, Pencil, Pen, and Airbrush brushes to emphasize the outlines of a drawing, while preserving the subtlety of the original line work.

Related Techniques

Emphasizing a Misty Contour 44

Controlling Line Thickness through Brush Tracking 113

1 | Lightly Erase Background

Select the Small Eraser variant of the Eraser brush family from the Brushes palette. Select Controls→Size from the pull-down menu in the Brushes palette. Adjust the Size slider in the Controls: Size palette to suit the scale of your image. Lightly erase the background from around the central figures.

Note: It is a good idea to initially select File→Clone and then work on the clone (an identical copy), rather than the original scan. This way the original scan remains unaltered, and you won't accidentally alter that file.

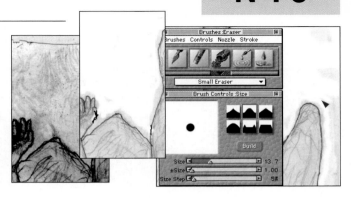

2 | Pencil in a General Outline

Select the 2B Pencil variant of the Pencil brush family. Select black in the Art Materials: Color Selector (located in the Art Materials palette). Reduce the Size slider to achieve a thin line, comparable to the original scanned line work. Carefully go over the general outline to emphasize it.

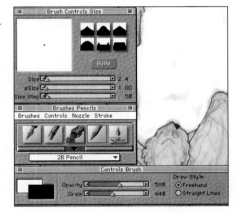

3 | Selectively Apply Ink Pen

Select the Smooth Ink Pen variant of the Pens brush family. Adjust the Opacity slider, located in the Controls palette, to 100%. Adjust the Size slider to a small enough value to give a solid black line equal to the same thickness as the original pencil lines. Use this pen selectively in parts of the image that you want to stand out from the rest.

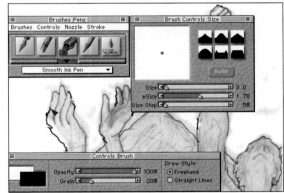

4 | Airbrush in Selected Areas

Select the Fat Stroke variant of the Airbrush brush family. Reduce the size to suit the scale of the image. Select the color you want to apply in the Color Selector. Apply the airbrush.

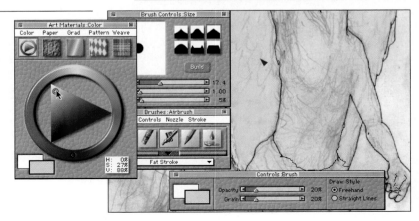

David Locke Higgins

Meerkats

Comments

Higgins captures moments in the lives of animals at the San Diego Zoo by recording the animals over a period of time using a regular VHS video camera. Then he selects a single frame that captures the feel of that particular animal. He uses that frame as a visual reference source on a separate monitor while he is painting his artwork. He begins directly on the computer with a quick freehand sketch that gradually gets built into a completed painting.

Studio Usage

This technique explains how Higgins creates the quick sketch: first, laying down a background; then using a Chalk brush variant to put down a rough outline; and subsequently filling in shading and adding highlights. The principles described here can be applied easily to concept visualization and animation or storyboard creation.

Related Techniques

1 | Fill Paper with Background Color

Open a new document. Keep the resolution at 72 dots per inch to minimize file size and keep the brush work as loose as possible. Select a color in the Art Materials Palette→Color Selector that picks up the hues in the image, is light enough to show up dark line work, and is dark enough to contrast with white highlights. Select Effects→Fill (⌘-F) {Ctrl-F}. Fill the image with the current color.

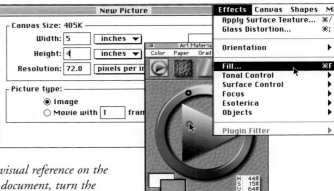

Note: *It is possible, instead of using the source image as a visual reference on the desktop, to clone the original source image, clear the clone document, turn the Tracing Paper on, and then work with a tracing paper reference image.*

2 | Modify Large Chalk for Line Work and Shading

Select the Large Chalk variant in the Chalk brush family of the Brushes palette. Expand the Brushes palette so that the Method and Method Subcategory menus are visible below the Variant menu. Change the Method to Buildup and the Method Subcategory to Grainy Soft Buildup. The Opacity slider in the Controls palette should be set to 100%. Select Controls →Size in the pull-down menu in the Brushes palette to access the Brush Controls: Size palette. Reduce the Size slider. Keep the default Basic Paper in the Art Materials→Papers Library. Adjust the color value to black by moving the inner triangle cursor in the Color Selector to the lower left-hand corner. Apply rapid, loose brush strokes and vary pressure while making your strokes.

Note: *If the Method and Method Subcategory menus are not visible, expand the Brushes palette by clicking on the square button in the top right-hand corner of the palette. The Buildup method gives translucent color that rapidly builds up to black if the color is not pure. The Grainy Soft subcategory gives a soft-edged brush stroke that is modulated by the currently selected Paper texture.*

3 | Add Highlights

Change the Method back to Cover and the Method Subcategory back to Grainy Hard Cover. Decrease the Opacity to 50% and increase brush size. Select white or off-white in the color selector. Apply rough highlights. Select Method Subcategory→Grainy Soft Cover for applying softer-edged highlights.

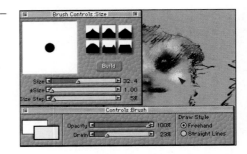

4 | Finish with Just Add Water

For final touches, smooth out and soften lines, shading, and highlights with the Just Add Water variant of the Water family of brushes in the Brushes palette.

Note: *Use the Broad Water Brush to add translucent water color washes to the image.*

Quick Sketches *Etched in Metal Look*

Jeremy Sutton

Jesse

Comments

The source for this image was a pencil sketch that was scanned and opened in Painter. The etched look was achieved by floating and lightening the darkest lines in the composition.

Studio Usage

This technique describes how to take a scanned sketch and give it the look of being etched into a metal plate. It involves the selection and subsequent floating of the very darkest lines in the drawing. This floater is then recolored with a lighter tone. The combination of the lighter tone line with a thin outline of darker tone gives the impression of an etched region, similar to embossing.

Related Techniques

1 | Clone Original Sketch

Select File→Clone to make an identical copy.
The scanned, original sketch should have
100% black in it for this technique to work
best. (Select Effects→Tonal Control→
Equalize). In the Equalize dialog box slide the
Black point to the right and the Brightness to
the left until the image shows black in the
darkest regions but is not too dark over all.
Click OK.

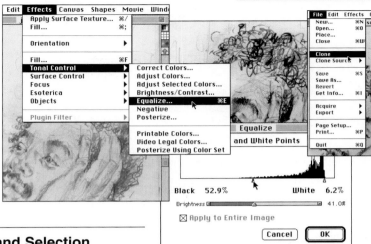

2 | Equalize Clone and Make Magic Wand Selection

With the clone image selected, select Effects→Tonal
Control→Equalize. In the Equalize dialog box, bring
the Black point to the right and slide the White point
toward it. Adjust these two points until the
image shows only the very darkest regions as
black and everything else as white. Click OK.
Select Edit→Select All followed by Edit→Magic
Wand. Click in the black. The black goes red.
Click OK.

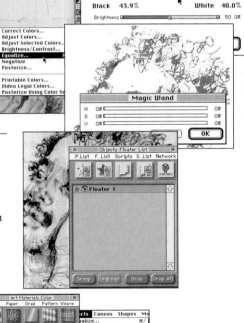

3 | Copy Selection and Paste Back into Original Sketch

Select Edit→Copy. Click on the original sketch image. Select
Edit→Paste→Normal. The selected black region is now pasted in as a
floater. Open the F. (Floater) List in the Objects palette by clicking on
the icon below the F. List pull-down menu. The floater name appears in
the list.

4 | Fill Floater with Lighter Tone

Open the Color Selector in the Art Materials palette. Select a
light-toned color of a similar hue to the image background. Select
Effects→Fill (⌘-F) {Ctrl-F}. The Fill dialog box should have the
option Fill With: Current Color checked. Adjust the Opacity slider in the Fill dialog box and look at the result in the preview window. Click OK when satisfied.

Applying Paint *Increasing Resolution during Painting Process*

Dennis Orlando

Old Boat with Early Morning Fog

Comments

This painting was built layer by layer, starting off as a low resolution image (72 pixels per inch or ppi) and working up to a higher resolution of 300 ppi during the painting process. Orlando started with a blank canvas, placed a source photograph under the acetate plastic flap on his Wacom graphics tablet, and roughly sketched in the main composition. He then used the Artist Pastel Chalk with Grainy Soft Cover method and Color Variability, as well as Just Add Water and Loaded Oil brushes, to build up the final image.

Note: *Pixels per inch (ppi) is also commonly referred to as dots per inch (dpi).*

Studio Usage

Traditionally, the painting process often begins with rough, quick sketching to outline the composition and fill in the main blocks of light and shadow. From that rough foundation, details are worked into the image, with finer and finer details being painted as the painting progresses. This process of working from broad outline to finer detail can be emulated in the digital world by starting with a low resolution image and, as you work into finer detail, increasing the image resolution. This process has the effect of creating a rich, layered look. The method of increasing resolution mid-painting is described here.

Related Techniques

Watercolor and Pastel   2

Replaying at Higher
Resolution   31

1 | Open New Image at 72 ppi

Select File→New (⌘-N) {Ctrl-N}. Set the initial file (canvas size) dimensions (pixel width and height) at the size you want to begin working. Set the resolution to 72 pixels per inch (ppi). Adjust the units pull-down menus from pixels to inches to see the physical size of the image when viewed at 100% magnification. Click OK.

Note: *You can initially set the width and height of the new picture in inches rather than pixels. In that case, it is critical to ensure that the resolution is set at 72 ppi.*

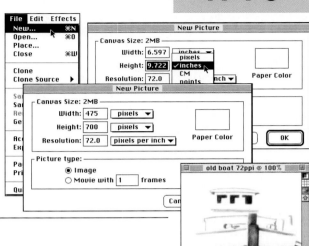

2 | Sketch Outline

Paint the rough sketch outlines for your composition. The file size is relatively small and thus there is very little, if any, noticeable time lag between moving your stylus and the response on the screen. This trick will help you achieve fluid, loose strokes.

3 | Resize to 150 ppi

Select Canvas→Resize. Click on the Constrain File Size box to uncheck it (you do not want the file size constrained). Change the Width and Height units from pixels to inches. Change the Resolution from 72 ppi to 150 ppi and click OK. The previous image now occupies more screen space when viewed at 100%. Select Window→Zoom Out to reduce the image to 50% magnification.

Note: *If you accidentally leave the file size constrained, when you increase the resolution, the physical width and height (in inches) will immediately be reduced so the total number of pixels remains the same.*

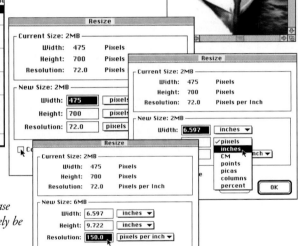

4 | Apply Sharpen and Paint in Finer Details

Select Effects→Focus→Sharpen. Click OK. If the sharpen effect is too pronounced, use the Edit→Fade command to fade it back by any percentage you choose. If you want more sharpening, repeat the sharpen effect. Paint in the finer details. For the final stage, repeat steps 3 and 4 using the resolution of 300 ppi, rather than 150 ppi.

Note: *Brushes that you were working with at 100% magnification at the lower resolution are now effectively reduced in size with the 50% magnification higher resolution image. To increase the effective brush size, select Controls→Size in the Brushes palette and increase the Size slider.*

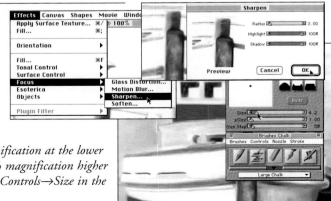

Mouse

Horishi Yoshii

Comments

This painting was started with a simple pencil sketch created directly in Painter. The major areas were filled with flat color. Yoshii then worked in many layers of chalk until he built up the appearance of a spongy, thick, powdery surface. It is this technique that is the focus of this section. The cheese holes in the mouse were all painted in by hand. The final stage was the application of Effects→Surface Control→Apply Surface Texture→Using Paper Grain to apply a texture across the mouse.

Studio Usage

This technique describes how to create the look of thick powdery chalk in your painting. It involves layering strokes from a slightly modified Chalk brush, working from darker to lighter tones. This particular example is an object, in this case a mouse, surrounded by white. The same principles of layering chalk can be applied in any region of a painting where you want to achieve this powdery effect.

Related Techniques

Using a Sketch as a
Template   1

Watery Chalk   16

Customized Chalk   20

Creative Cross-Hatching   26

1 | Select and Fill Main Areas

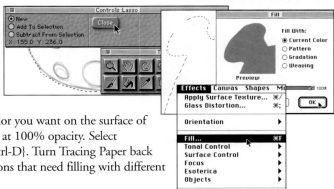

Sketch out the composition against a white background and use it as a visual template by cloning and turning on Tracing paper (see Technique #1). The sketch shows through the cleared Clone image. Select the freehand selection Lasso tool. Use Lasso to select the outer contour of the image. Choose a color darker than the final color you want on the surface of the image. Turn Tracing Paper off to view the filled region at 100% opacity. Select Effects→Fill. Click OK. Select Edit→Deselect (⌘-D) {Ctrl-D}. Turn Tracing Paper back on and repeat Lasso selection and Fill for any interior regions that need filling with different colors.

2 | Select Chalk Brush

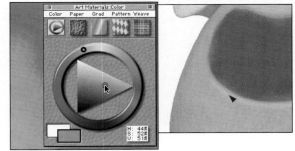

Make sure that the Brushes palette is expanded to show the Method and Method Subcategory below the Variant. Select the Large Chalk variant in the Chalk brushes family. Change the Method Subcategory from Hard Grainy Cover to Soft Grainy Cover. Adjust the Opacity slider to 50% in the Controls palette.

3 | Build up to Lighter Colors

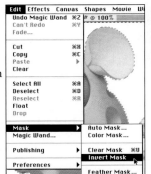

Select colors in a sequence building from darker to lighter tones while working within a given region of the image. Layer the chalk on top of the earlier chalk brush strokes. Use the tones to define form. Use the stroke directions (cross hatching) to suggest curvature.

4 | Select Mouse

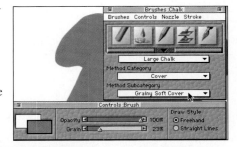

Select Edit→Magic Wand. Click on the white region surrounding the mouse. The white region will be indicated in red. Click OK in the Magic Wand dialog box. Select Edit→Mask→Invert Mask to invert the selection so that the mouse, not the white area, is selected.

Note: *If your mouse encloses regions of the white background, then select Edit→Select All prior to applying the Magic Wand. You'll ensure that white pixels anywhere in the image, rather than just contiguous pixels, are selected.*

5 | Apply Surface Texture

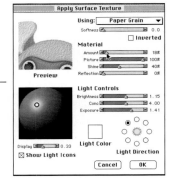

Select Effects→Surface Control→Apply Surface Texture. Using: Paper Grain is selected in the Apply Surface Texture dialog box. Note that in the preview box the effect is only being applied to the mouse. Adjust the Amount slider. Click OK and apply the selected texture.

Mario Henri Chakkour

Lenses of Sight

Comments

The imagery in this picture was inspired by the book *Window to the Soul, a Collection of Writings Influenced by Daheshism* by Mounir Youssef Murad. It was created from scratch using Chalks, Charcoal, Water, Liquid, and Airbrush brushes.

Studio Usage

This technique describes how to build a rich, painterly look using a combination of Painter brushes applied in a specific order. This particular technique was developed by Chakkour. He coined the name *Digital Wet-on-Wet* to describe it.

Related Techniques

1 Sketch with Chalk

Open your canvas at the maximum resolution you want.
Select the Sharp Chalk variant of the Chalk brush family in
the Brushes palette. Select Controls→Size from the Brushes
palette pull-down menu. Adjust the size slider until you get a
fine stroke to use for outlines. Select a dark hue and sketch
out the main structure and form of your painting.

Note: *If you are going to print, begin working at 300 pixels
per inch. You can always resize down at a later stage.*

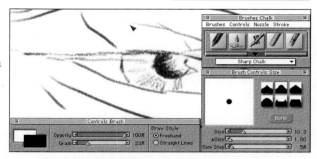

2 Apply Softer Lines with Charcoal

Select the Soft Charcoal variant of
the Charcoal brush family. Select
the Basic Paper grain in the Art
Materials Papers palette. Close the
papers library drawer and expand
the palette. Adjust the Scale slider
to a low value so the grain is fine.
Apply the charcoal softly over the
sharper chalk lines.

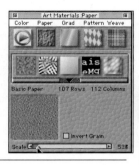

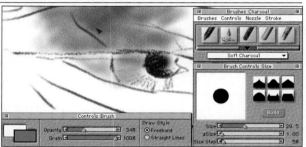

3 Blend with Water

Select the Just Add Water variant of the Water brush family.
Blend the charcoal and chalk lines together. Repeat Steps
1–3, adding more color until the hues melt together. This
painting now forms the foundation that you will build on,
using the Liquid and Airbrush tools.

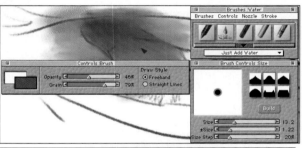

4 Apply Total Oil Brush

Select the Total Oil Brush variant of the Liquid brushes.
Reduce the Opacity slider in the Controls palette to about
10%. Use this brush to build up thick color masses. As in
Step 3, blend in with Just Add Water.

5 Detail with Airbrush and Distorto

Select the Fat Stroke variant of the Airbrushes. Adjust Size
to suit the dimensions of the details and highlights you
want to add to the image. Apply Airbrush lightly, stroking
back and forth as you gradually build
up soft-edged lines. Select the
Distorto Liquid brush variant. Use it
to pull the paint around the canvas.

Note: *To capture a style reminiscent of
traditional airbrush, create hard-edged
masks in your image by using the
Masking brushes or selection tools.*

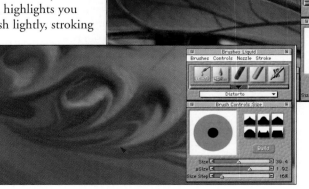

Applying Paint *Bright Colors on a Black Background*

Fiona Hawthorne, courtesy of Hong Kong Telecom

Hong Kong City Street

Comments

This painting, one of a series of five large murals, was originally commissioned by Hong Kong Telecom for an interactive exhibit. Hawthorne started with a plain black canvas and painted freehand directly in Painter, drawing from her years of experience as a traditionally trained fine artist. She worked at normal screen resolution (72 pixels per inch), using a variety of Painter brushes—some customized, some standard. In this image she made use of a customized Crayon described in this technique, Pen and Ink and Single Pixel variants of Pens, and the Artist Pastel Chalk. She worked from broader strokes to finer details.

Studio Usage

Working against a black, or dark, background provides a dramatic backdrop for the application of bright colors, such as those resulting from fluorescent lighting in a night scene. The Build Up Method brushes will not show up against a dark background. A customized Waxy Crayon, developed by Hawthorne specifically for the purpose of applying against a dark background, is described here. When creating a customized variant such as this, it is very useful to save the variant for future use. That process is also described in this technique.

Related Techniques

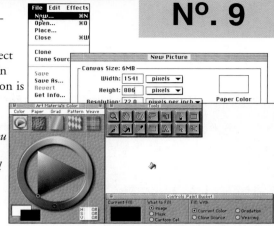

1 | Fill Background with Black

Open a new canvas. The standard default paper color is white. Select black in the Art Materials Color Selector. Select the Paint Bucket in the Tools palette. Make sure that the Fill With Current Color option is checked in the Controls Palette. Click in the new canvas with the Paint Bucket. The canvas is now filled with black.

Note: It is possible to define color in the New File dialog box when you first open the canvas. However, this will set the paper color for future new files until you change it. For that reason, the Paint Bucket is used here (the Effects→Fill command is another alternative to the Paint Bucket).

2 | Customize Waxy Crayon Method Category and Subcategory

Select the Waxy Crayon variant of the Crayon brush family. Change the Method Category from Build Up to Cover by clicking and then dragging on the pull-down menu in the expanded Brushes palette. Similarly, change the resulting Method Subcategory from Flat Cover to Grainy Edge Flat Cover. (The standard Waxy Crayon will not show up against the black background.)

3 | Adjust Brush Size and Opacity

Select Controls→Size in the Brushes palette pull-down menu. Adjust the Size slider to suit the scale of the brush stroke you want to apply. Adjust the Opacity slider in the Controls palette to 100%. Apply the brush stroke. Try going over the same stroke several times and observe how the brightness of the color appears to increase.

4 | Save Customized Variant

Select Brushes→Variants→Save Variant in the Brushes palette pull-down menu. Give the customized brush a new name in the Save Variant dialog box (don't replace the existing default variant). Click OK. The saved variant now appears in the Crayons variant list. Saving the variant enables you to return to exactly the same customized settings that you set in Steps 2 and 3. If you don't save the variant when you change brushes and then return to the Waxy Crayon, you have to reset all the settings.

5 | Change Paper Color to Allow Editing with Eraser

When working against black, it is useful to be able to edit your painting by applying an eraser that erases to the black background color rather than the default white. To do this, select black (or whatever the dark background color is) in your Color Selector. Then select Canvas→Set Paper Color. The Eraser variants now erase to black. Remember to reset Paper Color if you move onto other background colors.

David Locke Higgins

Cougar

Comments

Higgins began this painting with a freehand black-and-white sketch (in Painter) based on a video-captured image. When he had completed the initial sketch, he added a colored background to make the cougar stand out in a dramatic way. The highlights and further shadows were applied with Grainy Cover Method Brush Variants that covered up the background color. To give the finished painting a unified feel, he finished by applying a Dye Concentration Surface Control Effect Using Paper Grain.

Studio Usage

There may be situations where you want to preserve the lines of sketch but change the background color. This technique describes how to "float" the dark tones of a sketch and change the background color from white. This technique is applicable any time you want to isolate a black sketch from a white background.

Related Techniques

1 | 1. Select Dark Tones

Select Edit→Select All (⌘-A) {Ctrl-A}. Select
Edit→Magic Wand. Click in the white background. The
white background becomes red, indicating that it is
included in the Magic Wand selection. Hold down the
Shift key and click and drag through the unselected
lighter gray tones to include them in this selection. Click
OK. Select Edit→Mask→Invert Mask. You'll achieve the
effect of inverting the selection so that now the dark
tones are selected.

Note: *If you want, you can select the dark tones initially
and avoid the inverting of the selection.*

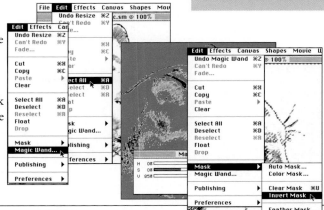

2 | Float Selection

Select Edit→Float to float the selection. Click on the
F.(Floater) List icon in the Art Materials palette. The floater
appears in the list.

3 | Fill Background

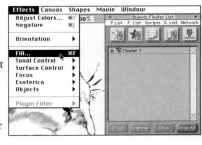

Select the color in the
Art Materials Color
Selector that you want
the background filled
with. Deselect the
floater by clicking
below it in the Floater
List (or use ⌘-D)
{Ctrl-D}. Select Effects→Fill (⌘-F) {Ctrl-F}. Make sure that
Fill With: Current Color is checked in the Fill dialog box.
Click OK. The background is now filled with the selected
color. Click on the Drop All button in the Floater List. The
floater is now dropped onto the background canvas. Begin
painting with Cover Method brushes over the image, inte-
grating the dropped line work as the foundation for the
painting.

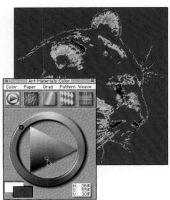

4 | Apply Dye Concentration Effect

As a final step to unify the background and painting, select Effects→Surface
Control→Dye Concentration. Select Using: Paper Grain. Select the Paper Grain in
the Art Materials: Papers palette. Adjust the grain scale in the Papers palette (the
papers library drawer must be closed and the palette
expanded to reveal the scale slider). In the Adjust Dye
Concentration dialog box, set the Maximum slider to
140% and the Minimum to 70%.

Note: *These Adjust Dye Concentration settings maintain
the values of the original paint, while creating the effect
of a uniform paper grain over the whole image (the
default settings tend to overlighten the image).*

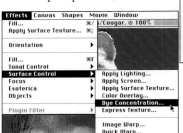

Four Elements

Sharron Evans

Comments

This four-component image was created from a simple black-and-white image, which was "floated" above the background canvas. A colored crayon was applied to the background, showing only through the white part of the floated image. The floater was finally "dropped" into the background canvas and then different effects were applied to different sections of the image. The bottom two elements were treated with a Glass Distortion effect, and the upper left element was treated with a softening effect.

Studio Usage

This technique emulates the effect of covering your paper with colored crayon followed by black paint, and then scratching through the black to reveal the colored underlayer. In this case, in order to get the colors corresponding to the composition, the process was reversed. The drawing scratched out of the black was created first, followed by the addition of the colored crayon below the scratched-away black surface. There are many variations you can try with this technique, including the effect of simply working in white on a black scratchboard.

Related Techniques

Hairy Rake   12

Working from a Layer   76

1 | Start with a Black Canvas

Select File→New (⌘-N) {Ctrl-N}. Open a 500 pixels wide by 400 pixels high canvas. Select black in the Art Materials Color Selector. Select Effects→Fill (⌘-F) {Ctrl-F} and fill the paper with black.

Note: You should fill with black rather than select black in the Paper Color Selector within the New File dialog box because changing the paper color will change the color revealed when selections are deleted or erasers used. The fill leaves the paper color as the default white.

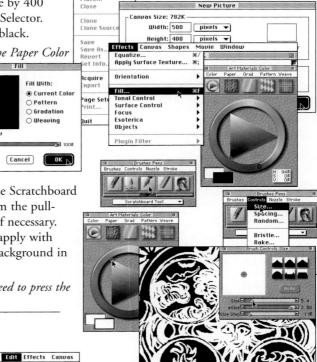

2 | Draw in White against Black

Select the Scratchboard Tool variant from the Pens family of brushes in the Brushes Palette. Change the Color Selector from black to white. Try out the Scratchboard Tool on your canvas. Select the Controls→Size palette from the pull-down menu in the Brushes palette. Adjust the Size slider, if necessary. Note how the brush width is affected by the pressure you apply with your stylus. Paint your design with white against a black background in this manner.

Note: To change the Scratchboard Tool brush size, you will need to press the Build button or (⌘-B) {Ctrl-B} before using the tool again.

3 | Float the Drawing

Click on the F. List icon in the Objects palette to reveal the Floater List. The Brush tool should still be selected in the Tools palette. Select Edit→Select All (⌘-A) {Ctrl-A} and then select Edit→Float. The image created in Step 2 is now floated above a plain white background canvas, and is listed as a floater in the Floater List.

4 | Apply Gel Composite Method

Select the Floater Adjuster tool in the Tools palette. Make sure that the floater is active by clicking on its name in the Floater List. Click on the Composite Method pull-down menu in the Controls palette. Change the Composite Method from Default to Gel. The Gel Composite Method tints the underlying image with the floater's color. In this case, because the floater is a black-and-white image, the white part of the floater becomes transparent to anything painted on the background canvas below.

5 | Deselect the Floater

Click below the floater name in the Floater List to deselect the floater. Go back to the canvas and paint in the background, selecting different colors and different tools. The color is now appearing wherever there was white in the earlier image.

Note: If you want to follow the traditional scratchboard process of creating the colored crayon underlayer first, followed by the scraping away of a black covering, then you start by floating the solid black paper created in Step 1. Click the Floater List "eye" icon closed to make the black floater invisible. Deselect the floater by clicking below it in the Floater List. Create the color on the white background canvas. Reselect the floater by clicking on its name again. Make the floater visible by clicking on the "eye" icon. Select the Gel Composite Method and paint on the floater in white with the Scratchboard tool.

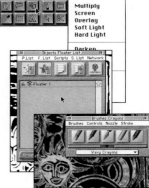

Applying Paint *Hairy Rake*

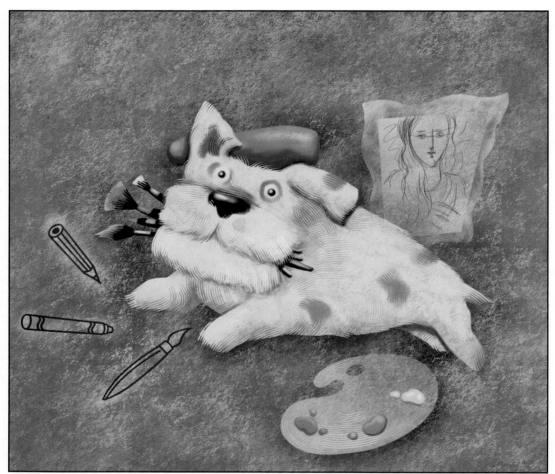

Art Dawg

Mark Jenkins

Comments

This painting was started as a hand-drawn sketch that was later scanned and used as a foundation for painting the final image. The various objects in the image, including the dog, were originally painted on separate digital canvases and then introduced into the composition as floaters. The floaters were repositioned and rescaled and finally dropped into the background.

Studio Usage

This technique describes how the effect of the dog whiskers and hairs was created in this image using one of Painter's rake brushes. The technique can be extended to include the look of paint thickly plastered onto canvas. The principles can be applied any time you want to have a hairy texture extending beyond the contour of an object.

Related Techniques

1 | Flatten Image

If there are any floaters in your image, then click the Drop All button in the Objects Palette→F. List (Floater List). This flattens the image into a single layer, which will be important if the hairy rake is going to work seamlessly beyond the contours of objects.

2 | Modify Scratchboard Rake

Select Scratchboard Rake variant in the Pens brush family. Select Brushes Palette→Controls→Rake. Adjust the Brush Scale slider in the Advance Controls: Rake palette to suit the size of brush marks required. Select the Dropper tool (hold down the ⌘ {Ctrl} key while in the Brush tool) and click on the region in the object where you want to pick the color of the hairy rake stroke. Apply brush strokes starting within the object and extending slightly beyond its edges.

3 | Sculpt Form with Color and Direction

You should continually adjust the color and the direction of the strokes to build up a varied and rich form within the object, as well as hairs projecting from the object.

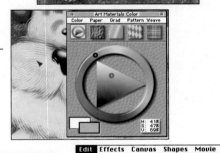

4 | Apply Texture

As a final stage, use the freehand selection Lasso tool to roughly select the object. Click close on the Controls palette to turn the path described by the Lasso into a selection (indicated by black-and-white "marching ants"). Select Edit→ Mask→Feather Mask. Set the feather to 10 pixels. The selection marquee now turns to green-and-white "dancing ants," indicating that the selection is now feathered (in technical terms the selection is now a representative path computed from the feathered mask). Select Effects→Surface Control→ Apply Surface Texture→Using Image Luminance. This effect gives an interesting, realistic, thick, oil paint look.

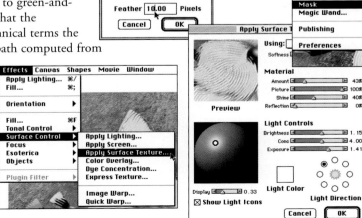

Applying Paint *Rough Sandstone*

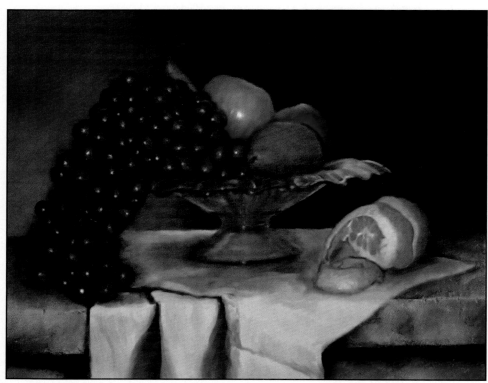

Pear Still Life

Nancy Vachini

Comments

This painting began as a QuickTake digital photograph of a still life with fruit. The photograph was then cloned. A variety of cloning brushes were applied. Further paint brushes were applied to create the final composition. Part of the pure painting process included forming the appearance of a rough sandstone ledge on which the fruit appears to be resting.

Studio Usage

There are a number of ways you can create the appearance of rock or stone surfaces in Painter. This technique deals with an approach using both grainy chalk painting and an application of surface texture effects. An alternative approach is looked at in Technique #22.

Related Techniques

1 | Paint Surface Background

Select the Large Chalk variant from the Chalk brush family in the Brushes palette. Select Controls→Size to access the brush size slider. Leave the Size slider in its default position. Leave the Opacity slider in the Controls: Brush palette at 100%. Click on the Paper icon in the Art Materials palette with the Basic Paper grain selected. Click on the Color Selector icon in the Art Materials palette. Select a tan color for the primer coat (the foundation for the sandstone surface). Expand the Color Selector palette and adjust the hue Color Variability slider to a low value of about 1% (to add a subtle color variance as you paint). Apply brush strokes on your canvas until you have filled the stone surface region.

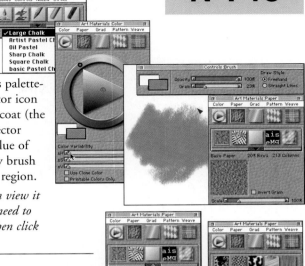

Note: It is advisable to tear off the Papers palette so that you can view it and the Color Selector simultaneously. To tear off palettes you'll need to have an icon selected other than the one you want to tear off. Then click and drag the appropriate icon off in a single operation.

2 | Paint Surface Texture Details

Select the Square Chalk variant of the Chalk brushes. Reopen the Papers palette. Open the Papers Library drawer by clicking on the horizontal bar. Click on the Library button. Select the Texture Sampler papers

library file in the Painter 4 applications folder. Select the Mountains grain from within this library. Close the library drawer so that you can access the grain Scale slider. Adjust grain scale to suit the scale of the image. Lower the Opacity slider to about 10%. Set the hue variability to about 4%. Select, alternatively, colors that are lighter and darker than the background color applied in Step 1, and apply these over the background, changing the brush size as appropriate.

3 | Apply Embossed Relief Effect

Select Effects→Surface Control→Apply Surface Texture. Select Using: Image Luminance in the Apply Surface Texture dialog box. Reduce the Amount and Shine sliders until you see the desired stone surface look in the Preview window. Click OK.

Note: For both this and the next step you may need to first select your stone surface region within your image so the effects are only applied to the stone. You can do this by using the Lasso selection tool for a freehand selection.

4 | Apply Lighting

The final step is to select Effects→Surface Control→Apply Lighting. Set up one or two light sources. Adjust their light colors, orientation, and brightness. Click OK.

Note: It is easy to overdo the lighting effect and end up overpowering your original image, losing a lot of surface detail in the process. If you find this happening, select Edit→Fade and scale back the lighting effect for more subtlety.

Applying Paint *Ancient Egyptian Fresco*

Mark Jenkins

Oisiris and Tutor

Comments

This painting was created totally with digital paint. No photographs were used. Jenkins began with considerable historical research and developed an initial pencil line sketch on paper, which was then scanned and used as a template upon which the fresco wall design was built. To achieve the ancient fresco look, he painted in the main forms. The hieroglyphs, Painter can, and lotus blossoms were introduced as shapes and image floaters. They were positioned, scaled, painted, and finally dropped into the background canvas. The final stage was the addition of cracks and effects to simulate the aging of a hard surface. (This image was used on the poster enclosed with Painter 4.0.)

Studio Usage

Fresco is the historic method of applying paint directly on a wall surface. This technique explains how to achieve an ancient Egyptian fresco look. The approach used in this image starts with a scanned sketch (which could be created directly in Painter). A clone is made in which the fresco base texture is laid down. Then the linework, solid blocks of color, and watercolor washes are painted. Finally, the surface texture, color, and lighting are modified using the Effects menu. You may find this a useful technique whenever you want to create the appearance of a weathered, worn surface.

Related Techniques

1 | Clone Scanned Sketch

Scan the preliminary sketch and open it in Painter. Select Canvas→Resize to resize the canvas to the desired final resolution (typically 300 dpi). If you want to add to your sketch, use the Soft Charcoal variant of the Charcoal brush family with the Method Subcategory (in the expanded Brush palette) set to Soft Cover. Select File→Clone. Select Edit→Select All (⌘-A) {Ctrl-A} followed by Delete to clear the Clone canvas.

Note: *Remember to uncheck Constrain File Size in the Resize dialog box before adjusting size. You can set absolute width and height in pixels or inches while adjusting Resolution in Pixels Per Inch.*

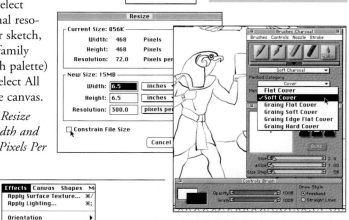

2 | Fill Background

Select a dark gray base color from the yellow family of hues in the Color Selector (accessible in the Art Materials palette). Select Effects→Fill (⌘-A) {Ctrl-A} and fill the Clone canvas with the dark gray.

3 | Build Up Fresco Texture

Select Brushes→Brush Looks from the drop-down submenu in the Brushes palette. Select Sponge from the current Brush Looks library. Select a lighter hue and set a few percent in the Hue and Value Variability sliders in the expanded Color Selector. Paint over the dark gray background. Select the Soft Charcoal variant from the Charcoal brushes family. Keep the paper texture the same as the Sponge look. Reduce the Paper Texture scale. Paint over the canvas with even lighter hues. Continue building up layers in this manner until the fresco look is achieved.

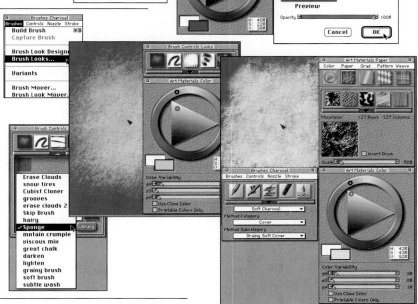

4 | Add Washes, Details, and Apply Surface Texture

Select Canvas→Tracing Paper (⌘-T) {Ctrl-T}. The original sketch now shows through the fresco texture. Use this tracing paper image to paint in the main compositional elements. Select the Broad Water Brush variant of the Watercolor brushes family to lay down translucent washes behind the figures. Use the Soft Charcoal brush with Watercolor 2 Paper Texture from the More Paper Textures library for the skin tones. Paint cracks in the wall. Select Effects→Surface Control→Apply Surface Texture. Select Using→Image Luminance. Adjust the Amount slider between 50%–60%. Check the final effect in the Preview window.

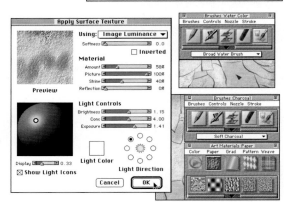

Applying Paint *Smeary Distorto*

Jeremy Sutton

Eagle

Comments

This Eagle was created using a customized variant of the Liquid brush family to smear color around within the image, while at the same time adding fresh color to the canvas. In this image Sutton used stylus pressure to reduce the size of the brush according to the level of detail involved. For example, a much smaller brush size was used around the eye compared to the brush used for the feathers.

Note: *Refer to Technique #27 for a detailed description of how to save a customized brush variant and add it to the variant list of an existing brush family.*

Studio Usage

Although the Distorto variant of the Liquid family of brushes is commonly used for smearing purposes, it can also be turned into an effective painting tool. For example, in this technique small adjustments to the standard Distorto brush create the effect of both smearing existing colors and imbuing new color to the canvas. This tool is useful for producing smooth liquid strokes in your paintings. You can use this brush to transform an existing image, say a photograph or company logo, into a totally different image.

Related Techniques

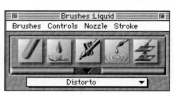

1 | Open Canvas and Select Distorto

Select File→New (⌘-N) {Ctrl-N}. Set the new canvas size to 600 pixels by 600 pixels. Select the Distorto variant from the Liquid family of brushes in the Brushes floating palette. The standard behavior of this brush is to smear paint around that already exists on the canvas, but not to add any new color.

2 | Adjust Brush Size and Opacity

Select Controls→Size from the drop-down sub-menu in the Brushes palette. Adjust the Size slider, located in the Brush Controls: Size palette, to suit the scale of your image. Press the Build button (⌘-B) {Ctrl-B} after the size is adjusted. Then adjust the Opacity slider in the Controls palette from 0% (the default for Distorto) to about 10%.

3 | Adjust Control Sliders

Select the Controls→Sliders from the submenu in the Brushes palette. Set the Size to vary with Pressure (the default is Velocity) and the Opacity to None (default is Pressure). Then paint with this brush. It produces a smooth liquid stroke, as well as smearing existing paint. The size of the brush is modified by the pressure you apply with your stylus, allowing fine control.

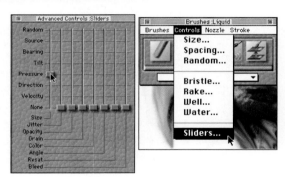

4 | Save Variant

At this stage, it is a good idea to save the brush as a customized variant so that you do not need to repeat these set-up steps every time. Select Brushes→Variants→Save Variant from the submenu in the Brushes palette. The brush will now appear in the Liquid family variant list.

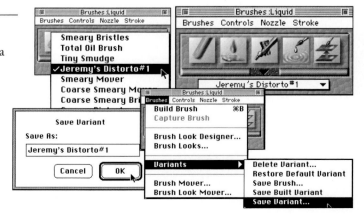

Applying Paint *Watery Chalk*

Lol Creme

Man in Sky

Comments

Creme created this piece as part of a series on dancers. It was painted from his imagination by using a combination of Chalk and Water brushes. He gradually built up the forms, the clouds and the figure, in Chalk and then completed the work with the application of Water to soften and diffuse the chalk, giving a misty translucent feel to the image.

Studio Usage

This technique describes how to achieve a watery chalk look in your painting by using a simple Chalk brush followed by using a Water brush. Although this painting has a limited color palette, the same technique can be applied to create complex and colorful imagery in a simple manner.

Related Techniques

1 | Fill Image with Background Color

Open a new document. Work initially at a low resolution of 72 pixels per inch. Working this way gives you the benefit of a small file size and loose, responsive strokes. Select blue color in Art Materials Palette→Color Selector. Select Effects→Fill (⌘-F) {Ctrl-F}. Fill the image with the current color.

2 | Select Large Chalk

Select the Large Chalk variant of the Chalk brush family in the Brushes palette. Reduce the Opacity slider in the Controls palette to 60%, which gives you more subtlety and control in the build up of pigment on the canvas. Select white in the Color Selector. Adjust the brush Size slider in the Brushes palette→Controls→Size palette to suit the scale of the image. Apply linework and shading, varying the brush size as appropriate. Build up to bright white by going over a stroke repeatedly and applying greater pressure.

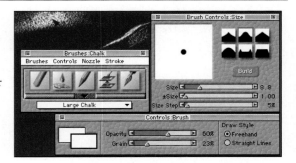

3 | Apply Just Add Water

Select the Just Add Water variant of the Water brush family. Keep the Opacity at 60% for more control. Adjust the brush size so that it's small enough for fine lines. Gently stroke lines that need diffusing. Decrease the Opacity to 14% and increase the brush size to encompass broad regions of the image in a single stroke. Apply very light pressure across the regions that need softening and the addition of a watery look.

4 | Fine-Tune with Dodge and Burn

As a final touch, select the Dodge brush, which has the effect of bleaching the lighter tones. Reduce the brush size to suit yourself. Increase the Opacity to 8%. Use the tool to emphasize highlights. Select the Burn tool, which has the effect of darkening colors in the image. Again, reduce the brush size to suit yourself. Apply in the regions where you want to deepen shadows and increase the contrast between lights and darks. The Burn tool is good for emphasizing contours where a dark region meets a lighter region.

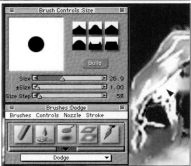

Applying Paint *Impressionism*

Dennis Orlando

Monet Study

Comments

In this painting, inspired by Monet's *The Oat Field*, Orlando explores the way that Monet used color and brush strokes. Orlando built up this painting almost entirely by application of a single, modified Liquid brush (Total Oil).

Studio Usage

Painter's Natural Media brush tools offer different ways of achieving an impressionistic look. In this technique, two approaches are explained that can be used together to produce an expressive, impressionistic painting. One approach is the customization of the Total Oil brush. The other approach uses the Impressionist brush provided in the Artists Brush family. Both approaches utilize the HSV variability sliders in the Color palette.

Related Techniques

Expressionism 24

Bristly Oil Brush Effect 27

1 | Select Total Oil Brush

Select the Total Oil Brush variant of the Liquid brushes family in the Brushes palette. Select Controls→Size from the Brushes palette pull-down menu. Adjust the Size slider to suit the scale of your canvas and the level of detail you want to apply.

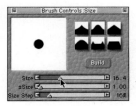

2 | Add Color Variability

Open the Color selector in the Art Materials palette. Expand the palette so that the Color Variability sliders are visible. Adjust the Hue and Value sliders (top and bottom) to about 18% and the Saturation slider (middle) to about 5%. Try out the brush stroke. Adjust the sliders to see the difference they make. Build up your painting from larger strokes and larger brush size to smaller ones.

3 | Compare to Impressionist Artists Brush

Select the Impressionist variant of the Artists Brush family. Adjust the brush size as in Step 1. Paint strokes whose direction follows the flow of the composition.

Note: *To blend the individual dabs, select the Smeary Mover Liquid brush variant and run it over the Impressionist brush dabs. Then select Edit→Fade to partially undo the Smeary Mover effect to match the look that you want.*

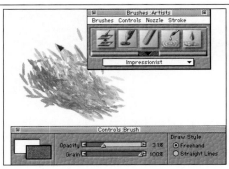

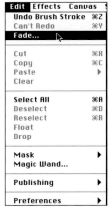

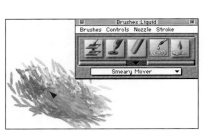

Applying Paint *Watercolor Cloning*

© '96 LOVATO

Richard Lovato

Judy

Comments

This painting was a traditional wash drawing that was scanned and reworked on the computer by using a number of cloning brushes in Painter. A glass distortion effect was applied as a final step.

Studio Usage

Pastel and watercolor cloning brushes can help strengthen a composition that is started with traditional media. This example shows one way to apply these brushes.

Related Techniques

1 | Create Clone

Open the scanned painting. Select File→Clone. A duplicate of the original scan is created. The original scan is automatically assigned as the Clone Source.

Note: You can confirm the assigned clone source by selecting File→Clone Source. There is a check by the name of the original image that indicates it is assigned as a clone source. If no clone source is assigned, then the current pattern in the Pattern library is the default clone source.

2 | Apply Pastel Clone

Select the Artist Pastel Chalk variant from the Chalk brush family in the Brushes palette. Click on the icon below the word Color in the Art Materials palette to open the Color Selector. Expand the Color Selector. Check the Use Clone Color box. Apply the Pastel Cloning brush in the Clone image.

Note: Click on the small square icon in the upper right corner of the palette to toggle back and forth between the expanded and shrunk state of the palette.

3 | Apply Watercolor Clone

Select the Broad Water Brush variant of the Water Color brushes. Check the Use Clone Color box in the expanded Color Selector. Apply the Water Color Cloning brush to the Clone image. The Water Color brushes paint into the Wet Layer above the canvas, whether the color is being selected from the Color Selector, a Color Set, or a clone source. To "dry" the water color; paint into the background canvas and select Canvas→Dry. If you do not dry the Water Color, then that paint will remain as an independent layer above any other paint added to the canvas. The Wet layer is only preserved in files saved in RIFF format.

4 | Flip Original Image

Select the original scanned image by clicking back on it. Select Effects→Orientation→Flip Vertically. The original image, still assigned as the Clone Source, is now upside down. Click back on the Clone image and apply the Cloning brushes in the background.

5 | Apply Glass Distortion

Select Effects→Focus→Glass Distortion. Select Using: Image Luminance in the Glass Distortion dialog box. Adjust the Amount and Softness sliders until you get the desired result in the Preview window. Click OK.

Applying Paint *Capturing Texture*

Helen O'Dea

Comments

O'Dea began this picture working at a low resolution with a customized Scratchboard Tool to outline the composition. She sketched in the colors with Chalk brushes and then resized the image to a higher resolution. She then added Airbrush strokes and painted in further detail.

Studio Usage

The pattern visible in the frog's vest was created by capturing a simple customized texture, or Paper Grain, and applying it with a grainy Chalk brush. The Invert option, Scale slider, and Color were all varied to enhance the final pattern.

Related Techniques

Creative Cross-Hatching 26

Weathered Gold 33

Using a Border as an Image Element 34

Grainy Wood 35

1 Paint Texture

Select File→New (⌘-N) {Ctrl-N}. Open a 100 pixel by 100 pixel canvas. Select the Scratchboard Tool variant from the Pens brush family in the Brushes palette. Make sure that black is the currently selected Primary Color in the Art Materials: Color Selector palette. Access the Brush Size slider by selecting Controls→Size in the Brushes palette pull-down submenu. Adjust the size to suit the thickness of brush strokes you want to create. Paint a simple pattern on the 100 by 100 pixel canvas.

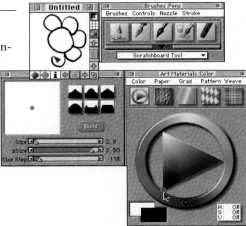

2 Capture Texture

Select the Rectangular Selection tool in the Tools palette. Create a selection around the pattern painted in Step 1. Select Paper→ Capture Texture from the pull-down menu in the Art Materials palette. Adjust the Crossfade slider in the Save Texture dialog box to zero (all the way to the left). Click OK. Open the Paper palette in the Art Materials palette. The new texture appears in the Papers library.

Note: The Crossfade parameter determines the amount of overlap of the repeating texture tiles into one another.

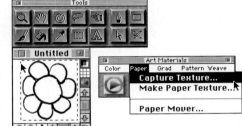

3 Apply Texture

Select the Square Chalk variant of the Chalk brush family. Make sure that the Paper palette library drawer is closed and the palette expanded so that a preview of the texture and a Scale slider is seen. Adjust the Scale slider until the preview shows the right scale of texture. Select a color that you want the lines to appear. Paint into the main image with the Chalk.

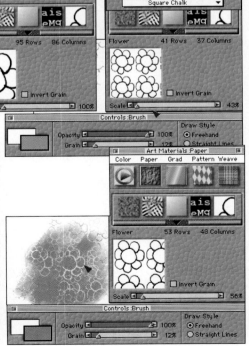

4 Invert Texture

Click the Invert box in the Paper palette. Select a different color. Apply the Chalk over the area already painted. Repeat Steps 3 and 4, adjusting Scale and Color. Build up a rich pattern in your painting.

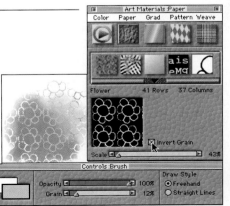

Applying Paint *Customized Chalk*

Horishi Yoshii

Sheep

Comments

This painting began as a simple sketch. The main blocks of color were then filled in, and a foundation was built up with chalk brush strokes. The hairs of the wool were individually painted using the technique described here.

Studio Usage

This technique describes how to create a thick, curly brush stroke effect that can be applied to clouds, textures, patterns or, in this example, sheep's wool. It involves using a slightly modified chalk brush. The principles used in this technique can be applied in many instances where a wool-like texture needs to be created. This example uses the case of an object, the sheep, surrounded by a white background. The technique could easily be applied to more complex imagery.

Related Techniques

1 | Lay Down Underlying Color

Use the freehand selection Lasso to select the region where the sheep's wool is to be painted. Click the Close button on the Controls palette. This makes the path described by the Lasso into an active selection, which will be filled in with dark gray. Click on the Color icon in the Art Materials palette to reveal the Color Selector. Select a dark gray in the Color Selector. Select Effects→Fill (⌘-F) {Ctrl-F}. The dialog box says Fill With Current Color. Click OK. Select Edit→Deselect (⌘-D) {Ctrl-D}. Follow the same procedure for other areas that need blocking out, such as the sheep's face and stalk.

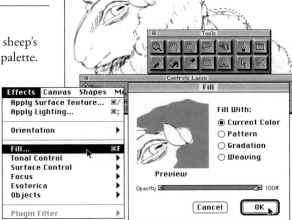

2 | Modify Large Chalk Advanced Controls

Select the Large Chalk variant of the Chalk brush family in the Brushes palette. Select Controls→Size in the Brushes palette pull-down submenu to reveal the Brush Controls: Size palette. Set the +/- Size slider to maximum. Reduce the Size slider to suit the scale of the sheep hair thickness. Open the Brushes palette→ Controls→Sliders palette. Change the left-hand slider from Velocity to Pressure. This change results in the stylus pressure determining the brush size (lighter pressure gives a thinner stroke, heavier pressure gives a thicker stroke).

Note: Adjusting the +/- Size slider to maximum will result in the brush diameter being visually represented by a small, inner, solid black circle surrounded by a larger diameter, gray circle. The black diameter represents the minimum, and the gray diameter represents the maximum brush diameter.

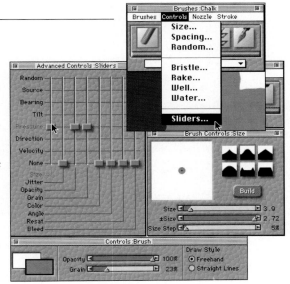

3 | Select Color and Paint Wool

Smooth out the sharp edge on the gray-filled region by painting the wool hair projecting beyond the sheep's body into white background. Make short brush strokes with lighter pressure at the beginning and end. Adjust the value in the Color Selector inner triangle to give a darker shade of color (drag the cursor down slightly) compared to the wool region background color (used to Fill in Step 1). Lighten the color value and increase the brush size to add broader, lighter wool hairs within the body of the sheep.

Note: It may be useful to save the customized chalk brush as a customized variant that can be recalled at any time in the future.

Note: Experiment to get the size and color correct. Make test brush strokes on the image and use Edit→Undo (⌘-Z) {Ctrl-Z} to undo test strokes.

Ilana

Jeremy Sutton

Comments

This portrait was created from life by using a variety of customized brushes to generate richness of texture and form. It is one of these brushes that is described in this technique.

Studio Usage

This technique is a simple way to achieve a textured effect that looks like crumpled paper. It involves a simple modification of a Watercolor brush. This is a good technique to combine with other textures, to be used to build up layers of paint. This technique also illustrates how you can save a Brush Look for future use.

Related Techniques

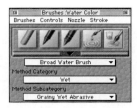

1 | Select the Broad Water Brush

Select the Broad Water Brush variant from the Watercolor family of brushes in the Brushes floating palette. This brush produces a broad translucent wash that shows the Paper Grain. Expand the Brushes palette so the Method Category and Method Subcategory pull-down menus are visible.

2 | Select Mountains Texture

Click on the Paper icon in the Art Materials floating palette and then on the horizontal bar to open the Paper library drawer. Click on the Library button to access a new library of textures. Select the library called Texture Sampler, which is located in the Painter 4 applications folder. Click OK. Select the Mountains texture from this library.

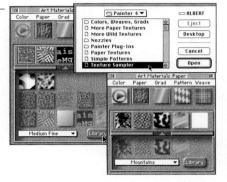

3 | Change Method

In the expanded Brushes palette, change the Broad Water Brush variant Method Category from Wet to Build Up. Change the Method Subcategory from Soft Buildup to Grainy Soft Buildup. Observe the way this new customized brush lays down the texture in your image. Select Controls→Size in the Brushes palette to access the Brush Controls: Size palette. Adjust the Brush Size slider to suit the scale of your image. Adjust the Opacity and Grain sliders, located in the Controls: Brush palette, until you get the effect the way you want.

4 | Save Brush Look

Save this customized brush as a Brush Look that can be recalled at any time in the future. Select Brushes→Brush Look Designer from the pull-down submenu. Paint a brush stroke in the Brush Look dialog box preview window. Make sure that the white background square in the Brush Look dialog box is selected. You can see a brush look based on the current brush settings, color, and texture. As you change any brush settings, color, or texture, the look changes accordingly. With your settings determined by Steps 1–3, click Save. Name the Brush Look. Click OK. Click Done in the Brush Look Designer dialog box (you need to do this before you can have access to any other functions in the program). Select Brushes→Brush Looks in the Brushes palette pull-down submenu to reveal the Brush Controls: Looks palette. Click on the horizontal bar to open the Brush Looks library drawer. The saved Brush Look is now included in the Brush Looks library. Click on its icon any time you want to reuse it.

Note: The Brush Look Designer is a very convenient way to check out brushes prior to using them. The saved Brush Look includes texture information as well as the customized brush settings. Saving a customized variant, only saves the brush settings, not the texture information.

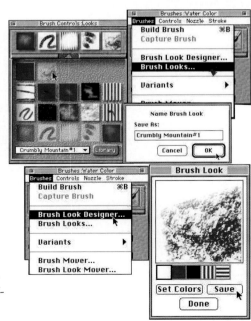

Applying Paint *Rock Texture*

Adam Sadigursky

Rock Solid

Comments

In this painting, Sadigursky has successively applied a variety of rock-like textures, varying the scale of textures as well as applying Surface Texture effects. He has used both standard textures supplied with Painter and textures that he has created himself. This technique looks at one aspect of the rocky relief that he has succeeded in building in this composition.

Studio Usage

This technique describes how to create a rock-like texture using standard Paper Grain provided with Painter. It involves modifying a texture and then applying it with different colors and at different scales of magnification. The same principles can be usefully applied to other Paper Grains.

Related Techniques

1 | Paint Basic Texture

Click on the Paper icon in the Art Materials palette. Click on the horizontal bar to open the paper library drawer. Click on the Library button located in the lower right corner of the open papers library drawer. Select the More Paper Textures library. Select Fine Grain paper texture from the More Paper Textures library. Click on the horizontal bar again to toggle the paper library drawer closed. Make sure that the Art Materials: Paper palette is expanded so that you can see a preview of the texture and a Scale slider. Select the Large Chalk variant from the Chalk family of brushes. Adjust the Grain slider in the Controls palette to 19%. Make sure that black is the currently selected color. Paint grain onto the canvas.

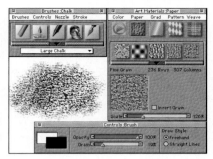

Note: To expand a palette, click on the small square icon in the top right corner of the palette.

2 | Rotate Texture

Select Rectangular Selection tool. Select a region with the texture painted in. Select Floater Adjuster tool (keyboard shortcut "F"). Click on the selection with the Floater Adjuster tool to make a floater. Then select Effects→Orientation→Free Transform. You now have handles around the floater that allow it to be rotated, rescaled, and distorted. Hold down the Command key and drag the corner handle on the floater to rotate the floater. Click the Drop button in the Objects palette Floater List. The rotated texture is now part of the background canvas.

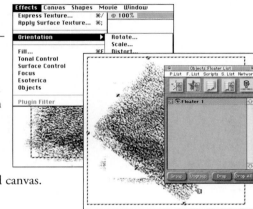

3 | Capture Custom Texture

Use the Rectangular Selection tool to select a square section of the rotated texture. Select Effects→Surface Control→Express Texture→Using: Image Luminance. In the Express Texture dialog box, put Contrast to maximum and adjust the Gray Threshold and Grain until the preview shows a distinct, well-defined, high contrast texture. Click OK. Select Papers→Capture Texture from the Papers pull-down submenu in the Art Materials palette. Name the texture. It is now part of the current papers library.

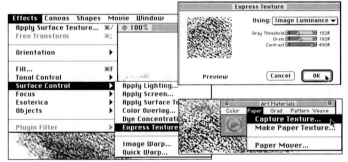

4 | Apply Custom Texture

With the Large Chalk variant selected, apply the new texture using a dark color. Check the Invert Grain box in the expanded Paper palette (the Paper Library drawer must be closed). Then paint with lighter colors. Adjust the Scale slider and repeat the process. In this image a custom texture at large scale was used to give the coarse features.

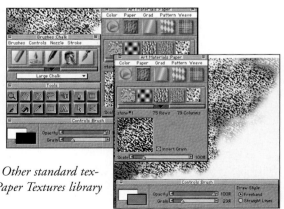

Note: Applying Effects→Surface Control→Apply Surface Texture→ Using:Image Luminance can also have interesting effects. Other standard textures that work well for rock are the Surface 1 texture in the More Paper Textures library and the Mountains texture in the Texture Sampler library.

Applying Paint *Acrylic Colors*

Bonny Lhotka

Real Paint

Comments

Lhotka frequently works with the integration of "traditional" (non-digital) and digital media in her creative process. She often starts with scanned monotypes and ends by adding "real" paint to her prints. This palette of scanned "real" acrylic paint was composed as a tool for selecting colors that reflected her traditional paint palette, rather than the standard Color Selector in Painter or the range of available Color Sets. She wanted to avoid the look of "computer colors."

Studio Usage

This technique describes how to construct a convenient color palette based on scanned paint. The palette is based on piecing together sample squares into a single "patchwork quilt" image. The colors in this image can then be directly sampled by using the Dropper tool from the Tools palette. While working on a painting with the Brush tool, you can hold down the Command {Ctrl} key and click in the region of the scanned paint image from which you want to sample color. This color then becomes the currently selected color.

Related Techniques

1 | Create New File

Select File→New (⌘-N) {Ctrl-N}. Select the size of the new file according to how many sample paint squares you want to include. In this case, an 8" by 10" image was selected to accommodate 80 one-inch squares. A resolution of 100 pixels per inch (ppi) gives slightly more detail than a screen resolution of 72 ppi. Click OK.

2 | Set Grid Options

Select Canvas→Grid→Grid Options. Set the Horizontal and Vertical Spacing to 1 inch. Leave the rest of the settings in their default values. Click OK. Select Canvas→Grid→Snap to Grid and make sure that it is selected (check mark by it). The pasted one-inch squares will now align neatly in columns and rows.

3 | Show Grid

Select Canvas→Grid→Show Grid if your grid is not visible. The grid is now visible and is superimposed on the image.

4 | Create One-Inch Square Selection

Open one of the scans from your artwork from which you want to sample color. Select the Rectangular selection tool. Using the superimposed grid as a reference, drag to select a one-inch square selection from within the image.

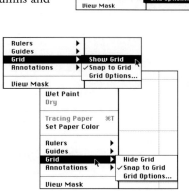

5 | Paste Square into Color Sampling Image

Select Edit→Copy (⌘-C) {Ctrl-C}. Click on the blank canvas created in Step 1. Select Edit→Paste→Normal (⌘-V) {Ctrl-V}. The sample square from your scanned artwork is now introduced as a floater. Using the Floater Adjuster tool, drag this into position in the new canvas. Repeat this process for other color samples until the patchwork sampler is full.

Note: *It is possible to sample colors and convert them to a customized Painter Color Set. By doing this, you can isolate specific colors you may want to regularly reuse and make it easier to select that particular color. (See Technique #50 for an explanation of how to create a custom Color Set.)*

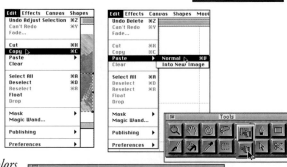

Applying Paint *Expressionism*

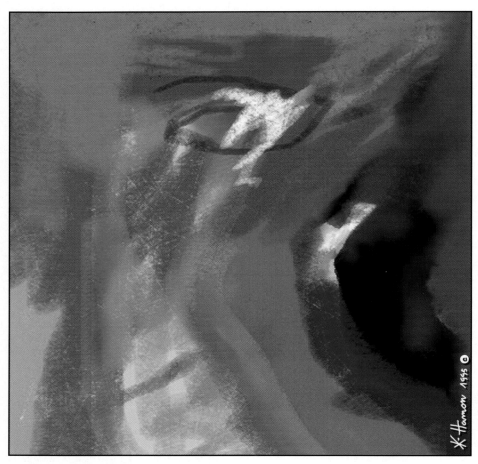

La Femme Qui Avance

Comments

This painting was created directly on a blank white digital canvas in Painter. Hamon worked primarily with Chalks, Water, Burn, and Dodge brushes. She made extensive use of the Paper grain.

Studio Usage

This technique describes a simple approach to building an expressionistic painting (in this case almost abstract) through the use of a few brushes and papers.

Related Techniques

1 | Apply Square Chalk

Select the Square Chalk variant of the Chalk brush family. Click on the icon below the Paper pull-down menu in the Art Materials palette to access the Paper palette. Open the Papers Library drawer by clicking on the horizontal bar with the arrow in the middle. Click on the Library button. Select the Wild Textures Papers Library. Select the "rice paper" grain from within this library. Close the Library drawer. Make sure that the Paper palette is expanded so that you see a preview of the grain, an Invert box, and a Scale slider. Adjust the Scale slider to suit the scale of your painting. Click on the icon below the Color pull-down menu in the Art Materials palette. Select the base color you want as a "primer" for your canvas. Apply the Chalk on the canvas.

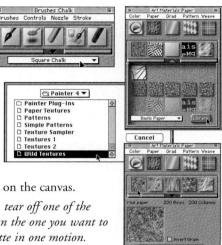

Note: *If you want regular access to both the Color Selector and the Paper palette, tear off one of the palettes from the Art Materials palette. Remember to first select an icon other than the one you want to tear off and then drag the icon you want to tear off out of the Art Materials palette in one motion.*

2 | Change Paper Grain and Apply Charcoal

Open the Paper palette Library drawer and click on the Library button. Select Paper Textures Library (the default Library). Click Open. Select the Basic Paper grain. Change color in the Color Selector. Slightly lower the Opacity slider in the Controls: Brush palette. Apply more Square Chalk. Select the Default variant of the Charcoal brush family in the Brushes palette. Select Controls→Size in the Brushes palette pull-down menu. Adjust the Size slider to suit the scale of brush strokes you want to apply. Apply the charcoal over the paint laid down in Step 1.

Note: *Adjusting the Grain slider, located in the Controls: Brush palette to the right, gives a flatter, less grainy look, and adjusting to the left gives a grainier look.*

3 | Use Just Add Water for Blending

Select the Just Add Water variant of the Water brush family. Reduce the Opacity to about 42%. This gives you more control. Apply this brush to regions where you want to gently blend, or smear, the colors.

4 | Bring Out Highlights and Shadows with Dodge and Burn Brushes

Select the Dodge brush. Reduce the brush Size and slightly increase the Opacity (10% Opacity is usually a good value to work with). Apply it to regions where you want to lighten the colors or bring out a highlight. Select the Burn brush. Similarly adjust Size and Opacity. Use them to bring out the shadows.

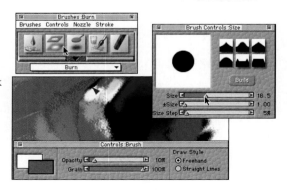

Judy York Copyright © 1995 Harlequin Enterprises Limited. Used With Permission

Unicorn Vengeance

Comments

This painting, created as a book cover, started off with the two photographed figures. The landscape immediately surrounding them was then painted into the picture. The starry sky was created next, along with the star reflections. Trees and candles were then painted over the sky and water.

Studio Usage

This technique shows you how you can use Painter 4.0 to easily achieve a starry night in your own composition. You can create realistic night sky scenes with the effect of far-flung galaxies, the milky way, and familiar star patterns, or you can capture the atmosphere of twinkling stars, slightly diffuse, fading into the night sky. The same principles used here can also be applied in other areas of painting (for example, the final step of softening and adding noise to your art can be useful in making a surface look natural).

Related Techniques

1 | Create Gradient

Open the image in which the starry sky will be added. Leave the sky region white. In the Color Selector, choose the darkest blue that you want the sky to be. Then select the Secondary Color rectangle and choose a lighter blue.

Open the Gradient Library drawer within the Gradient Editor in the Art Materials palette. Select the Two Point Gradient and close the drawer. Move the red rotation slider until the gradient preview shows dark at the top and light at the bottom. The gradient type should be linear. Select the Fill Bucket tool and click in the white region that is the sky. It now fills with the two color gradient.

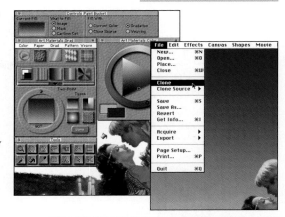

2 | Create Clone and Select Texture

Select File→Clone. Working from a clone rather than the original provides flexibility in removing unwanted stars. Open the Paper Library drawer in the Art Materials palette. Click on the Library button. Select the Painter 4 CD-ROM→GOODIES→PAPERS→ Textures 1. Select the texture Starry Sky from this Library. Close the drawer. Check the Invert Grain box. Adjust the Scale slider until the star sizes are a suitable scale for your painting.

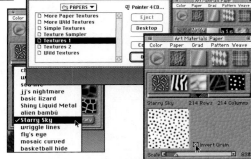

3 | Paint Stars

Select the Artist Pastel Chalk variant from the Chalk family of brushes in the Brushes palette. Set the Grain slider to 10% and keep Opacity at 100% in the Controls palette. Select an off white color in the Color Selector, with either a slight red or blue hue. Adjust the Brush Size slider (Brushes Palette →Controls→Size) to be small enough so that it only paints in one or two stars at a time. Paint in the stars against the gradient background. To remove stars, select the Soft Cloner variant from the Cloners family of brushes. Adjust the Brush Size so you can remove one star at a time. Set Opacity to 100%. Paint out unwanted stars.

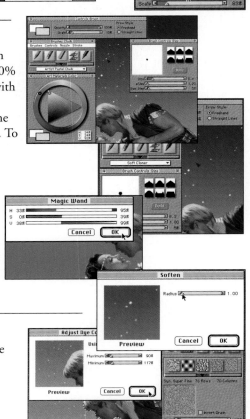

4 | Select Sky

Select Edit→Magic Wand. Drag the Magic Wand through your sky from the darkest to the lightest blue, including several of the stars. Press OK. The sky is now selected for application of effects.

Note: If the Magic Wand selection preview shows portions missed, then hold the Shift key while dragging the Magic Wand over the missing regions.

5 | Soften and Add Noise

Select Effects→Focus→Soften. Adjust the Radius slider to 1.0. Apply the soften effect. Select the Syn. Super Fine texture from the More Paper Textures library. Select Effects→Surface Control→Dye Concentration. Adjust the Maximum and Minimum sliders until you get a sufficiently subtle noise effect.

Hiroshi Yoshii

Stove

Comments

This image was painted using Chalks, Water, and Watercolor brushes. The painted regions were selected and a customized cross-hatching texture was applied to the selected painted region. Most of the shadowing was painted towards the end, with some subtle lighting effects being applied in the final stages.

Studio Usage

This technique describes how to create and apply your own customized cross-hatching relief and incorporate it in part or all of your image. The cross-hatching is first captured as a Paper Texture and then applied as a Surface Texture.

Related Techniques

1 | Create Cross-Hatching

Select File→New (⌘-N) {Ctrl-N}. Set the new canvas size to 400 pixels by 400 pixels. This canvas will be used to create the cross-hatching texture. Select black in the Color Selector. Select Effects→Fill (⌘-F) {Ctrl-F} and fill the canvas with black. Select white in the Color Selector. Select the Scratchboard Rake variant of the Pens brush family. Select Controls→Size→Spacing and→Rake from the submenu in the Brushes palette. Experiment on the black canvas, adjusting the Bristles, Brush Scale, and Brush Size sliders until you are satisfied with the cross-hatching look. Repeat the Fill command with black to clear your trial marks.

Note: *You need to click the Build button in the Size palette (⌘-B) {Ctrl-B} every time you adjust the sliders.*

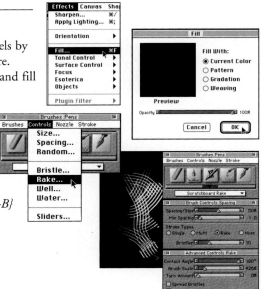

2 | Capture Texture

Use the Rectangular Selection tool, with the Shift key held down, to select a square region of the cross-hatching image. Select Paper→Capture Texture from the submenu in the Art Materials palette. Give the texture a name. It is now part of the current Paper library. You may want to repeat this process, selecting different regions of the image, and then see which captured texture works best.

Note: *If you generate several trial textures, it is a good idea to select Paper→Movers and create a new Paper library especially for your customized textures. See Technique #72 for a detailed explanation.*

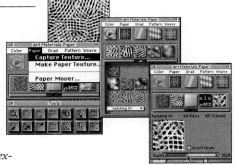

3 | Apply Surface Texture

Choose which texture works best. Open the painting to which you want to apply the cross-hatching. Select the region of the painting to be affected by the texture. (In this case Yoshii used the Edit→ Magic Wand to select the white surrounding the painted image and then Edit→Mask→Invert Mask to reverse the selection.) Select Effects→Surface Control→Apply Surface Texture. Select Using→Paper Grain. Adjust the Amount, Shine, and Brightness sliders to achieve the desired effect.

Note: *As a final step, Effects→Surface Control→Apply Lighting, applied subtly, may enhance the image.*

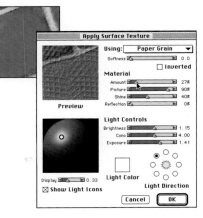

Applying Paint *Bristly Oil Brush Effect*

David Locke Higgins

DAVID LOCKE HIGGINS '95

White Rhino

Comments

This painting was created directly in Painter, starting with a white canvas and using a frame from a video as a visual reference (see Technique #4 for a more detailed description of the process). Higgins used a customized brush, which he saved as a specially named variant in the Brushes palette.

Studio Usage

This technique describes how to achieve the effect of dabbing or dragging a bristly oil brush on the canvas, giving a "stippled" look close up and a soft painterly look from afar. Also described here is how to save a customized brush variant. When you save a variant, it is added to the list of variants associated with a particular brush family, which is useful when you want to repeatedly go back to using the same customized variant.

Related Techniques

1 | Select Loaded Oils Brush

Select the Loaded Oils variant of the Brush family in the Brushes palette. Select Controls→Size from the pull-down menu in the Brushes palette. Adjust the Size slider to suit the scale of brush-strokes you want to make.

Note: *Make trial brush strokes with different Size settings. After each brush stroke, select Edit→Undo Brush Stroke (⌘-Z) {Ctrl-Z} to remove the last brush stroke.*

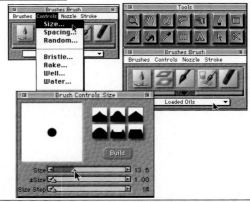

2 | Open the Brush Controls: Spacing Palette

Select Controls→Spacing from the pull-down menu in the Brushes palette. The Brush Controls: Spacing palette appears on the desktop. The standard Loaded Oils variant gives a smooth, slightly smeary, oily stroke.

3 | Increase Minimum Spacing

Drag to the right the Min Spacing slider in the Brush Controls: Spacing palette. A value of 19 works well.

4 | Save Brush Variant

Select Brushes→Variants→Save Variant from the Brushes palette pull-down menu. In the Save Variant dialog box give this customized Loaded Oils variant a name that is different from the default variant name. Click OK. The saved customized brush variant now appears as the currently selected brush variant. If you change brushes and then come back to the Brush family, this customized brush will still be listed in the variant list. By saving the variant, you do not need to repeat all the customized settings of this customized brush every time you want to use it.

Note: *Be careful not to accidentally select Save Built Variant instead of Save Variant. If you do, you alter the default variant rather than creating a separate, customized one with a different name. Restore the original default settings of any brush variant by selecting Brush→Variants→Restore Default Variant.*

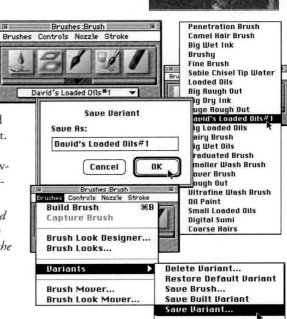

Applying Paint *Wax Resist Effect*

Jeremy Sutton

Lisa

Comments

This portrait was created from a live sitting. The background was first built by using a variety of brushes. The spongy regions that look like an oily surface, such as wax causing a watery paint to form bubbles, were produced with the customized Felt Marker described here. Chalks, Burn, and Dodge brushes were used to complete the image.

Studio Usage

One of the benefits of working with digital paint is the fact that virtually everything can mix with everything and remain wet forever. However, that can also be a disadvantage—for example, you might actually want the effect of an oily surface rejecting a water-based paint and causing it to form small bubbles. The technique described here was created in order to duplicate that bubbly effect, reminiscent of viscosity rejection in traditional media. The technique involves a simple modification of the Felt Marker variant in the Felt Pen family of brushes.

Related Techniques

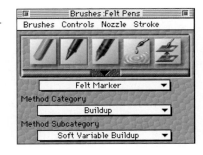

1 | Select the Felt Marker

Select the Felt Marker variant from the Felt Pen family of brushes in the Brushes palette. This results in a stroke that builds up to black, if the color is not 100% saturated, and that is "muddied" by darker colors that it runs through.

2 | Select Wet Method

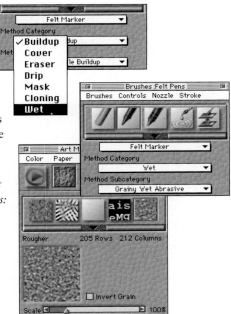

If the Brush palette is not expanded, that is, showing the Method Category and Method Subcategory below the Variant, then click the Expander button in the top right-hand corner to expand it. The default method is Buildup. Drag down from Buildup to Wet. The Method Subcategory now becomes Grainy Wet Abrasive. The word Grainy indicates that this brush is affected by the paper grain. Try different paper grains. The default Rougher grain works well.

Note: This brush paints in the Wet layer, which means that until the paint is dried, it is in a separate layer above the background canvas. To preserve the Wet layer, save the file in RIFF file format. To dry the Wet layer, either select Canvas: Dry from the top menu or save in any other file format.

3 | Select Colors

Click on the Color icon in the Art Materials palette to reveal the Color Selector. Select a dark color from the Color Selector and cover some of the canvas with this color. Then select a lighter color and apply more brush strokes over the same area. Add more colors and note the interesting effect as the colors mix and mingle.

Note: You may want to save this customized brush either as a saved variant (see Technique #27) or as a saved Brush Look (see Technique #21).

Applying Paint *Constructivism*

Dynnamic Mann

Patrick Lichy

Comments

This painting was inspired by the constructivist philosophy of Wassily Kandinsky. It was constructed using a combination of the Bézier Pen tool for the geometric shapes and the Pen, Chalk, and Charcoal brushes for the rest of the composition.

Studio Usage

This technique explains how to utilize flat (uniform colored) geometric shapes to divide the canvas into sections that are to be painted independently of each other. It makes use of the Bézier Shape tools and the Mask Drawing icons.

Related Techniques

Zig Zag Border   39

Paper Cutouts   78

Smooth Metallic Interface   109

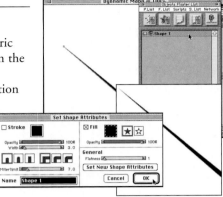

1 | Create a Bézier Shape

Select the Bézier Pen tool in the Tools palette. Create the first of the geometric shapes. Be sure to complete the shape so that it forms a closed outline. Open the Floater List (icon beneath F. List) on the Objects palette. The Shape name appears in the list. Double-click on the name. Make sure that the Stroke option is unchecked and the Fill option is checked in the Set Shape Attributes dialog box.

Note: Also check the Fill color, as required (in this case black). If the color is not what you want, click on the Fill color square and select the desired color.

2 | Create Other Shapes

Repeat the process in Step 1 for all the other geometric shapes of the same color. They will all appear as separate names in the Floater List. When they are completed, click the Drop All button in the lower right of the Floater List to merge (flatten) the floaters into the background.

3 | Apply Auto Mask

Select Edit→Mask→Auto Mask. Make sure that Using: Image Luminance is selected in the Auto Mask dialog box. Click OK. Drag the Mask Visibility icons to the center one. The mask will now be displayed in red and will cover the region that was black.

4 | Fill Mask Layer

Select black in the Color Selector. Select the Paint Bucket in the Tools palette. Select What to Fill: Mask and Fill With: Current Color in the Controls: Paint Bucket palette. Click in the region out-side the region you want to isolate for painting. It fills with red, indicating it has been added to the mask.

5 | Edit Mask and Apply Paint

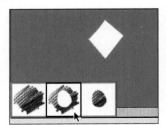

Step 4 may leave a thin, white line within the region you want masked out. To eliminate this, select the Masking Pen variant of the Masking brushes. Black should still be the current primary color. Apply the Masking brush over the areas where the mask is missing. Select the middle of the Mask Drawing icons to protect the masked region from the effect of the brushes. Select the left-hand of the Mask Visibility icons so that you can see the whole image unobscured by the red representation of the mask (the mask is still there, just not visible). Paint in the unmasked region. Repeat this process for all the areas you want to paint in independently of the rest of the image. Selecting white as the current color will cause the Masking brush to take away from, rather than add to, the mask.

Applying Paint *Versatile Chalk*

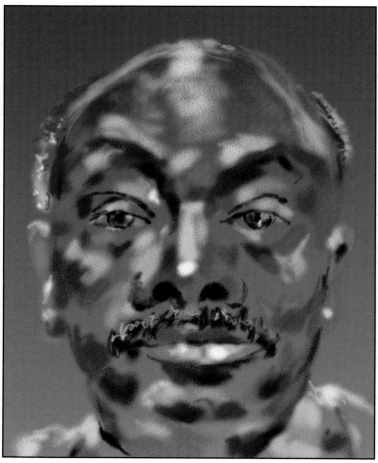

Jeremy Sutton

Willie L. Brown, Jr.

Comments

This portrait was created from life in about 20 minutes. Sutton used a customized variant of the Large Chalk brush that gave versatility of stroke and minimized the need to go back and forth between the canvas and the floating palettes.

Studio Usage

This technique utilizes a pressure-sensitive stylus to achieve fine brush control and a versatile range of effects with a single customized brush. The Advanced Controls: Sliders were adjusted so that the stylus pressure determined the diameter of the brush stroke produced by the Large Chalk brush variant. The same procedure described here for the Large Chalk can also usefully be applied to many other brush variants.

Related Techniques

1 | Select Large Chalk

Select the Large Chalk variant from the Chalk family of brushes in the Brushes floating palette. Adjust the +/- Size slider in the Brushes→Controls→Size palette to the right as far as it can go (value is 2.7). Adjust the Size slider to suit the scale of your painting.

Note: The gray outer diameter represents the maximum brush diameter, and the black inner circle represents the minimum brush diameter. When the +/- Size slider has a non-zero setting, the Build button must be clicked (⌘-B) {Ctrl-B} after changing any of the parameters in the Brush Controls: Size palette.

2 | Adjust Pigment Distribution

Click on the visual representation of diameters. You'll get a depiction of how pigment will be distributed in the stroke. (It's determined by the six icons to the right.) Select the pointed option, top left, to get the most pigment concentrated in the center. Click again on the visual representation, and it toggles back to the gray and black circles.

3 | Adjust Sliders

Select Brushes→Controls→Sliders in the Brushes palette to reveal the Advanced Controls: Sliders palette. Along the left of the Advanced Controls: Sliders palette, you'll see a list of input parameters followed by output parameters that affect brush behavior. Set the first sliding control to Pressure. Set all other sliders to None.

Note: Both Pressure and Size will be highlighted in red. The brush size is now regulated by pressure.

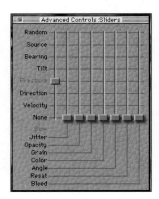

4 | Adjust Pressure and Opacity

Set the Opacity slider in the Controls palette to 100%. Leave the Grain slider at its default position. Select a dark color from the Color Selector and make a stroke on your canvas by applying very light pressure. Reduce opacity to about 7%. Make a series of overlapping strokes on the canvas with heavy pressure so that you'll get maximum diameter. You'll create a diffuse, soft shading in contrast to the fine line associated with 100% opacity and light pressure.

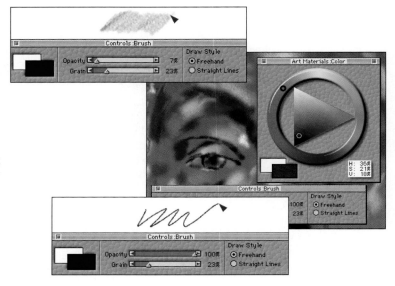

Pablo Picasso

Jeremy Sutton

Comments

This image was initially created at 72 pixels per inch (ppi) resolution and was then replayable at 300 ppi resolution. The starting point for the creation of this portrait was the creation of a painted background inspired by two Picasso paintings, *The Bullfight* and *The Dream*, that represented the aggressive and sensual sides of his character. The final portrait was then built over this background using a variety of standard and customized Cover Method brushes.

Studio Usage

It's often useful to paint an image at screen resolution (72 ppi) because the file size is relatively small, and there is little time lag between the stylus movement and the corresponding brush stroke. You can also achieve more fluid and spontaneous brush strokes. However, if the final image is to be printed, then a resolution of about 300 ppi is needed for the optimum quality. These competing factors can both be addressed by using the recorded script to replay a painting at a higher resolution (the technique described here).

Related Techniques

1 | Open a Low Resolution Canvas and Select All

Select File→New. Set the pixel width and height of your low resolution canvas. The resolution setting should be 72 ppi. Click OK. Select Edit→Select All (⌘-A) {Ctrl-A}. Select File→Save As and name the file.

2 | Begin Recording

Click on the Scripts icon in the Objects palette. With the scripts library drawer closed, the scripts controls are visible. Click on the central red Record button to begin the script recording. Select Edit→Deselect (⌘-D) {Ctrl-D} to get rid of the black-and-white "dancing ants" marquee.

3 | Stop Recording and Save Script

While you are recording, you can use any Painter brushes and effects. However, you should not select, open, or create any other document on the desktop while recording the painting process. When you have finished painting, click on the left-hand square Stop button in the Scripts palette. Name the script in the dialog box that results.

Note: Because the script is a list of commands, not a frame by frame saving of the actual bit map image, it is a very small file size.

4 | Create New High Resolution Canvas and Select All

Select File→New (⌘-N) {Ctrl-N}. If the low resolution canvas was the last New document, you should see the pixel values you set in Step 1. Select "inches" instead of "pixels" in the Width and Height units pull-down menus. Change the resolution from 72 to 300 ppi and click OK. Select Edit→Select All (⌘-A) {Ctrl-A}.

5 | Replay Script

Click on the horizontal bar in the Scripts palette to open the scripts library drawer. Click on the thumbnail version of your painting (also listed by script name in the library pull-down menu). Click once again on the horizontal bar to close the drawer. The script you just recorded is now selected and its icon appears above the bar enclosed in a red square contour. Click the Play button in the Scripts palette (black arrow, second from left). The script of your low-resolution painting is now replayed, resulting in a duplicate at a higher resolution. The replayed brush strokes are the same as if you had originally created the image at the higher resolution.

Note: You can choose to stop the playback at any time by clicking on the Stop button, or just pause it by clicking on the Pause button (second from the right).

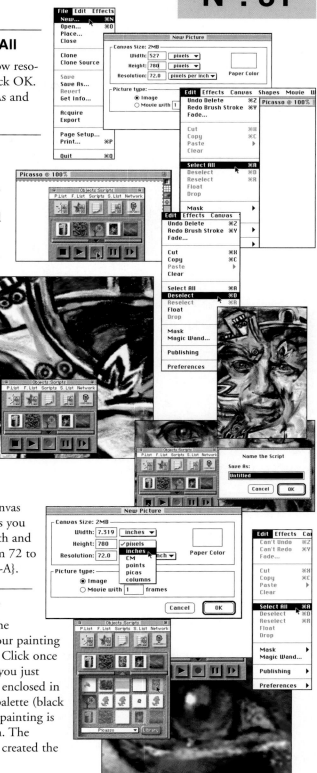

Applying Paint *Paint on Papyrus*

Flynn De Marco

The Egyptian

Comments

The figure in this painting was created separately from the background and introduced as a floater. The background writing was created by using a font family called DesertCrypt. The piece of papyrus was created by applying surface texture using a Painter Paper Grain. The painted figure was created separately from the background and the papyrus. It was introduced as a floater and its composite method was adjusted to give the effect of being painted directly on the papyrus. The final stage was to flatten the image and apply lighting effects.

Studio Usage

The Darken Composite Method can be useful when you want to introduce an image into a composition with the appearance of being painted directly on a grainy paper already in the background of the composition. The image is introduced as a floater. By using this technique, you'll have the flexibility to try out different papers or easily change the image without affecting the background. This example shows one application of the technique.

Related Techniques

1 | Apply Auto Mask

Create a black-and-white line drawing with solid black lines completely enclosing the regions of the image that you want to fill with color. This is the image that will be transposed onto the papyrus, as if it was originally painted directly on the papyrus. Select Edit→Mask→Auto Mask. Make sure that Using: Image Luminance is selected within the Auto Mask dialog box. Click OK. You'll generate a mask based on the luminance in the image (100% mask for black and 0% for white).

Note: Select the middle of the Mask Visibility icons. You can now see the image with red where there was black (red indicating the mask). Go back to the left-hand Mask Visibility icon so that you see the image without the red indication of mask.

2 | Use Cartoon Cell Fill

Click on the icon below the word Color in the Art Materials palette to reveal the Color Selector. Select a color to use to begin filling in the image. Select the Paint Bucket tool in the Tools palette. Check the What to Fill: Cartoon Cell and Fill With: Current Color options in the Controls: Paint Bucket palette. Click in the region you want to fill with the selected color. Continue this process for other regions of the image.

Note: If the initial fill "leaks" out of the region you want to fill, then double-click on the Paint Bucket icon in the Tools palette. Adjust the Mask Threshold slider to the right and try again. If the leak continues no matter what value you set the Mask Threshold to use, then use the Masking Pen brush with black as the selected color to ensure that a solid line of mask surrounds the area you want to fill. The advantage of using Cartoon Cell Fill rather than regular Image Fill is that the fill color goes right into the black lines and doesn't leave any white or gray gaps.

3 | Copy Image and Paste into the Main Image

Select Edit→Select All. Select Edit→Copy. Click on the main image that contains a light colored textured ("papyrus") background. Select Edit→Paste→Normal. The image prepared in Steps 1 through 3 is now introduced over the papyrus as a floater.

4 | Change Composite Method

With the Floater Adjuster tool selected in the Tools palette, change the Composite Method pull-down menu in the Controls: Adjuster palette from Default to Darken.

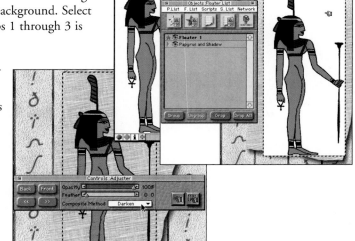

Frames and Borders *Weathered Gold*

When There is Hope

Judy York

Comments

This painting was originally created as cover art for a paperback novel. The central image was created first, utilizing three sets of photographs for the couple, the sea scene, and the angels. They were composited using floaters and cloning. Painting techniques were then applied across the entire image, including the addition of gold dust in the woman's hair (using the Pixel Dust variant of the Pens brush family). The beaten gold frame was created last to enhance the image and complete the composition.

Studio Usage

This technique describes how to create the look of a beaten, gold frame within your artwork. The rich, weathered, natural look of the gold is built up by application of a number of varied paper textures, followed by applying a surface embossing effect, adjusting the lighting and, finally, painting in the cracks. This technique can also be applied within your image to create natural looking surfaces.

Related Techniques

1 | Select the Border

Select the Rectangular Shape tool to select the interior of the border. The rectangle created may fill with the currently selected color. Double-click on the Shape listed in the Objects Palette→Floater List and uncheck the Stroke and Fill boxes in the Set Shape Attributes dialog box. Select Shapes→Convert to Selection from the top menu. Select the middle Mask Visibility icon in the Objects Palette→Path List. You will see a red mask indicated in the border. Select Edit→Mask→Invert Mask. Select the right-hand Mask Visibility icon. You now have the border selected.

2 | Fill with Gold and Apply Paper Textures

Click on the Color icon in the Art Materials palette. Select a gold color in the Color Selector. Apply Effects→Fill with Current Color checked in the Fill dialog box. Select the Brushes Palette→Chalks→Artist Pastel Chalk variant. Set the Controls Palette→Grain slider to 10% and keep the Opacity at 100%. Adjust the Brush Size slider (Brushes Palette→Controls→ Size) to be about half the width of your border. Click on the Paper icon in the Art Materials palette to reveal the Art Materials: Paper. Click on the horizontal bar. Start painting into the border region by using different paper textures and different hues and values from the gold family. Try overlapping textures, inverting them, and changing their scale.

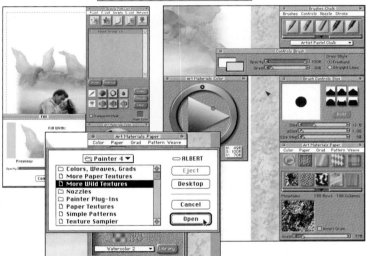

3 | Apply Effects and Paint Cracks

Select Effects→Surface Control→Apply Surface Texture. Select Image Luminance. Adjust the Amount slider and press OK. Select Effects→Surface Control→Apply Lighting. Move the light sources by clicking and dragging on the larger end and rotate their direction by dragging on the small end. Add sources by clicking in the Preview window and remove them by clicking on an existing source and then deleting. Adjust Light Color. Click OK. Keeping the Artist Pastel Chalk variant, adjust the Grain slider to 100% and the Opacity to 20%. Make the Brush Size about 6.2. You can paint in the cracks with the appropriate colors. Use the background color to paint in the frame to simulate the chipped gold leaf effect on the frame.

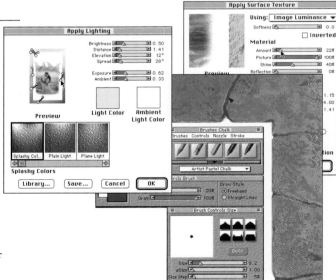

Frames and Borders *Using a Border as an Image Element*

Transform

Stephen Rock

Comments

This image combines various manipulated photographic elements with a smaller version of a separate, secondary image entitled *Hand*. The border of the Hand image is repeated in another section of the main image, reversing out color in that section (around the mountain). This artwork is an example of one way that a border, in this case from a secondary image, can be used as an image element within a composition.

Studio Usage

The border motif of the Hand image within the main composition was reused to frame the mountain. In order to use the border within the image, the artist first created a floater and then adjusted the Composite Method. This technique describes how the original white border in the Hand image was created, and then how it was floated and used to interact with another part of the composition.

Related Techniques

1 | Enlarge Canvas Size of Secondary Image

Open the secondary image. Select Canvas→Canvas Size. Increase the size all over. Click OK. By doing this, you'll add pixels to the canvas around the original image, effectively creating a plain white border (assuming your choice for paper color was white when creating the secondary image).

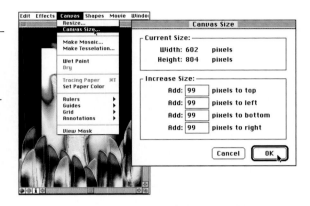

2 | Adjust the Hard Edges of the Secondary Image

Select the Coarse Smeary Mover variant of the Liquid brushes family in the Brushes palette. Use this, and other Liquid variants, to smear the edges of the original image into the newly created white border.

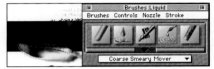

3 | Select the Border Region of the Secondary Image

Select Edit→Magic Wand. Click in the white border region and click OK. The white border region is now selected. Select Edit→Copy (⌘-C) {Ctrl-C}. The border region is now copied to the clipboard and is ready for pasting.

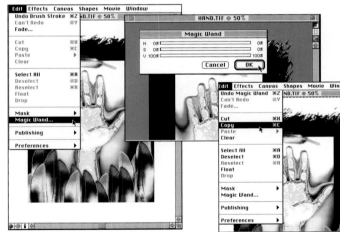

4 | Position Border and Change Composite Method

With the main (primary) image open, select Edit→Paste→Normal (⌘-V) {Ctrl-V}. The border is now pasted into the main image as a floater. Select the Floater Adjuster tool. Drag the floater into position. Select Reverse Out in the Composite Method pull-down menu in the Controls palette. Try out other Composite Methods for effect.

Note: *If the border needs resizing or orienting, select Effects→ Orientation→Free Transform. Grab the corner handles, holding the Shift key down for resizing proportionally, or hold the Command {Ctrl} key down for rotating. Select Effects→Orientation→Commit Transform.*

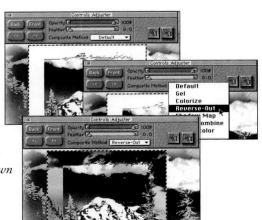

Frames and Borders *Grainy Wood*

Jen with Flower

Corinne Okada

Comments

This painting started out as a black-and-white pencil sketch on paper. After scanning in the sketch, a light brown color overlay was applied, followed by a gradient background in selected regions of the image. The details were then built up in paint. Okada employed a rich variety of customized paper textures.

Studio Usage

You can enrich your paintings and achieve the look and feel you want by creating and applying your own customized textures. In this example, Okada scanned an authentic wood surface, used a Cloner brush with the Patterns feature to make it a seamless tile, and then added it to the Papers library so that it could be applied to the image using a grainy brush. She filled the frame with a dark brown using the Fill Bucket. She then chose a light brown with which to apply the wood texture.

Related Techniques

1 | Select the Texture

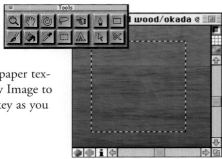

Scan the wood surface at the same resolution as the image. Open the scanned image in Painter. Use the Rectangular selection tool to select the square region of the scanned image that you'll use as the basis of a repeating paper texture tile. Use Edit→Copy (⌘-C) {Ctrl-C} followed by Edit→Paste Into New Image to create an image cropped to the square selection. By holding down the Shift key as you drag the Rectangular selection tool, you can select a perfect square.

2 | Create a Seamless Tile

Select the Pattern pull-down menu in the Art Materials palette and choose Pattern→Define Pattern. Choose the Soft Cloner variant from the Cloners family of brushes in the Brushes palette. Hold down the Control key and click once on the far left of the square wood image. Paint on the far right, right up to the edge. Do the same for the top and the bottom of the image. Hold down the Space bar and Shift key and click and drag in the image. You will see the image scroll seamlessly and can easily observe any hard edges that need softening. Select File→Save As.

3 | Capture the Texture

Choose Effects→Surface Control→Express Texture. Adjust the Gray Threshold, Grain, and Contrast sliders until you get a good definition of grain (64%, 64%, and 200% in this example). Click OK. You have now converted your color image into a high contrast, grayscale image.
Choose Edit→Select All (⌘-A) {Ctrl-A}. Choose the Paper pull-down menu on the Art Materials palette and select Paper→Capture Texture. Press OK after naming your texture. Your customized wood texture has been added to the paper library and is the currently selected texture.

4 | Choose a Grainy Brush

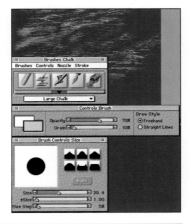

Choose the Large Chalk variant of the Chalk family of brushes in the Brushes palette. Adjust the brush size to suit the region of image to which you are applying the texture. Move the Grain slider in the Controls palette to 10% and the Opacity to 70%.

Note: You can change brush size while in Brush mode by selecting Option ⌘ {Ctrl-Alt} while dragging on the image.

5 | Apply the Texture

Paint directly on the image with the Large Chalk and the wood texture grain will appear.

Frames and Borders *Ornamental*

Judy York Copyright © 1996 Harlequin Enterprises Limited. Used With Permission

Fool's Paradise

Comments

This painting, created as a book cover, was formed in four stages. First, the central image was generated, utilizing a combination of photography and painting. This was followed by the construction of the ornamental frame (the techniques described in this section). The final stages were the addition of the fabric background pattern and the painting of the fruit spilling over the frame.

Studio Usage

This technique enables you to conveniently construct detailed ornamental frames within your paintings. The ornamental patterns and designs can be scanned easily from source books and photographs, or drawn from scratch. In this image two different designs were used, one for the horizontal and vertical bars and another one for the corner pieces. An important aspect of successfully creating a frame like this is prior planning. It is advisable to work out in advance your precise frame and image dimensions.

Related Techniques

1 | Clean Up Pattern

Scan the black-and-white pattern you want to use in the horizontal and vertical bars of the frame at the same resolution as the final image. Open Painter. Select Effects→Tonal Control→Equalize. Adjust the black-and-white sliders. Use the Rectangular selection tool to select the repeating region of pattern. Select slightly more, rather than less, of the region. It is easier to overlap the pattern elements later than to make up for a gap. Select Edit→Copy.

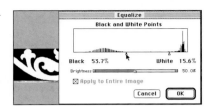

2 | Apply Gel Composite Method

Open a new canvas that is as wide as the width of the frame needed. Introduce a floater of weathered gold. Select Edit→Paste→Normal. Position the floater over the gold. Click on the F. List icon. Drag the gold floater above the pattern floater in the Objects: Floater List. With just the gold floater active, set the Composite Method to Gel in the Controls: Adjuster palette. The dark pattern shows through, but gold fills the white space around the pattern. Select Drop All.

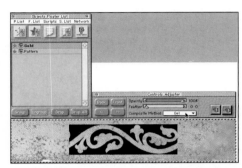

3 | Construct Frame

Use the Rectangular selection tool to select the repeating pattern element with the gold. Copy and paste it back into the same canvas and position the resulting floaters so they form a seamless length of ornamental frame. Select Canvas→Rulers→ Show Rulers. Then select all floaters, group them, and collapse them into a single floater.
Select Edit→Copy. Open up the canvas that you want framed. Make sure that you have sufficient white space around the image. Select Edit→Paste→Normal and drag the floater to the upper frame position around the image.

4 | Replicate, Flip, Rotate the Floater, Add Corners, and Apply Lighting

Drag the floater by holding down the Option {Alt} key to position the lower side of the frame. Select Effects→Orientation→Flip Vertical. Hold down the Option key and drag a third floater into the image. Select Effects→ Orientation→Rotate and type in 90 degrees. Position the new vertical floater on the left side of the image. Drag a fourth floater from this vertical floater while holding down the Option {Alt} key. Position it on the right side. Apply Effects→Orientation→Flip Horizontal to make a mirror of the left part of the frame. Create corner pieces following the same process and introduce them to the image as floaters. Select all the floaters and then select Group, followed by Collapse in the Floater List. Select Effects→Surface Control→Apply Lighting.

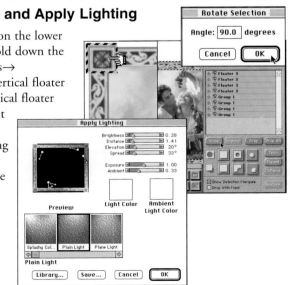

Frames and Borders *Brush Stroke*

David Locke Higgins

Borneo Orangutan Baby

Comments

This painting was created entirely in Painter using a video grab as a visual reference. The primary tools used were chalks. The final step was to add a border around the edges to soften them. The border prevents an otherwise soft and expressive work from having harsh straight edges in the final print. If the edges are left hard, the image looks like it is pasted on the paper rather than being an integral part of it.

Studio Usage

This technique describes how to add a very simple line border around your painting that softens the contrast with the paper on which the image is printed. By using this tip, you can avoid the stark contrast and mechanically clean straight edge that is otherwise present at the edge of your composition when it is printed.

Related Techniques

1 | Pick Color from Image

Select the Dropper tool from the Tools palette. Click on a light tone in the image. This is the color that will be used for the border. The Dropper tool can also be selected by holding down the Command key while the Brush tool is selected.

2 | Match Paper Grain

Click on the Paper icon in the Art Materials palette. Click on the horizontal bar to open the paper library drawer. Click on the Library button. Select the More Paper Textures library from the Painter 4 application folder. Select the Big Canvas grain from that library by dragging down to the grain name on the pull-down menu that is visible when the Paper library drawer is open. After selecting Big Canvas grain, close the library drawer and make sure that the palette is expanded so you can see the Papers scale slider. Adjust the grain scale to match the image grain.

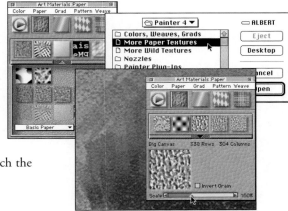

3 | Select Square Chalk

Select the Square Chalk variant from the Chalk brush family in the Brushes palette. Select Controls→Size in the Brushes palette submenu. Adjust the Size slider to give the right diameter of stroke for the border. Because the cross section of the Square Chalk in the Brush Controls: Size palette is not circular, the brush must be "built" every time you change its size. Click on the Build button or use the keyboard shortcut ⌘-B {Ctrl-B}.

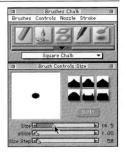

4 | Draw Straight Edge

Use a conventional ruler on the tablet surface and vary the stylus pressure as you draw the border over the top of the existing image. This may take some experimentation to get it right. The modulation of stylus pressure avoids a mechanical straight border. An alternative is to select Edit→Select All (⌘-A) {Ctrl-A}. Select P. List→Stroke Selection in the Objects palette submenu. You've now formed a perfect border using the chalk stroke. The stroke appears at maximum opacity—unlike making a brush stroke with a pressure sensitive stylus, where the opacity is determined by pressure. If the stroke is too strong, select Edit→Fade to partially undo the effect. If the stroke is too weak, repeat the P. List→Stroke Selection command a number of times.

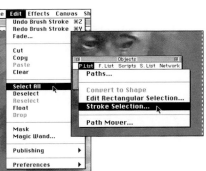

Frames and Borders *From Polaroid Transfer Prints*

Dorothy Simpson Krause

Dragon Lady

Comments

This image combines diverse elements including an old wood engraving, a piece of Japanese fabric, and a section of the Rosetta Stone. The various components have been integrated into a whole by using floaters and by applying cloning brushes. The gold is applied using Kai's Power Tools. The border is taken from the rough black border of a Polaroid transfer print. The original transfer print was scanned and sections of the border applied in different images. Krause reuses these borders, picking up frames from one image for use in another.

Studio Usage

The imagery for creating frames within your digital artwork can come from many diverse sources. A Polaroid transfer print is one potential source. In this example you'll see how Krause uses and reuses the rough edge left by the chemical gel that is squeezed from the outer edge of a Polaroid transfer. Although she used a very large 20" by 24" Polaroid film (there are only four Polaroid cameras of that scale in the world), this can also be done with some of the smaller standard Polaroid films.

Related Techniques

1 | Select Edges

Scan the Polaroid transfer print at a resolution at least as high as the final image you intend to create. This ensures the maximum quality of the image. Select the Rectangular selection tool in the Tools palette. Make a rectangular selection around an edge section in the Polaroid scan. Select Edit→Copy.

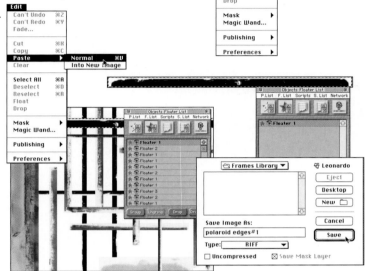

2 | Paste Edges into New Canvas and into Final Image

Open a new file at least as large as the final image you want to create. Select Edit→Paste→Normal. The scanned edge now appears as a floater on the new canvas. Click on the F. List icon in the Objects palette. The floater is listed in the Floater List. Repeat Steps 1 and 2 for other interesting edges in the same scan or in other Polaroids. Don't worry about rescaling or reorienting the edges at this stage. Select an edge you want to use in your image by clicking on it with the Floater Adjuster tool. Following the procedure described above, copy and paste the edge into the final image.

3 | Manipulate Edge to Form Frame

Select Effects→Orientation→Free Transform. Rotate the floater by holding down the Command {Control} key while dragging a corner control handle on the rectangular yellow-and-black marquee surrounding the floater. Select Effects→Orientation→Flip Horizontal or Flip Vertical. Resize the floater, maintaining the aspect ratio, by holding down the Shift key while dragging the corner control handles. Position, orient, and scale the floater to suit your image. Then select Effects→ Orientation→Commit Transform.

4 | Repeat for Other Edges

Repeat Steps 2 and 3 for the other three edges needed to complete the frame. Each of the four sides of the frame can be made up of more than one floater. You can try changing the floater Composite Methods (in the Controls: Adjuster palette) at this stage. When satisfied, click the Drop All button in the Floater List so the floaters merge with the background canvas. Now apply paints to integrate the frame into the rest of the image.

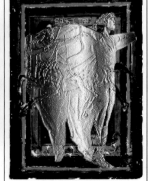

Frames and Borders *Zig Zag Border*

Horishi Yoshii

Boy

Comments

This painting was created primarily in chalk. The composition had a zig zag border region built into it. Refer to Technique #7 to see a description of how the powdery chalk effect was created.

Studio Usage

This technique describes a simple way to mask off a border region, in this case a zig zag-shaped region, for the creation of a painted border to frame the artwork.

Related Techniques

1 | Create Bézier Shape

Select the Bézier pen tool from the Tools palette to draw the outline of the border shape. Expand the canvas window by dragging on the expander square. Take the Bézier shape outside the canvas where you want the border to intersect with the edge of the image. When the shape is completed (closed), it appears in the Objects palette Floater List (click on the icon below the F. List pull-down menu).

2 | Convert Shape to Selection

Select Shapes→Convert to Selection from the top menu. The shape is now seen as a selection with a black-and-white "dancing ants" marquee. It is listed in the Objects palette Path List (accessed by clicking on the icon below the words P. List).

3 | Invert and Feather the Selection

Selecting Edit→Mask→Invert Mask inverts the selection, which now appears to be surrounded by a green-and-white "dancing ants" marquee. Select Edit→Mask→Feather Mask. The default feather is 3 pixels. You may want to increase this to 5 pixels. Click OK.

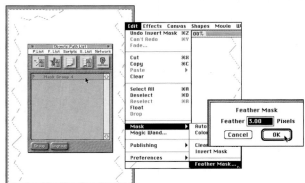

4 | Apply Paint

Select the Artist Pastel Chalk variant of the Chalk brushes in the Brushes palette. Apply this, and other brushes, in the border region. When you are ready to apply paint in the opposite region (that is now masked), simply repeat Step 3.

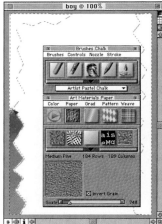

John Derry

Can

Comments

This painting was created by using a photograph of a can as a source image. The image was cloned and the Make Mosaic mode applied to the clone. With Use Clone Color checked in the Color Selector, Derry created mosaic tiles that reflected the clone source color. In addition, he painted some tiles with colors unrelated to the source image.

Studio Usage

This technique describes how to transform a photograph into a mosaic by using the clone and mosaic features of Painter. The principles can be applied to any situation where you have an image, not necessarily a photograph, and you want to transform all or part of it into a mosaic representation of the same image.

Related Techniques

1 | Make Clone of Source Photograph

Open the source photograph that will be transformed into a mosaic. Select File→Clone. An identical copy of the original photograph appears.

2 | Select Make Mosaic Mode and Adjust Settings

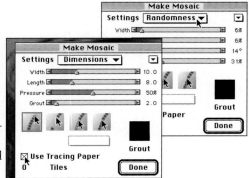

Select Canvas→Make Mosaic. The clone image goes black, the default color of the grout. Select Randomness from the pull-down Settings menu in the Make Mosaic mode dialog box. Adjust the width and length settings to give moderate randomness. Make sure that the left-hand Apply Tiles icon is selected. Test out the effect of changing the Randomness settings by painting tiles onto the image. Select the Dimensions Settings. Adjust the Width and Length sliders while painting mosaics on the image. Select Reset Mosaic from the pop-up menu in the top right-hand corner of the Make Mosaic dialog box to clear all the tiles.

3 | Use Clone Color

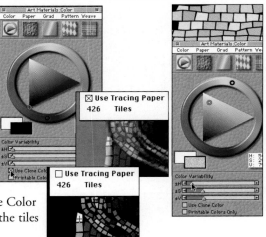

Check the Use Tracing Paper option in the Make Mosaic dialog box. The original photo shows through with 50% opacity, and the grout and mosaic tiles also are viewed at 50% opacity. On the basis of the trials in Step 2, adjust the mosaic tile dimensions to suit the scale of the section of image you want to paint. Delineate the outlines in the composition. Expand the Art Materials: Color Selection palette to see the Color Variability sliders. Check the Use Clone Color box. Paint in the mosaic tiles, following the contours of the underlying original image. Toggle tracing paper to view the mosaic tiles at 100% opacity. Adjust tile dimensions according to the region you are painting tiles onto. To add tiles in the background that do not correspond to the original image, uncheck the Use Clone Color box. Increase Hue Variability to add interesting variation in color as the tiles are laid down. Use larger tiles for flat areas of color.

4 | Render Mosaic into Mask and Apply Surface Texture

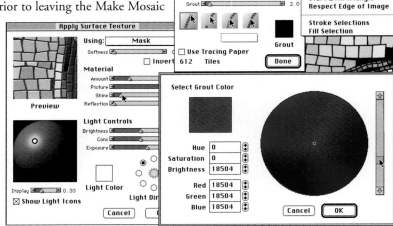

When you are satisfied with the mosaic design, select Render Tiles into Mask in the Make Mosaic pop-up menu. Prior to leaving the Make Mosaic mode, adjust the grout color by double-clicking on the grout color square. Press Done to leave Make Mosaic mode. Select Effects→Surface Control→Apply Surface Texture→Using: Mask. Reduce the Amount and Shine sliders slightly until the preview window shows the mosaic tiles rendered as three-dimensional looking tiles. Press OK.

Aleksander Jensko

Fiddler

Comments

This image was based on a photograph Jensko took of a fiddler, Thomas J. Blank. He applied a series of effects to the photograph, ending with a highly textured and posterized looking image. Posterization refers to the limiting of the color palette. Normally on a computer, you are seeing either thousands or millions of potential colors. In a posterized image, you may only be seeing a few levels of color.

Studio Usage

The application of the Posterize command in Painter, which allows you to reduce the number of levels of color in the image, can be enhanced by combining it with other effects, such as Color Overlay, Equalize, and Sharpen. Painter is a 24-bit color program. If your computer's display supports 24-bit color, each pixel in each image has 24 bits of binary information defining color. Thus, over 16 million distinct colors can be defined. Posterization in Painter approximates the effect of working with less color. Every pixel still has 24 bits defining color and the image is still a 24-bit color image.

Related Techniques

1 | Apply Color Overlay

Open up a scanned photograph. Click on the Color icon in the Art Materials palette. Select a color in the Color Selector that you want to imbue the image with. Select Effects→Surface Control→Color Overlay. Select Using: Uniform Color and Model: Hiding Power in the Color Overlay dialog box. Adjust the Opacity slider until you are satisfied with the Preview. Click OK.

Note: *Hiding Power means that the color covers up the image behind it.*

2 | Equalize

Select Effects→Tonal Control→ Equalize (⌘-E) {Ctrl-E}. Adjust the Black and White points and the Brightness slider (which actually adjusts the gray point or gamma). Click OK. Equalize has the effect of boosting contrast and giving you the control over which regions of the image become pure black or pure white.

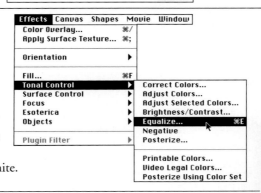
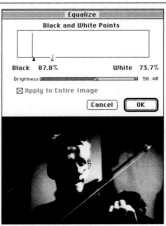

3 | Posterize

Select Effects→Tonal Control→Posterize. Select the number of levels of color. Experiment with different numbers and observe the difference they make in the Preview window. In this case, six levels were used. Click OK.

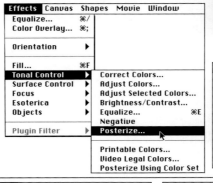

4 | Sharpen

Select Effects→Focus→Sharpen. Adjust the Radius slider slightly. Observe the contrast difference that that setting makes in the Preview window. When satisfied, click OK.

Note: *As a way to further enhance your image, you can now create a clone (File→ Clone) and clone the image into itself using, for example, a Chalk cloner to give a more textured effect.*

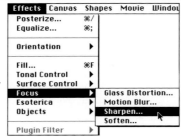
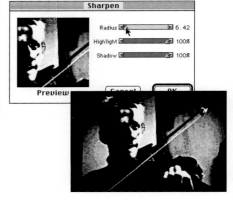

Transforming Photographs *Glowing Globe*

Judy York

Summons

Comments

This image was primarily painted from scratch. The lady holding the glowing globe was introduced from a photographic source and then painted over. Many interesting techniques using Painter were employed in this image to create effects such as the stone texture of the stairwell, the atmospheric lighting, and the eerie moon in the background. This technique focuses on the way that York achieved the glow around the globe.

Studio Usage

This technique shows how to create a luminous glowing effect around a lighted globe. You'll learn how to select the globe and rod, copy them to the clipboard for later use, and then repeatedly fill the feathered globe selection with a luminous yellow hue. The globe and rod are finally pasted back into the image. The glow appears to be emanating from the globe. The procedure described here can be applied to any situation where you wish to introduce a glowing effect around a lighted object.

Related Techniques

1 | Select the Globe

Select the Oval Selection tool. Drag over the globe while holding down the Shift key to achieve a perfectly circular selection. The position and the size of the circular selection are unlikely to precisely match the globe. Select the Selection Adjuster tool. Click and drag within the selection to move its position above the globe. Hold down the Shift key and drag a corner handle to adjust its size.

2 | Select the Rod

Select the Lasso freehand selection tool. Drag a selection around the portion of the rod immediately below the globe, making sure that it overlaps into the globe. The result may be an open shape with linked Bézier points instead of a closed selection. If that is the case, click the Close button in the Controls palette to produce a closed selection. The selection appears in the Path List as Shape 2, or something similar. Select Edit→Copy.

3 | Feather the Globe Selection and Fill It with Glow

Click once on the black dotted circle symbol to the left of the path name in the Path List that signifies the selection around the rod (Shape 2 or similar). The symbol now appears as a faint gray circle. This inactivates that selection (it can be reactivated at any time by clicking again on the circle symbol). Click on the globe selection path name. Select the Path Adjuster tool. Slide the Feather slider in the Controls palette to the right (about 40). Select Effects→Fill. The default will fill with the current color. Set the color in the Color Selector to the desired glow color. Apply the Fill. Repeat this as many times as necessary to achieve a sufficient glow. In this example it was repeated 6 times.

4 | Paste Back the Original Globe and Rod

Select Edit→Paste→Normal. The original selection of the globe and rod now reappear as a single floater. Use the floater Adjuster tool to reposition the floater precisely over its original location. The glow now appears to be emanating from the globe. Click the Drop button in the Floater List to merge the floater with the background canvas.

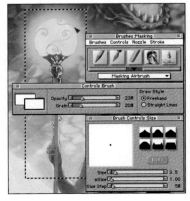

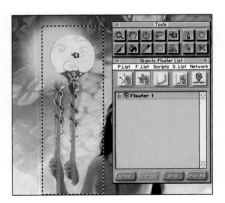

Banana Blossom

© S. Swaminathan, Golden Light Imagery

Comments

This painting was based on a photograph of a banana blossom that inspired Swaminathan. He wanted to bring out the dramatic beauty and brilliance of the blossom and achieved that effect by increasing the contrast between the blossom and the background.

Studio Usage

This technique describes how to create a controlled increase in contrast for dramatic effect. It involves isolating the two main elements in the composition, in this case the blossom and the surrounding leaves, and then applying different effects and brushes to each section in turn, building up to a more dramatic image.

Related Techniques

1 | Equalize

Open the source photograph. Select Effects→Tonal Control→ Equalize (⌘-E) {Ctrl-E}. There is an automatic contrast adjustment that occurs as the Equalization dialog box appears. Slide the black, white, and gray points slightly in both directions to see how they affect the image. Select OK when satisfied with this initial increase in contrast. The Equalization effect gives more control than the Brightness/Contrast sliders

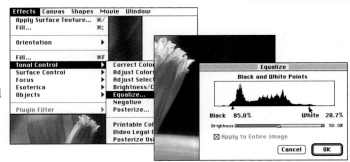

2 | Select the Blossom

Select Edit→Magic Wand. Drag the Magic Wand through the blossom. It is likely that the selection, as indicated in red, will be incomplete. In that case, continue dragging the Magic Wand in the holes (those areas that were not included in the initial selection), while holding down the Shift key. This will enlarge the selection of contiguous pixels to include a wider range of color. When the blossom is completely selected, press OK.

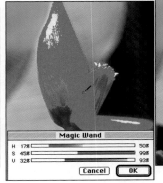

3 | Increase Saturation

Select Effects→Tonal Control→Adjust Colors. Keep the default Using: Uniform Color. Move the Saturation slider all the way to the right to transform the pale pink into a bright pink and add a yellow tint to the blossom contour.

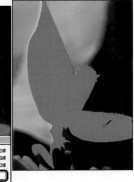

4 | Deepen Shadows with Burn Tool

Select the Burn tool in the Brushes palette. Increase the Opacity slider in the Controls palette to 18%. Apply the Burn tool to the shadowy areas in the blossom. Because the blossom is selected, you can use this tool to sharpen the contrast with the surrounding leaf.

5 | Invert Selection and Adjust Dye Concentration

Select Edit→Mask→Invert Mask to invert the selection to include everything except the blossom.
Open the drawer in the Art Materials: Papers palette. Click on the Library button. Select the Papers library called Wild Textures. Select the paper grain called Angle Weave. Select Effects→Surface Control→Dye Concentration→Using: Paper Grain. Adjust the maximum and minimum sliders to see their effect. Click OK. This effect results in the textured look of the background.

Transforming Photographs *Emphasizing a Misty Contour*

Miller Creek

Ken Milburn

Comments

This painting was created from a photograph of Miller Creek in Marin County, California. Milburn worked considerably with the Distorto and Water brushes to enhance the atmosphere of the picture.

Studio Usage

This technique describes how to emphasize a contour while maintaining the feel of a misty morning. It involves moving the dark tones toward the contour, selectively darkening the edges, softening details within the forms, and applying a subtle grain to the final artwork.

Related Techniques

1 | Push Dark Pixels to Edge

Select the Distorto brush variant from the Liquid brush family in the Brushes palette. Drag from the lighter regions in the mountain toward the horizon where the mountain meets the sky, in the process pushing darker tones to the edge.

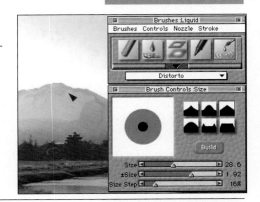

2 | Apply Burn Tool

Select the Burn tool in the Brushes palette. Increase the Opacity slider in the Controls palette to about 18%. Access the Brush Size palette from the Brushes→Controls menu. The default Burn brush size is quite large. Reduce it to about 26. Gently stroke the very edge of the horizon, bringing out darkness and saturation around the contour.

3 | Smooth with Just Add Water

Select the Just Add Water variant from the Water brush family. Soften the structure within the mountain by applying the Just Add Water. This gives a watery smooth blending of color.

4 | Adjust Dye Concentration

As the final stage in the artwork, open the Papers library drawer in the Art Materials palette. Click on the Library button. Select More Paper Textures library. Select the grain called Syn. Super Fine. Select Effects→Surface Control→Dye Concentration to get the effect of adding "noise" to the image, helping produce the misty atmosphere.

Note: *If the noise is too strong, use the Edit→Fade function to reduce the amount of application of the effect.*

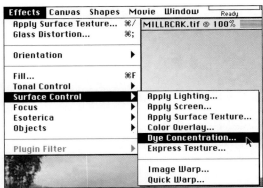

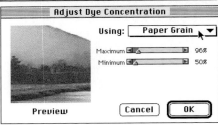

Transforming Photographs *Adding Drama through Use of Lights and Distortion*

Richard Noble

Tropical Palms

Comments

This is part of a series of paintings based on color slides taken by Noble in southern California. Noble scanned the slide and opened it in Painter. He experimented with the Effects→Tonal Control→Correct Colors by using the Curve and Freehand adjustments. When satisfied with the result, he made a clone of the image and applied a variety of clone brushes to give a painterly look. His final stage in this image was to apply the Lighting effect, throwing brightly colored spots on his painting, and then to distort the painting's proportions, stretching it width-wise.

Studio Usage

The dramatic atmosphere in a painting can be enhanced by the application of colored lights and by altering the proportions of the image. Both operations are explained in this technique.

Related Techniques

Transforming Lighting
from Day to Night   51

Transforming Images
to Shadowy Forms   57

1 | Apply Lighting

Open an image that has been partially completed but needs a final dramatic touch of color and reproportioning. Select Effects→Surface Control→Apply Lighting. Select the Splashy Colors lighting option in the Apply Lighting dialog box. Move the light sources by dragging the larger circles in the Preview window. Change the angle at which the light is projected by dragging the smaller circle (limited to rotational movement). Adjust the light color by double-clicking in the box entitled Light Color. In a similar way, make the Ambient Color a warmer color. To add light sources, simply click in the Preview window. To remove light sources, click on them and then press the Delete key. For each light source, experiment with the sliders to fine-tune their effect. Click OK.

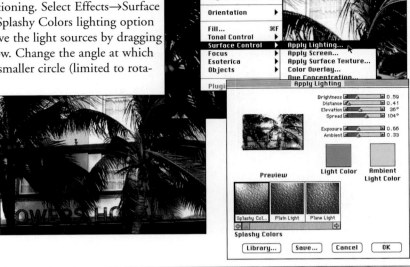

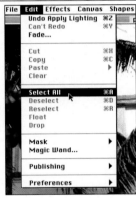

2 | Select All

Select Edit→Select All (⌘-A) {Ctrl-A}.

3 | Resize Canvas

Select Canvas→Canvas Size. Add the same number of pixels to the left and to the right. In this case, 100 pixels were added to each side (about 30% total increase in the canvas width). Click OK.

4 | Scale Selection

Select Effects→Orientation→Scale. The selection is now converted into a floater, with control handles appearing around the perimeter of the selection. Uncheck the Constrain Aspect Ration option in the Scale Selection dialog box. Leave the Preserve Center option checked. Drag the small control handle in the middle of either side of the selection to the edge of the canvas. Click OK. The image has now been stretched to fill the resized canvas.

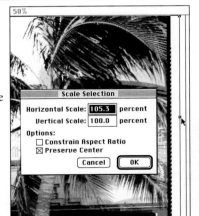

Transforming Photographs *Replacing Sky with a Two-Point Gradient*

Birds of Rio del Mar Beach

Comments

This dramatic image of seagulls was based on a less dramatic photograph. Swaminathan isolated the seagulls from the sky and increased their contrast to make them stand out. He then replaced the original sky with a two-point gradient and finished by lightly applying the Burn tool around each bird while the birds were masked.

Studio Usage

This technique describes how to modify a photograph by replacing the sky with a gradation and emphasizing the foreground objects. The principles applied can be useful in many different circumstances where the background of an image can be replaced to enhance the elements in it.

Related Techniques

1 | Select Birds

Select Edit→Select All. Select Edit→Magic Wand. Click in one of the birds. Some of the birds now appear red, which indicates that those regions are included in the Magic Wand selection. Hold the Shift key and drag through the unselected parts of the bird until all the bird regions appear red. Click OK.

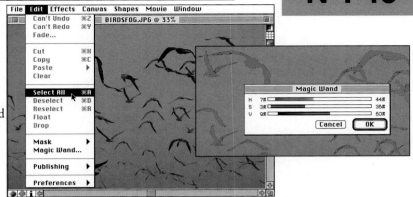

2 | Increase Contrast and Reverse Selection

Select Effects→Tonal Control→Equalize. Adjust the Black-and-White points until you see the birds reach optimum contrast. Click OK. Select Edit→Mask→Invert Mask to reverse the selection. The selection is now surrounded by green-and-white "marching ants."

3 | Fill Sky with Gradation

Select Primary and Secondary colors, that you want to be the two end points of the sky gradation. Use the Color Selector. Open the Gradation library in the Art Materials palette. Select the Two-Point Gradation and close the library drawer. Drag the small, spherical slider in the Gradation palette to orient the gradation, which uses the Primary and Secondary colors as its end points. Orient the gradation at an angle with the red in the lower right. Select Effects→Fill. The Fill With: Gradation should be selected in the Fill dialog box. Click OK.

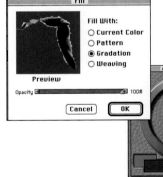

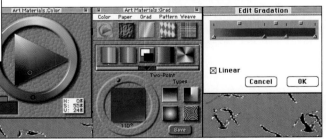

4 | Finish with Burn Tool

Select the Burn brush in the Brushes palette. Increase the Opacity slider in the Controls palette to about 30%. Decrease the Size slider in the Brushes: Size palette. Lightly apply the Burn brush around the birds. The birds remain unaffected because they are outside the active selection and are therefore masked from the effect of brushes.

Transforming Photographs *Color Enhancement with Multiple Floaters*

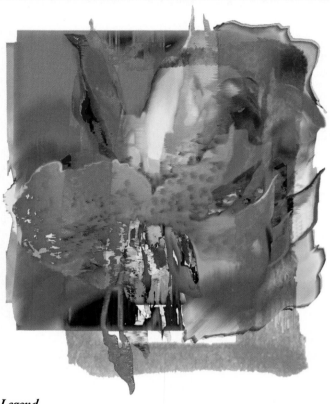

Judith Moncrieff

Legend

Comments

This image was created as part of a triptych entitled *Legend, Myths and Lilies* (see the illustration next to Step 5). *Legend* was based on a photograph of a lily. Identical copies of this photograph were layered on top of each other as floaters. Moncrieff then took two or three layers at a time and adjusted their hues, saturations, and values and changed their Composite Methods. She flattened the group of floaters into a single layer and repeated this process with other layers. She ended up with six layers with various Composite Methods. The final step was to drop all floaters and apply small amounts of the Smeary Mover Liquid brush and the Ultrafine Eraser.

Studio Usage

Painter offers a vast array of ways to enhance and alter colors in an image. The use of multiple identical floaters stacked up on one another is a powerful way to control and experiment with color. This technique describes a basic manipulation of two floaters to create highly saturated bright colors from an original photograph. This process can be repeated with more floaters, layered on top of each other, as in this example by Moncrieff. Interesting series of related images can be created in this way.

Related Techniques

1 | Select Original Image

Select the Bézier Pen tool in the Tools palette. Create a shape that completely outlines the image you want to use as a basis for a floater. When the shape is closed, click on the Make Selection button in the Controls: Shape Design palette. Select the Lasso Selection tool. Check the Subtract From Selection in the Controls: Lasso palette. Draw around any regions within the outline that should not be part of the image selection.

2 | Make Multiple Floaters and Change Composite Method of Top Floater

Select Edit→Copy. Open and select the canvas on which you want to build the final image. Select Edit→Paste→Normal. Repeat this Paste command a second time. There are now two identical floaters layered on top of one another. Click on the F. List icon in the Objects palette to reveal the Floater List. Click on the floater name at the top of the Floater List. Make sure that the Floater Adjuster tool is selected in the Tools palette. Select Pseudocolor from the Composite Method pull-down menu in the Controls: Adjuster palette.

3 | Adjust Colors in the Bottom Floater

Select the bottom floater. Select Effects→ Tonal Control→Correct Colors. Select Curve in the Color Correction dialog box. Click on each color square in turn and adjust the appropriate curve. Click OK.

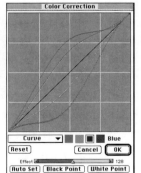

4 | Collapse Floaters into a Single Floater and Adjust Colors

Select both floaters by clicking on their names in the Floater List while holding down the Shift key. Click on the Group button followed by the Collapse button, both in the Floater List palette. Then apply Effects→Tonal Control→Adjust Colors by using either Uniform Color or Image Luminance. The Hue Shift slider can give dramatic changes in color.

Transforming Photographs *Heavy Oil Look*

Tea Kettle

Ken Milburn

Comments

This painting was created from the photograph of a tea kettle and then transformed into the look of a thick oil painting.

Studio Usage

This technique describes how to create the effect of thick oil painting based on a photographic source image. It clones an image into itself by using a thick oil brush and then applying an embossing surface texture effect to give the paint the look of standing out in three dimensions.

Related Techniques

1 | Clone Photograph

Open the digital photographic image. Select File→Clone to create an identical copy of the original photograph. Select File→Clone Source and note that the original image name has a check by it and is assigned as the source of clone color.

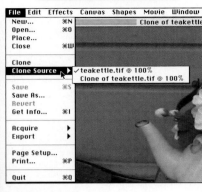

Note: *Save the clone image (File→Save As) onto the hard drive of your computer so that you can easily update the working document by selecting File→Save (⌘-S) {Ctrl-S}.*

2 | Create Black Outline

Select the Artist Pastel Chalk variant in the Chalk brush family of the Brushes palette. Make sure that the Brushes palette is expanded (upper right square icon) so that you can see the Method and Method Subcategory menus below the Variant menu. Select Buildup from the Method pull-down menu followed by Grainy Soft Buildup from the Method Subcategory. Select black in the Color Selector. Select Controls→Size in the Brushes palette submenu. Adjust the brush size slider to give a medium thick black brush stroke. Use this brush to outline your composition in black.

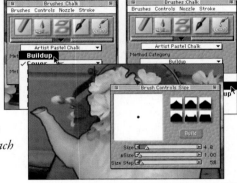

Note: *You can check how the actual brush stroke thickness on your image varies as you adjust the brush size slider by doing a series of test strokes, each followed by Edit→Undo Brush Stroke(⌘-Z) {Ctrl-Z}.*

3 | Apply Loaded Oils Using Clone Color

Select the Loaded Oils variant from the Brush family of brushes in the Brushes palette. Expand the Color Selector in the Art Materials palette to show the Color Variability sliders below the hue wheel. Check the Use Clone Color box. Start painting over the clone image with this brush. Note that the Loaded Oils brush picks up color from the point where the stroke begins and then drags that color through the stroke. You can use this to emphasize highlights or shadows. Adjust the brush size to suit the region of the image you are working in.

Note: *The Use Clone Color option directs the currently selected brush to look at the clone source, in this case the original photograph, for determining color.*

4 | Apply Surface Texture Using Image Luminance

When completed with the application of the Loaded Oils brush over the whole image, select Effects→Surface Control→Apply Surface Texture. Select Using: Image Luminance in the Apply Surface Texture dialog box.

Note: *Save your clone image prior to applying the surface texture effect. This gives you the flexibility to go back to the pre-effect stage. It also enables you to create multiple versions of a painting with different effects settings.*

Transforming Photographs *Enhancing a Polaroid Transfer Print*

Photography: Lisa Fenwick; Digital Enhancement: Jeremy Sutton

Madonna and Child

Comments

This image is based on a 3" by 3.75" Polaroid transfer print on watercolor paper. The original image was very washed out. The mother and child's faces were not tonally crisp or well defined. After scanning the print at high resolution (600 pixels per inch), a series of effects were applied to the image to enhance the overall image quality and, in particular, make the mother and child stand out from the background. The final step in creating this image was selecting the central portion of the image and expressing a gradation in that selected region.

Studio Usage

This technique explains how to create a more visual focus in a washed out photographic image and make the central figures more prominent. This is achieved by applying the Just Add Water brush to selectively soften and blend; applying the clone brushes to bring out darks; applying the eraser to bring out highlights; and muting background tones and colors.

Related Techniques

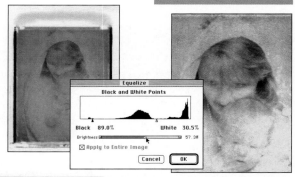

1 | Apply Equalize Effect

With a clone of the original scanned image open, select Effects→Tonal Control→Equalize. Adjust the Black and White points and the Brightness slider until the contrast is optimized. Click OK.

2 | Use Just Add Water to Blend Skin

Select the Just Add Water variant of the Water family of brushes in the Brushes palette. Select Controls→Size in the Brushes palette pull-down submenu. Adjust the Size slider to give a reasonably sized brush diameter. Reduce the Opacity slider in the Controls: Brush palette to about 14%. Gently apply the water to the skin regions of the image, stroking in the direction of the face contours. This softening creates contrast with the grainy background. Reduce the Size slider and increase the Opacity to 100%. Apply this thin water brush in the hair.

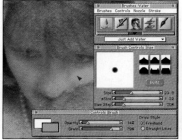
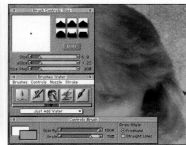

3 | Apply Cloning for Darkest Tones

Select the Soft Cloner variant of the Cloners brushes. Adjust the Size slider to make the brush diameter small in comparison with the details you want to emphasize by bringing out the darkest tones. Reduce the Opacity slider to about 8%. Hold down the Control {Shift} key and click in the darkest region of the image. Carefully clone in the dark tones into the pupil and other regions in the face. You will need to go back and reset the clone starting point every time you move to a new position.

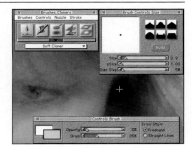

4 | Apply Eraser for Highlights

Select the Dropper tool and click on a point in the image with a light hue. Select Canvas→Set Paper Color to determine the color that appears when any of the eraser brush variants are applied. Select the Small Eraser variant of the Eraser brush family. Select a medium size brush diameter and low opacity (about 3%). Gently stroke regions where you want highlights.

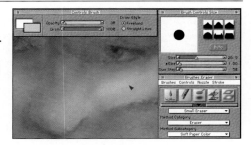

5 | Apply White Color Overlay to Background

Select white in the Color Selector. Select the Lasso selection tool and create a selection around the central figures. Select Edit→Mask→Invert Mask to invert the selection. Select Effects→Surface Control→Color Overlay. Select Using: Image Luminance and Model: Hiding Power in the Color Overlay dialog box. Adjust the Color Overlay Opacity slider to about 5% for a subtle overlay of white. Click OK.

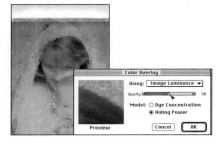

Rosemary Hendler

Poinsettias

Comments

This painting was based on a photograph that was transformed by using a combination of cover brushes, cloning brushes, and the application of the Leaky Pen splattering effect. Hendler likes to use customized color sets from which she can easily sample and go back to specific colors repeatedly without the need to duplicate them on the Color Selector or use the Dropper tool (or Command key) every time. In this case, she created a custom color set based on colors sampled from the original photograph, as well as others she added independent of the original image. The color set can also have the advantage of giving a clear visual summary of the color range of the painting.

Studio Usage

When you want to use a consistent color palette for a particular painting, or series of paintings, it can be useful to create a customized Color Set. The colors can then be selected just by clicking in the Color Set without needing to change the tool or hold down any keys to pick a color. The technique of creating, adding to, and saving a Color Set is described here.

Related Techniques

Acrylic Colors   23

1 | Open New Color Set

Select Color→Adjust Color Set from the pull-down submenu in the Art Materials palette. Click on New Set. A small palette top bar appears with Color Set written on it.

Note: Because the empty Color Set to bar is so small, it is possible to think that nothing has happened when you click on New Set. If you have a visually cluttered desktop, you may have to look carefully to locate the new Color Set.

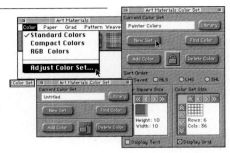

2 | Sample Color to Add to Color Set

Select the Dropper tool in the Tools palette. Open the source image from which you will sample the colors. Click on the first color you want to add to the color set.

3 | Add Color to Color Set

Click on the Add Color button in the Color Set palette. The color sampled in Step 2 now appears as the first color square in the new Color Set. Continue this process of sampling colors and then adding them to the Color Set. When you are ready to save the Color Set, click the close button on the top left corner of the Color Set. The Color Set closes and is no longer visible.

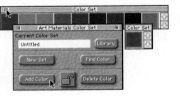

4 | Save Color Set

Click on the Library button. A dialog box asks if you want to save changes made to the current Color Set. Click Save. Name the Color Set and save it in the Color, Weaves, Grads folder within the Painter 4 applications folder. Click Save. A dialog box appears asking you to select a Color Set to open. Select the newly named, custom Color Set and reopen it.

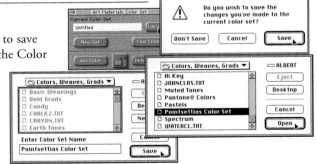

5 | Apply Colors

The new Color Set reappears. Click on the color squares in the new Color Set to select that particular color.

Note: The expanded Color Set palette gives you the ability to control the size and arrangement of the colors. By double-clicking on each color in turn and checking the Display Text box, you can individually identify each color by name.

Transforming Photographs *Transforming Lighting from Day to Night*

The Crossword Puzzle Doer

Nancy Vachani

Comments

This composition was created from a digital camera image of an early morning coffee shop scene near the University of California campus at Berkeley. The original canvas size was enlarged and the composition extended out to fill in the blank space around the original photo. The atmosphere was radically changed by adjusting tones and colors in the image and applying lighting effects. Cloning with oil brushes was also used extensively to create a more painterly feel to the image in the manner of Edward Hopper.

Studio Usage

This technique describes how to alter an ordinary daytime lighting photo to a more dramatic evening lighting effect. Unwanted glass reflections and other distracting elements in the photo were changed or removed. Fuzzy background details, originally obscured by sunlight reflections, were enhanced. Colors of specific image elements were changed to suit the new lighting conditions. The Apply Lighting effect was used to change the light source and ambient light color.

Related Techniques

Adding Drama through
Use of Lights and Distortion   45

1 | Clone Image and Remove Reflections

Open an image. Select File→Clone to make a clone copy of the image. With the Dropper tool, select nearby colors and sketch over the image lightly with the airbrush. Select the Thick Oil variant of the Liquid brushes family in the Brushes palette. Work over the same area with that brush, bringing out the part that you want to highlight.

Note: Working on a clone copy has the added benefit of keeping the original photo unaltered and allowing the convenient application of oil brushes with or without the use of the clone color.

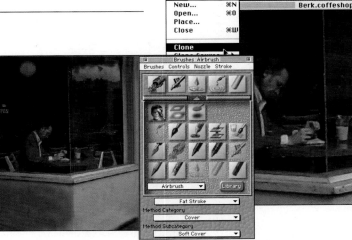

2 | Apply Lighting Effect

Open Effects→Surface Control→Apply Lighting. In order to highlight the central figure, select the lighting option called Center Spot lighting. Each light source is represented in the Apply Lighting Preview window by two circles, one slightly larger than the other, joined together by a short line. Click on the larger circle of one of the light sources and drag it close to the ceiling light fixture. Click on the smaller circle of the same light source and rotate its position so the light is directed downwards. Repeat this for other light sources. In this manner you'll create a realistic lighting effect that fits in with the picture. Double-click on the Light Color box. A color selector appears. Select a warm yellow. Click OK in the color selector dialog box. Double-click on the Ambient Light Color box. Select a warm beige. Move the sliders for Brightness, Distance, Spread, Exposure, and Ambience to different positions until the right effect is achieved. Click OK.

Note: If the Apply Lighting effect is too strong, the Edit→Fade menu can be applied afterwards.

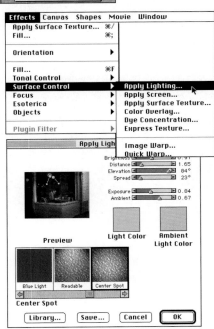

3 | Adjust Color

With the Rectangular or Lasso Selection tool, select an area that needs its color adjusted to reflect the change from daytime to evening lighting. In this example, the white bricks were selected. Select Effects→Tonal Control→Adjust Colors. Select Uniform Color from the Using pull-down menu in the Adjust Colors dialog box. Adjust the Hue, Saturation, and Value sliders until an appropriate red color is found, more appropriate to an evening lighting effect.

Note: A similar process was applied to the jacket of the crossword doer, changing it from brown to blue.

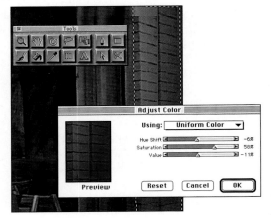

Lilith

Judith Moncrieff

Comments

This image combines a background of trilliums with a multilayered lily. The background was created by using two identical layers, or floaters, and applying the Glass Distortion effect. The resulting pattern was then taken into Adobe Photoshop and color adjusted, using Image→Adjust→Variations. The lily was made into multiple identical floaters, which were then set to have different Composite Methods to achieve the final look. Moncrieff likes to work with multiple floaters for the greater flexibility and room for experimentation that they allow.

Studio Usage

This technique describes one way that you can introduce variation into a photograph, primarily using the Glass Distortion effect. The source image, in this case a photograph of trilliums, is made into two layers (floater and background), each of which is treated differently to achieve the final result.

Related Techniques

Color Enhancement with Multiple Floaters   47

Pumping Up Highlights with Pure White   71

Texturizing Photographs   94

Torn Paper   104

1 | Create Floater

Open your background image. Select Edit→Select All
(⌘-A) {Ctrl-A}. Select Edit→Float. Copy (⌘-C) {Ctrl-C}
and then paste (⌘-V) {Ctrl-V} the floater to create a second identical one. Click on the F. List icon in the Objects
palette to open the Floater List where the floater is listed.

*Note: An alternative way to generate a duplicate floater is to
click on the floater with the Floater Adjuster tool while holding down the Option {Alt} key.*

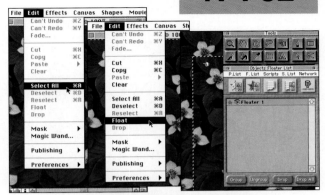

2 | Reverse Out

With the floater active (highlighted in the Floater List) and the Floater
Adjuster Tool selected, change the Composite Method in the Controls:
Adjuster palette to Reverse Out.

*Note: This step is equivalent to applying Effects→Tonal Control→Negative
to a flat (single layered) image.*

3 | Apply First Glass Distortion

Click on the eye icon next to the floater name in the Floater
List. You'll make the floater invisible so that you just see the
underlying background. Click in the gray space below the
floater name in the Floater List to deselect it (it should no
longer be highlighted). Select Effects→Focus→Glass
Distortion. Select Using: Image Luminance and Map: Angle
Displacement in the Glass Distortion dialog box. Adjust the
Softness slider slightly. Click OK.

*Note: After the floater is deselected, any effects applied are applied to
the background canvas, not to the floater.*

4 | Apply Second Glass Distortion

Click on the Paper icon in the Art Materials palette. Make sure that
Basic Paper is the selected grain. Repeat Step 3, but this time select
Using: Paper Grain and Map: Refraction in the Glass Distortion
dialog box. Adjust the Amount slider until the desired amount of
distortion is achieved. You can see in the Preview window how the
effect will look when applied. Click OK.

*Note: It is advisable to save a version of the file in RIFF format
with all the floaters preserved before you click Drop All in the
Floater List to flatten the final image, or save it in a format other
than RIFF (which also flattens the image). The advantage of saving the floaters is the flexibility you have to try out different effects
with the image.*

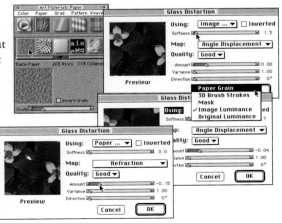

Transforming Photographs *Applying Texture with Variations*

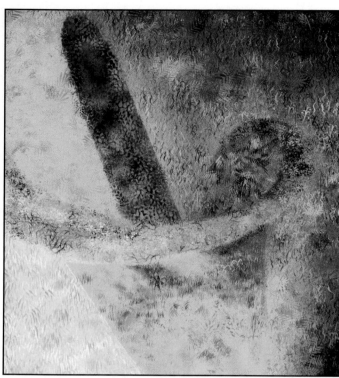

© S. Swaminathan, Golden Light Imagery

Calla Lily

Comments

This painting is a combination of cloning from an original photograph of a Calla lily blossom and the addition of painted texture. A lot of different textures were used in this image, including many from the Trees and Leaves collection. The opacity, scale, and color of the textures was varied as they were applied, building up a richness of the image.

Studio Usage

This technique describes how to vary the orientation, opacity, scale, and color of paper grain as it is applied to an image using a Chalk brush. The original photograph is transformed into a rich, textured composition that preserves the main forms but is much more colorful.

Related Techniques

1 | Open New Document for Rotating Texture

Select File→New (⌘-N) {Ctrl-N} and open a new document 100 pixels by 100 pixels. This is going to be used to rotate a texture for use in cloning from a photograph. Open the Papers library drawer in the Art Materials Palette. Click on the Library button and select the Wild Textures library. Select the Long Grain paper grain from that library.

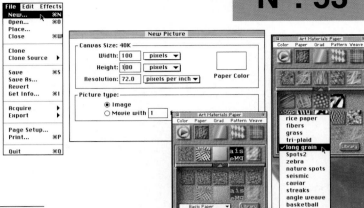

2 | Rotate Texture

Select Pattern→Define Pattern from the Art Materials palette pull-down menu. Select the Large Chalk variant of the Chalk brush family in the Brushes palette and select black in the Art Materials Color Selector. Apply brush strokes in the small document until the grain is uniformly visible in all regions of the square. Select Edit→Select All. Select Effects→Orientation→ Rotate. Type in 90. The grain pattern is rotated through 90 degrees. Open the F. List in the Objects palette. Click on the Drop All button.

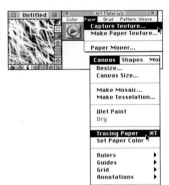

3 | Capture Texture and Clone Photograph

Select Edit→Select All. Select Paper→Capture Texture from the Art Materials pull-down menu. Name the texture. It is now part of the current texture library. Open the photographic source image. Select File→Clone. Select Edit→Select All and then Delete {Backspace}. Select Canvas→Tracing Paper to activate the Tracing Paper and see the underlying source image showing through.

4 | Apply Color, Scale, and Opacity Variability

Expand the Art Materials Color Selector. Adjust the sliders to give variability of hue, saturation, and value. Click on the Use Clone Color box. Apply the Large Chalk to the image. Open the expanded Papers palette with the library drawer closed to access the grain scale slider. Vary the grain scale as you apply paint. Also vary the Opacity slider in the Controls palette. Try inverting the texture, as well.

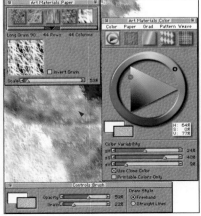

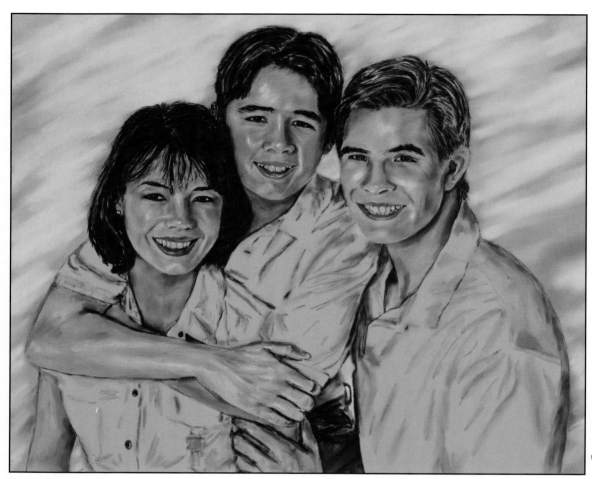

Nomi Wagner

The Hillman Kids

Comments

This drawing is an example of how a photograph can be transformed into a sepia tone drawing. The original photograph was adjusted to increase its contrast and sharpness. This adjustment allowed the details to be more easily visible when used as a visual reference with tracing paper. A freehand drawing was then created. The outline was established by using the original image as a visual reference. A Masking brush was used to mask out the figures in the composition and work on the background.

Studio Usage

This technique explains how to create a freehand sepia tone drawing based on a photograph. It involves the creation of a clone image of the original photograph. This clone image is then cleared and filled with a background sepia tone. The freehand drawing is then drawn by using the original image in tracing paper mode as a visual reference.

Related Techniques

1 | Increase Contrast and Sharpness in Scanned Photograph

Open the original scanned photograph. Select
Effects→Tonal Control→Equalize (⌘-E) {Ctrl-E}.
Adjust the black-and-white point sliders to increase
contrast in the image without losing detail. Click OK.
Select Effects→
Focus→Sharpen
and click OK.

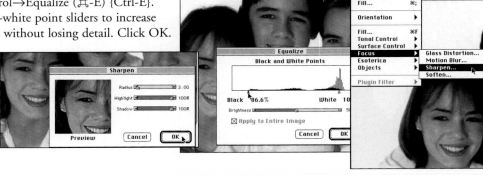

2 | Make Clone and Turn On Tracing Paper

Select File→Clone to make a clone copy of the image. Select Edit→Select
All followed by the Delete key to clear the clone image. Select Canvas→
Tracing Paper to turn the tracing paper on. You can now see the underlying
image at 50% opacity.

3 | Fill with Sepia Tone Background and Apply Crayon

Select a light sepia tone in the Art Materials Color Selector. Select
Effects→Fill. The Fill With Current Color option should be checked.
Click OK. The clone image now fills with the sepia tone. Open the
Papers palette within the Art Materials palette. Select the Basic paper
grain. Select the Default Crayon variant in the Brushes palette. Access
the Brush Size adjuster from the Controls→Size pull-down menu in the
Brushes palette. Adjust the +/- Size slider to the right and
reduce the Size slider to suit the scale of the image. Select
Controls→ Sliders. In the Advanced Controls: Sliders
palette, drag the leftmost slider up to Pressure so that the
brush size varies with stylus pressure. Choose a darker sepia
tone in the Color Selector and use the tracing paper image of
the original photograph to make an outline. Select
Canvas→Tracing Paper to turn the tracing paper off.
Continue applying sepia tones in the shading.

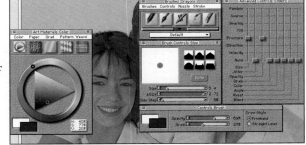

4 | Add Highlights with Eraser and Blend with Water

Select the Small Eraser variant of the Eraser brush
family. Lower the Opacity slider in the Controls
palette to about 9%. Apply the eraser with light
pressure to create soft highlights. Select the Just
Add Water variant of the Water brush family to
blend differing tones together in the skin.

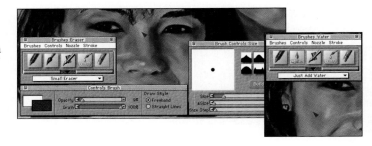

Transforming Photographs *Expressionistic Brush Strokes*

Gary Clark

Deja' View

Comments

This painting combines the painting over of a photograph with the cloning in of textures and colors from other photographs and imagery. The main source image on which the composition is based was a photograph taken with a high quality, digital back camera. The photograph was opened as a grayscale image, and the Painter's Water, Chalk, and Liquid brush tools were used to build up the main areas of tone and color. The finer details and textures were added later with small, grainy brushes. Highlights were brought out with controlled application of the Dodge and Bleach tools.

Studio Usage

This technique describes how to transform a grayscale landscape photograph into a rich, expressionistic painterly scene. The principles can be applied to any photographic image. The photograph serves as a compositional base from which the painting is subsequently built.

Related Techniques

1 | Convert Photograph to Grayscale

Open the color photographic image. Select Effects→Surface Control→Express Texture. Select Using: Image Luminance in the Express Texture dialog box. Adjust the Gray Threshold, Grain, and Contrast settings until the preview image shows an appropriate amount of grayscale detail and tone. Click OK.

Note: Click and drag on the image in the preview in the Express Texture dialog box to check all regions of the opened image. Be wary of adjusting for one section of the image while another section becomes too dark or too light.

2 | Apply Just Add Water

Select the Just Add Water variant of the Water brush family in the Brushes palette. Select the Controls→Size in the Brushes palette pull-down menu. Adjust the Size slider to give a brush stroke width that suits the scale of the painting. At this stage the brushes are being used to form rough areas of common tone so the brush need not be too small. Blur similarly toned adjacent regions of the image into one another. Be loose with your brush strokes because details can be added later.

3 | Apply Chalk

Select the Large Chalk from the Chalk brushes family. Change the shape of the brush (as defined by the icons in the Brush Controls: Size palette) to the flat-topped one. Click the Build button. Adjust the size as in Step 2. Click on the Color icon in the Art Materials palette to reveal the Color Selector. Expand the Art Materials: Color palette by clicking on the expander button in the top right-hand corner. Add Hue, Saturation, and Value variability by adjusting the sliders. Pick a color in the Color Selector to suit the area of the image you want to work on. Apply the chalk in that area. Work around the image going back and forth to the Color Selector. Click and drag the Paper icon from the Art Materials palette to tear off the Art Materials: Paper palette. Vary the selected paper grain as you paint. Expand the Paper palette. Close the Papers library drawer and adjust the scale of the paper grain as you paint.

4 | Apply Smeary Brushes

Select the Smeary Bristles variant in the Liquid brush family. Select the flat-topped brush shape. Hold down the Command {Control} key, which turns the Brush temporarily into the Dropper tool, and then sample color in the image. Apply the Smeary Bristles brush in that region. As in Step 3, change the paper grain as you paint to add richness and variety to the brush strokes.

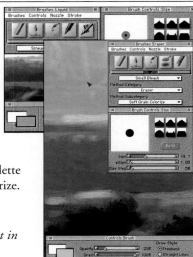

5 | Apply Bleach

Select the Small Bleach variant of the Eraser brush family. Expand the Brushes palette and change the Method Subcategory from Soft Paint Remover to Soft Paint Colorize. Sample lighter colors in the image and apply the bleach in areas that you want to highlight.

Note: The Dodge and Burn tools are useful at this stage for adding additional contrast in the image.

Transforming Photographs *Customized Cubist Blurring*

Cicero Civil Rights Riot

Comments

Swaminathan took the original slide transparency, on which this image was based, in 1966 during a civil rights march through Cicero, Illinois. He caught the moment when the antagonistic crowd threatened a black National Guardsman. Swaminathan's own experience of racism when he revisited Cicero 30 years later led him to create this painting. Swaminathan wanted to emphasize the Guardsman and applied a cubist blur, via a cloning brush, to the surrounding figures in the photograph. He also adjusted brightness, contrast, and color balance.

Studio Usage

When you want to create the effect of some part of your image being in focus while the rest of the image is out of focus, you have a number of alternatives, each of which has its own characteristics. You can select the region to be out of focus and apply Effects→Focus→Soften; you can use the Just Add Water variant of the Water brushes to blend colors and soften contours; or you can make a clone copy of the image and selectively apply some form of "clone filter."

In this last case you can either use standard brushes and paper textures or customize your own. Here you can see how to customize your own paper texture and apply it with a cloning brush. This technique offers incredible versatility and control.

Related Techniques

1 | Create Texture Template

Select File→New. Set the width and height to be 100 pixels. Click OK. Click on the Paper icon in the Art Materials palette. Select the Gradient paper texture from the standard paper textures library. Ensure the library drawer is closed and the palette expanded so the paper preview window and Scale slider are visible. Click on the Color icon in the Art Materials palette to view the Color Selector. Make sure that black is selected. Select the Large Chalk variant of the Chalk brushes. Paint lightly in the 100 pixel by 100 pixel texture template.

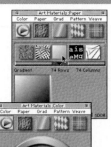

Note: Paper textures are made up of repeating grayscale tiles where black represents the parts of the paper that stick up ("mountains") and pick up pigment, and white represents the "valleys" that avoid picking up pigment.

2 | Successively Reduce Texture Scale

Reduce the Scale slider in the Art Materials: Paper palette to about 71%. Paint in the template. Reduce the Scale further to about 43% and paint in the template. Repeat this for various texture scales until you reach the minimum scale of 25%. You should now have built up a cubist-like grayscale pattern within the template.

3 | Save Customized Cubist Paper Texture

Select Edit→Select All. Select Paper→Capture Texture from the pull-down menu in the Art Materials palette. Name the texture and click OK. The texture now appears in the current papers library as the currently selected paper texture.

4 | Clone Main Image and Apply Chalk Cloner

Click on the main image where you want to apply the cubist blur. Select File→Clone. Open the Color Selector and expand the palette so that you can see the Color Variability sliders at the bottom of the palette. Check the Use Clone Color box. Select Control→Size in the Brushes palette and adjust the Size slider according to the level of detail you are blurring. Apply the Large Chalk brush in the clone image where you want to have the blur effect.

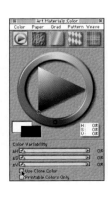

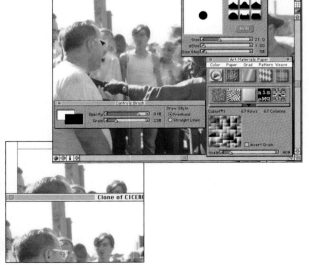

Transforming Images to Shadowy Forms

Avebury Hominin

Comments

This picture is based on the super-position and collage of three source images: a photograph of the ancient stone circle in Avebury, England; a video grab of a tree (Sequoia); and a video grab of the artist's cat. Paint was applied to the Avebury photo-graph, as well as a number of textur-izing and color adjustment effects. The photograph was distorted and cropped to achieve a more dramatic composition. The two video grabs were then introduced as floaters, and the Composite Method changed for each one.

Studio Usage

This image illustrates how you can incorporate imagery as an underlying shadowy form behind another dominant image. The technique makes use of low opacity floaters with Difference and Shadow Map Composite Methods. The principles discussed can be applied with many variations in opacity and Composite Method. In addition, after the shad-owy form is achieved, you can flatten the whole image and continue to apply effects to modify the overall color and texture.

Related Techniques

1 Distort Photograph

Select Effects→ Orientation→Distort. Drag one of the central control handles that appear around the perimeter of the image. Drag the handle until the rectangle is elongated. Click OK. Applying this effect automatically floats the image. Click on the F. List icon in the Objects palette.

Note: For the best quality of image, check the Better (Slower) option in the Distort Selection dialog box. If your image is very large you may want to initially leave that option unchecked to try out the distortion and then select Edit→Undo Distortion and repeat the distortion with the Slower option checked.

2 Equalize

Select Effects→Tonal Control→ Equalize. Bring the Black-and-White points closer together to increase contrast in the image. Adjust the Brightness slider and select a position that gives the required level of brightness in the image.

3 Correct Colors

Select Effects→Tonal Control→Correct Colors. Select Freehand in the pull-down menu in the Color Correction dialog box. Select each of the four color squares in turn and experiment with different freehand curves to adjust color levels. Click OK.

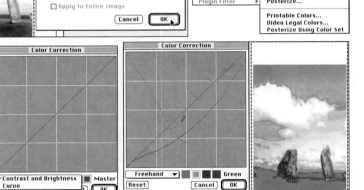

4 Introduce Tree Image

Paste in the tree image as a floater. Select Effects→ Orientation→Free Transform. Drag the control handles to distort the floater so that it fits in with your composition. Lower the floater opacity slider in the Controls: Adjuster palette to 10%. Change the Composite Method from Default to Difference. Select Effects→Orientation→ Commit Transform.

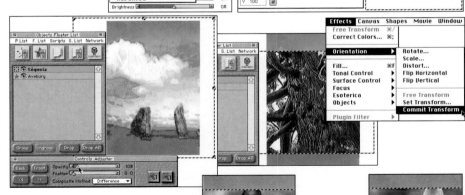

5 Introduce Cat Image

As in Step 4, introduce the cat image as a floater. Distort it in Free Transform, if necessary. Reposition it to suit your composition. Select Effects→Tonal Control→Negative. Reduce its opacity to 30%. Change its Composite Method to Shadow Map.

Transforming Photographs *Watery Ripples from Marble and Warp*

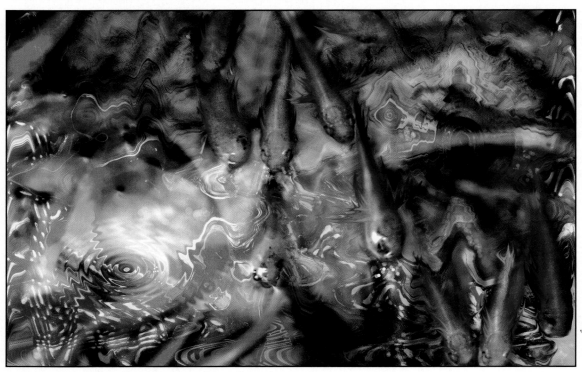

Gary Clark

One Thin Paradigm

Comments

This painting consists of many layers with the suggestion of light reflecting off the surface of water and revealing a layer of reality below the surface. The base image is a photograph in which a pair of eyes has been superimposed over a telescope viewing eye piece. Clark distorted this base image into an almost unrecognizable form by flipping it vertically and then applying effects such as marbling and warping. The fish were photographed in a local pet store, and then the images were used as a visual reference and as clone sources for copying colors and textures. Other photographs were used as clone sources as well. The image was color adjusted. Finally, the saturation and contrast were enhanced by use of the dodge and burn tools.

Studio Usage

It can be useful to transform a photographic image into an abstract, distorted image that has the look of watery ripples. You can then use the image, in conjunction with clone brushes, as a basis for a new composition, as in this example. This technique describes how various Painter effects can be used in sequence to achieve this result.

Related Techniques

1 | Flip Base Image

Select Effects→Orientation→Flip Vertical. The image is now flipped upside down.

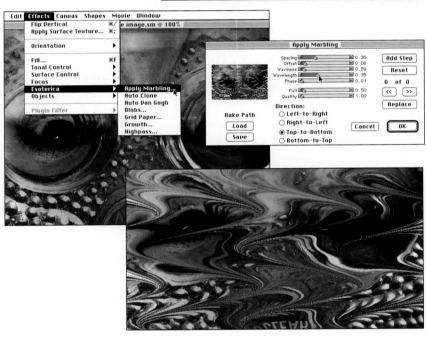

2 | Apply Marbling

Select Effects→Esoterica→Apply Marbling. In the Apply Marbling dialog box, adjust the sliders to achieve the required look. In particular, decide on a vertical or horizontal marbling and check the appropriate Direction option. The upper five sliders change parameters, which are indicated in the preview window by dashed lines. The Pull slider determines the "amount" of marbling that will be applied and how far from the original image the marbled image will end up being. Click OK when satisfied.

Note: *You may need to go back several times to adjust parameters by trial and error. In that case, use the Edit→Undo (⌘-Z) {Ctrl-Z} command followed by Effects→Apply Marbling. In the Apply Marbling dialog box, click on the Replace button when you have changed the sliders. You'll update the marbling parameters to reflect the new slider values.*

3 | Apply QuickWarp

Select Effects→Surface Control→Quick Warp. Select Ripple and increase the Power and Angle sliders slightly. When satisfied with the preview, click OK.

Note: *Quick Warp, with the Sphere option selected, is a useful way to generate "environmental maps" for applying as clone sources when using the Reflectance slider in the Apply Surface Texture effect dialog box.*

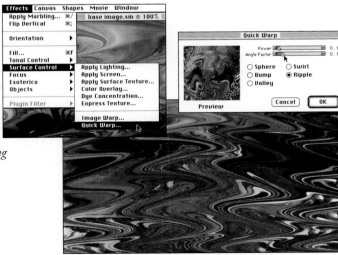

John Derry

Woman with a Paint Can

Comments

This painting was created for the Painter 4.0 poster that comes with each can. It was based on a scanned painting by Vermeer. The woman's face was taken from a video grab of someone posed in the right position, and then the face was introduced as a grayscale floater. The floater was rescaled and reoriented in Free Transform mode and feathered and dropped into the background canvas.

A Big Wet Oil cloner was used to unify the whole image with consistent brush strokes, and, in the process, obliterated the original fine cracks visible in the varnish of the original painting. These fine cracks were recreated by applying the Dye Concentration effect.

Studio Usage

A scanned historical oil painting may have fine cracks in the varnish. Adding image elements that lack the cracked varnish creates an inconsistent surface. This inconsistency can detract from the unity of the painting. The lack of brush strokes in added photographic elements also can be a problem. When clone brush strokes are applied to the whole image, the original varnish cracks are obliterated. This technique addresses these issues and shows you a way to easily add consistent brush strokes that appear to be covered by cracked varnish.

Related Techniques

1 | Clone Composited Image

Select File→Clone to create a clone of the composited image. You'll automatically "flatten" the clone picture; that is, merge any floaters into the background canvas.

2 | Apply Clone Brush Strokes

Click on the Paper icon in the Art Materials palette. Click on the horizontal bar in the Art Materials: Paper palette. Click on the Library button. Select the More Paper Textures library in the Painter 4 folder. Select the Small Canvas paper. Close the drawer, make sure that the palette is expanded, and adjust the grain Scale slider to match the scale of your image. Select the Big Wet Oils variant from the Brush family of brushes. Expand the Brushes palette to show the Method Category and Method Subcategory. Change the Subcategory from Flat Cover to Grainy Flat Cover. Click on the Color icon in the Art Materials palette. Expand the Art Materials: Color palette. Check the Use Clone Color box. Select Controls→Size in the Brushes palette pull-down menu and adjust the Size slider. Apply brush strokes all over the image.

3 | Select Paper and Apply Dye Concentration

Following the same procedure as in Step 2, select a paper that has a crackled look to it. Close the Paper library drawer. Select Effects→ Surface Control→Dye Concentration. Change the Using menu in the Dye Concentration dialog box to Paper Grain. Adjust the Maximum and Minimum sliders to see the effect as shown in the preview window. Click OK.

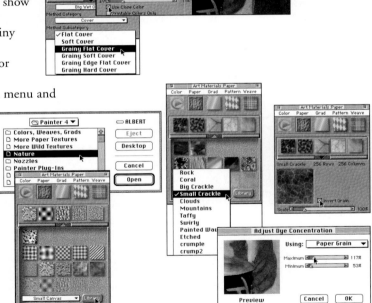

4 | Fade

The Dye Concentration effect may be a slight overkill, in which case you can partially scale back the effect by selecting Edit→Fade. Adjust the Undo Amount slider until you are satisfied with the image seen in the Preview window. Click OK.

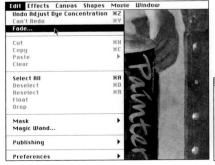

Transforming Photographs *Applying an Image Element as a Full Size Texture*

Nadja couchée sur son drap de littoral onirique

Jean-Luc Touillon

Nadja dos au Littoral Onirique

Comments

This image, as a sister image of Wagon Nadja seen in Technique #103, is comprised of three main elements: the photograph of the woman, Nadja, the photograph of the man in sunglasses, and a handwritten letter. The two photographs were cloned together, and their colors and tones were adjusted. A warm red color overlay was applied. The handwriting was introduced as a paper texture. The typed lettering at the bottom of the image says: "Nadja lying down on the sheet of the legendary coastal line."

Studio Usage

There are several ways you can integrate a high contrast image element into the fabric of your artwork. You can make the image element into a clone source. You can then get an embossed effect by applying Effects→Surface Control→Apply Surface Texture and selecting the Using: Original Luminance option. Alternatively, you could use the image element to generate a paper texture. This allows you not only to get an embossing effect by selecting Using: Paper Grain in the Apply Surface Texture dialog box, but also to apply grainy brushes to color selected regions of the embossed image. By making the paper texture tile the same size as your final image, you can accurately place the image element into your composition and consistently apply different grainy brushes.

Related Techniques

1 | Copy Image Element to Clipboard

Create directly on the computer, or scan, the image element you want to introduce into your picture, in this example handwriting from a letter. Open up that file and select Edit→Select All. Then select Edit→Copy.

2 | Clone the Main Image

Click on the main image into which you want to integrate the image element from Step 1. Select File→Clone. Select Edit→Select All (⌘-A) {Ctrl-A} and press the Delete key {Backspace on PC}. You'll clear the clone image so that it is now a plain white canvas. Select Canvas→Tracing Paper, or click on the black-and-white overlapping rectangles Tracing Paper icon in the upper right of the image frame. You'll now see a 50% opacity view of the underlying clone source (the original main image).

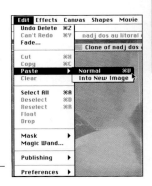

3 | Paste and Position Image Element in Clone

Select Edit→Paste→Normal. The image element from Step 1 now appears as a floater in the clone image created in Step 2. Use the Floater Adjuster tool from the Tools palette to drag and position the floater. Use the Tracing paper image for visual reference. Click on the F. List icon in the Objects palette to access the Floater List. Click on the Drop (or Drop All) button at the bottom of the Floater List to flatten the image.

4 | Capture Entire Clone as Paper Texture

Select Edit→Select All. Select Paper→Capture Texture from the pull-down menu in the Art Materials palette. Name the texture and click OK. Click on the Paper icon in the Art Materials palette to reveal the Papers palette. The new texture now appears as the currently selected paper texture.

5 | Apply Surface Texture Effect and Grainy Brushes

Click back on the main image to reselect it as the active document on the desktop. Select Effects→Surface Control→Apply Surface Texture. In the Apply Surface Texture dialog box, make sure that the Using menu is set to Paper Grain, check the Inverted box, set Softness to about 0.7, set Amount to about 15%, and set Shine to about 30%. Adjust these settings and click OK. Select the Artist Pastel Chalk variant of the Chalk brushes in the Brushes palette. Lower the opacity to 13%. Access the Color Selector. Select a color that you want to paint on the embossed structure in your image. Lightly stroke the chalk brush over the embossed areas to which you want to add color.

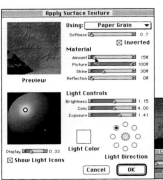

Transforming Photographs *Creating a Duotone from a Color Photograph*

Jeremy Sutton

Frank and Peter

Comments

This image illustrates the application of expressing a two-point gradation to create a duotone effect in a color photograph. When the source photograph was originally scanned and opened in Painter, the Effects→Equalize effect was used to increase the contrast. The background was then selected by using the Freehand Selection tool and softened. The selection was then inverted and the two figures sharpened. The spectacle lenses were excluded from the express gradation effect. In the final stage the two figures were selected and the equalization applied selectively to make them stand out from the background.

Studio Usage

This technique describes how to apply the Gradation: Express in Image command to transform a scanned, color photograph into a duotone image. It presents a convenient route to try out different duotone color combinations and selectively leave portions of the image with their original color. By using black and white as the gradation colors, this also offers an easy way to transform your photograph into grayscale.

Related Techniques

Posterization   41

Increasing Contrast
and Saturation   43

Sepia Pencil Drawing   54

Solarized Photographs   91

1 | Clone Original Photograph

Open the scanned photograph in Painter. Select File→Clone to create a copy of the original scanned photograph, which becomes your working document.

Note: Working from a clone in this way ensures that you do not accidentally alter the source file, and it also provides useful opportunities to experiment with cloning effects.

2 | Select the Two Colors of the Duotone

Select the lighter of the two colors you want to use in the Art Materials Color Selector. This lighter color becomes the currently selected primary color. Click on the Secondary Color rectangle in the lower left of the Color Selector (over-lapped by the Primary Color rectangle). Select the darker of the two colors.

Note: The lighter of the colors will end up being mapped to the lightest parts of the image, and the darker color to the darkest parts of the image.

3 | Mask Out Any Regions You Do Not Want Transformed to Duotone

Select the Freehand Selection Lasso. Carefully drag the cursor through the path around the objects you want to mask out. If there is more than one region, then click the Add to Selection option in the Controls palette. Select Edit→Mask→Invert Mask. The black-and-white "marching ants" will become green and white. The selection is now inverted and the objects are now masked off.

Note: If the freehand selection is not closed, you will see a shape described. In that case, click on the Close button in the Controls palette to convert to selection.

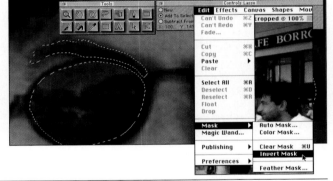

4 | Express Two-Point Gradation in Image

Open the Art Materials Gradient palette. Select the Two-Point gradation (overlapping black-and-white rectangles). The Two-Point gradation has the primary and secondary colors as the extreme end points of the gradation. Select Grad→Express in Image. The dialog box shows a preview of the duotone effect. Click OK.

Note: The bias slider alters the order of mapping of colors from the gradation according to luminance in the image.

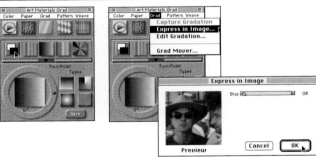

5 | Selectively Apply Equalize

The duotone image now has no deep black, unless the darker of the two colors was black. To give more "bite" to the image, it can be effective to selectively apply the Equalize effect to bring out contrast. To do this, use the freehand selection Lasso to select the prominent components of your image. If there are "holes," use the Subtract from Selection Controls option. Select Effects→Tonal Control→Equalize (⌘-E) {Ctrl-E} and click OK.

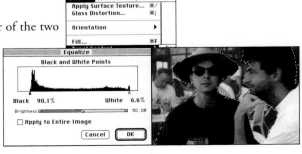

Transforming Photographs *Van Gogh Effect*

Victor Claudio

Coliseum

Comments

This image was created for the cover of a travel magazine. It was based on a color slide. The image was initially retouched to remove unwanted elements, such as the people. The original sky was too dark and was replaced with a hand-painted sky. The Auto Van Gogh effect was then applied to the whole image. Finally, the Apply Surface Texture effect was applied with the Using: Image Luminance option selected. This last step resulted in a thick, three-dimensional look to the paint.

Studio Usage

Painter's Auto Van Gogh effect offers a very convenient way to apply brush strokes whose direction is based on the brightness of an original image, and whose variable color is based on color in the original image. The resulting brush strokes appear to wind their way around the form of the picture, reminiscent of the way Van Gogh applied his paint. To achieve the best result from applying the Auto Van Gogh effect, you need to prepare your original image and adjust the Auto Van Gogh brush parameters. This technique describes the way Claudio has gone about doing both those tasks.

Related Techniques

1 | Clean Up Original Image

Select the Soft Cloner variant of the Cloners brush family in the Brushes palette. Select Controls→Size and reduce the brush size to about 7.8. Hold down the Control {Shift} key and click in the image where you want to clone from. Then go to a feature you want to eliminate and paint over that feature. Repeat this process around the image until it is clear of unwanted artifacts.

2 | Select Sky and Paint

Select Edit→Select All. Select Edit→Magic Wand. Drag the wand through the sky and sample as much color in the sky region as you can. Red will appear indicating which areas are currently included in the Magic Wand selection. If it does not cover a sufficient area, hold down the Shift key and drag the wand through unselected pixels to add new colors to the selection. If it covers too much area, click Cancel and select the Magic wand again. Click OK. Select Edit→Clear. Select the Loaded Oils variant of the Brush brushes in the Brushes palette. Apply brush strokes in the selected region.

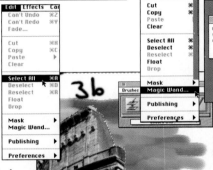

3 | Add Warm Wash

Click on the Mask Drawing icon in the bottom left of the document frame. Select the middle of the three Mask Drawing icons to restrict the brushes to painting outside the previously selected area. Select the Broad Water Brush variant. Apply a warm wash. Select Canvas→Dry. Select Edit→Deselect.

4 | Apply Auto Van Gogh

Select File→Clone. Select the Auto Van Gogh variant of the Artists brush family. Select Size = 16.4 in the Brush Controls: Size palette. Select Effects→ Esoterica→Auto Van Gogh. If you want to try it with different brush variables, select Edit→Undo Auto Van Gogh and try again.

Transforming Photographs *Combining Embossing with Partial Cloning*

Dorothy Simpson Krause

Dove

Comments

This picture was created from two source photographic images, one of the woman's face, the other of the dove. Krause utilized the Surface Texture effects menu and the Cloning brushes to modify and mix the images together in a unified composition.

Studio Usage

This technique describes how to achieve an interesting embossed effect by applying Surface Texture using Original Luminance to a metallic looking surface, followed by partial cloning of the original source photographic image. The result has a mysterious air to it, suggestive of the whole photograph but not explicit in detail.

Related Techniques

1 | Clone Original Photograph

Open the original photo-graph. Select File→Clone to create an identical copy of the original photograph.

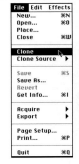

2 | Fill Clone

Select a gold color in the Art Materials Color Selector. Click on the Secondary Color rectangle in the Color Selector. Choose a darker shade of gold. Open the Art Materials Gradation palette. Select the Two-Point gradation (this reflects the current primary and secondary colors). Adjust the direction of the gradation. Select Effects→Fill (⌘-F) {Ctrl-F}. The Fill With Gradation option should be checked. Click OK. The clone image is now filled with gradation.

Note: *You can now apply Effects→Surface Control→Apply Surface Texture Using: Paper Grain to give the gold gradient a textured feel.*

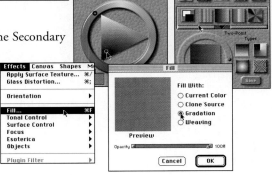

3 | Apply Surface Texture Using Original Luminance

Select Effects→Surface Control→Apply Surface Texture. Select Using: Original Luminance. Adjust the Amount and Shine sliders to get the appropriate embossed look. Use the preview window for real-time feedback. Click OK. You'll see an embossed version of the original photograph superimposed over the gold gradient.

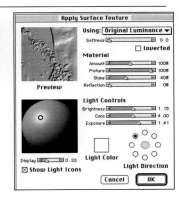

4 | Partially Clone Back Original Image

Select the Soft Cloner variant of the Cloners brush family in the Brushes palette. Select Controls→Size in the Brushes palette and adjust the Size slider to suit the scale of your image. Start cloning in some of the original photograph into the embossed gold surface. Use light pressure to get a soft translucent look. Press hard to completely replace regions with the original image.

Note: *By creating a clone in Step 1, the original photograph was automatically assigned as a Clone Source. You can veri-fy this by looking at the File→Clone Source pull-down menu. The original photograph file name has a check by it.*

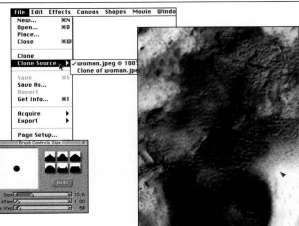

Aleksander Jensko

Bahnhof Delvaux

Comments

This picture was inspired by the artwork of the Belgian surrealist painter Paul Delvaux. It combines two source photographs, one of a Polish railway station and the other of a woman. The image of the woman was floated above the railway station image, repositioned, and then dropped. The whole image was then worked over, using the Flemish Rub Artist's brush. The final stage was the application of the Apply Surface Texture Effect.

Studio Usage

This technique shows one way to transform photographic images into paintings with the appearance of thickly applied oil paint. Refer to the Related Techniques to see the results of other approaches. In this case, after the collaging of two images together, the Flemish Rub variant of the Artists brushes was used to smear the colors and distort the forms in the image.

The Apply Surface Texture effect, with Using: Image Luminance, gave the final three-dimensional look to the paint.

Related Techniques

1 | Select Figure

Open an image. Select Edit→Magic Wand.
Click on the portion of the image you want to
select. Some of the figure goes red, indicating
that it is part of the Magic Wand selection.
Hold down the Shift key while dragging the
Magic Wand through variations of tone and
color contained within the region you want to
select. More of the figure now appears red.
Continue until most, if not all, the figure is
indicated as included in the selection. Click
OK.

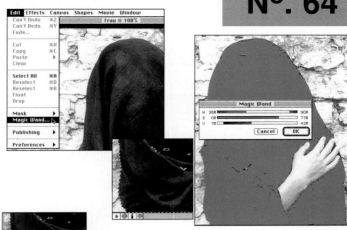

2 | Fine-Tune Selection

Select the middle of the Mask Visibility icons.
The region outside the selection is indicated in
red. The red represents the masked region. Select
the Masking Pen variant of the Masking brushes
in the Brushes palette. Click on the Color icon in the Art
Materials palette to access the Color
Selector. Select black. Paint in areas
that were excluded from the selection
that you wanted included. Select
white to take away from the selection.
When satisfied, select the right-hand
Mask Visibility icon. Select
Edit→Copy.

3 | Paste Floater

Open the other photograph into which you
want to add the figure selected above. Select
Edit→Paste→ Normal. Drag the floater
into position by using the Floater Adjuster
tool. Click on the F. List icon in the
Objects palette to reveal the Floater List.
When satisfied with the positioning of the
figure, click Drop in the Floater List.

4 | Apply Flemish Rub and Surface Texture

Select the Flemish Rub variant of the Artists brushes. Access
the Brush Controls: Size palette by selecting Controls→Size
in the Brushes palette pull-down submenu. Experiment
with the brush as you adjust the Size slider. Use the brush
to break up boundaries of different colors in the image.
Select Effects→ Surface Control→Apply Surface
Texture. Select Image Luminance from the Using
pull-down menu. Adjust the Amount and Shine sliders.
Click OK.

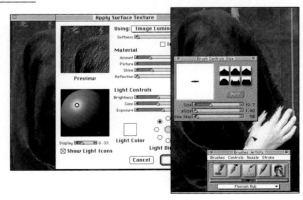

Transforming Photographs *Applying a Custom Pattern*

Ken Milburn

Heikke

Comments

This portrait was generated by applying background patterns and textures around the woman's face, leaving the face to emerge from the textures around it.

Studio Usage

This technique describes how to create a custom pattern and apply it to a selection within a photographic image. The use of a feathered selection gives the appearance of the unselected portion of the image, in this case the woman's face, emerging from a veil.

Related Techniques

1 | Open New Document

Select File→New and open a new document 200 pixels by 200 pixels. This document will be used for creating a customized, seamless, spattered paint pattern. Select the Spatter water variant in the Water Color brush family of the Brushes palette. Select Controls→Water from the pull-down submenu in the Brushes palette. Move the Wet Fringe slider in the Advanced Controls: Water palette all the way to the right (100%).

Note: *Since this is a Water Color brush it paints into the Wet layer and must be dried before it can be erased with Edit→Select All (⌘-A) {Ctrl-A} Delete.*

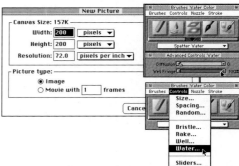

2 | Paint Seamless Pattern

Select Pattern→Define Pattern. Select Controls→Size from the Brushes palette and adjust the brush size slider to suit the size of spatters you want. To delete the spatters, select Canvas→Dry and then Edit→Select All, followed by Delete.

Note: *Paint right off the edge of the document. Note how the paint continues on the opposite side. If you hold down the Shift key and Space bar simultaneously, then you can scroll the pattern around seamlessly.*

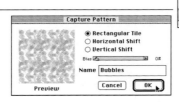

3 | Capture Pattern

Select Canvas→Dry. Select Edit→Select All. Select Pattern→Capture Pattern in the Art Materials palette submenu. Give the pattern a name and click OK.

4 | Create Feathered Selection

Select the photograph to which you want to apply the pattern. Select the freehand selection Lasso in the Tools palette. Delineate a selection contour around the face. Click on the Close button in the Controls palette when you have finished drawing the selection path. Select the Selection Adjuster tool from the Tools palette. Adjust the Feather slider to about 21 (or larger). Selecting Edit→Mask→Invert Mask inverts the selection so that everything except the woman's face is now selected.

5 | Fill Selection with Pattern

Select the expanded Pattern palette. Select the customized pattern created in Step 2. Close the drawer to reveal the scale slider. Adjust the slider to suit the scale of the image you are applying the pattern to. Select Effects→Fill. The Fill With: Pattern option is selected. Adjust opacity according to the degree you want the fill to cover up the image background. Click OK.

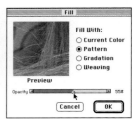

Transforming Photographs *Creating the Feel of Organic Movement*

©S. Swaminathan, Golden Light Imagery

Artichoke and Sunflower

Comments

The source photograph, on which this image is based, was a 35mm slide transparency that was digitized and then manipulated and painted over in Painter. Swaminathan started by experimenting with the color balance to brighten up the colors, ending up with an almost luminous effect. He sought to convey the feeling of ever-changing organic movement and growth in the artichoke and sunflower. He did this primarily by using the Liquid Distorto brush to pull light tones into dark and dark tones into light. The Dodge and Burn brushes were used in the final stage to add contrast.

Studio Usage

This technique describes an approach to convey the feeling of liquid, organic, ever-changing movement. It is based on the application of the Liquid Distorto brush. The effect is enhanced by application of the Dodge and Burn brushes. You may find it effective to apply this technique to any organic forms in your painting.

Related Techniques

1 | Smear Dark Tones into Light Tones

Select the Distorto variant of the Liquid brush family in the Brushes palette. Select Controls→Size in the Brushes palette to access the Brush Controls: Size palette. Adjust the brush size slider to suit the scale of detail in your image. Click the Build button (⌘-B) {Ctrl-B} after changing the brush size. Drag from the center of the dark tones in your image into regions of lighter tones. The directions of your brush strokes should reflect the forms in the image and the lines of motion you want to emphasize.

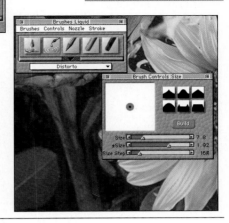

2 | Smear Light Tones into Dark Tones

Repeat Step 1, but this time drag from light tones into darker tones.

3 | Apply Burn Brush

Select the Burn brush. Apply this brush along borders where you want to increase the contrast between a light surface and a dark adjacent block of color and in regions where you want to deepen the shadows.

Note: This brush, as with the Dodge brush, can give quite dramatic effects. It is best to apply the brush strokes lightly, gradually building up to the effect you are seeking. In this way you can maintain more fine control.

4 | Apply Dodge Brush

Select the Dodge brush. Reduce the brush size. Apply the brush where you want to lighten areas of the image. Use this brush to bring out details in the highlights.

Note: The default brush diameters for Dodge and Burn brushes are relatively large and will usually need reducing before applying brush strokes. The default opacity settings for Dodge and Burn are both relatively low, and you may want to increase the Opacity setting in the Controls: Brush palette.

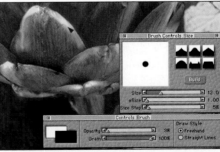

5 | Apply Broad Distorto

Select the Liquid Distorto variant again. This time make the brush size the approximate size of your main features in the image. Then gently apply this large Distorto brush within that particular feature.

Adam Sadigursky

Big City Love

Comments

This painting combines the use of direct brushwork on the background canvas with extensive use of floaters and selections. Many layers of effects have been applied in different areas to build up the rich variety of textures and looks that you see. This technique focuses on how the textured heart motif was generated. Similar techniques were also used in other parts of this composition. This painting won second place in the Fractal Design 1995 Art Expo Contest.

Studio Usage

This technique describes how to create a colored, crumpled heart motif by varying the Composite Method interactions of multiple floaters. The heart motif is built with three floaters—one rectangular and two heart-shaped. Each floater is colored and textured individually. The Composite Method for each of the floaters is set to give the required visual effect. The principles used in this example can be applied easily to any form from another image that you want to introduce into your composition. Using floaters gives you the flexibility to experiment with colors, effects, textures, and orientation between the forms.

Related Techniques

1 | Create and Paint Rectangular Floater

Open a new document (slightly larger than you want the rectangle around the heart to be). Click on the Paper icon in the Art Materials palette. Open the paper library drawer. Click on the Library button and select the More Paper Textures library. Select the texture called Surface 1. Select the Large Chalk brush variant. Use that brush to apply a light hue across the whole document. Close the Papers drawer to reveal the texture editor. Check the Invert Grain box. Lower the Grain slider to about 12%. Choose a dark hue and apply it across the whole document. Select Effects→Surface Control→Apply Surface Texture→Using: Image Luminance. Then select the Rectangular selection tool and create a rectangular selection. Select Edit→Copy. Click on the original artwork and select Edit→Paste→Normal. The rectangular selection is now pasted as a floater in the artwork image.

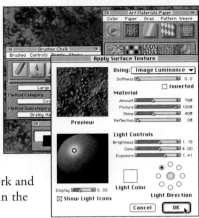

2 | Create Heart-Shaped Floaters

Open a new document for the creation of the heart shape. Select the Pen tool. Draw a heart shape. Click on the F. List icon in the Objects palette. Double-click on the shape name in the Objects: F. List palette. Check the Fill option. Click OK. Select Shapes→Convert to Floater. Click once on the heart with the Floater Adjuster tool while holding down the Option {Alt} key.

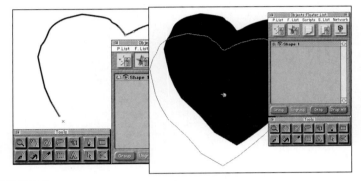

3 | Fill Heart Floaters with Color and Texture

Click on the top name in the Floater List. Select the Mountains texture. Lower the Grain slider to about 10%. Use the same Chalk brush as in Step 1 to apply a bright red to the heart-shaped floater. Click on the lower floater and drag it to the top of the Floater List. Select a bright yellow color. Select Effects→Fill with the Fill With: Current Color option selected. Click OK. Select Effect→Surface Control→Apply Surface Texture. Select the Using: Paper Grain option. Click OK. Select Edit→Copy. Select the original artwork document. Select Edit→Paste→Normal. Click back on the heart shapes document and select the lower (red heart) floater. Copy and paste this floater into the original artwork.

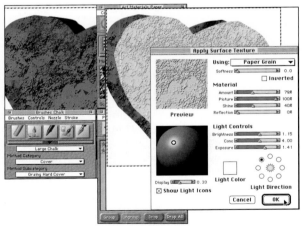

4 | Adjust Composite Methods and Floater Mask

Select the rectangular floater. Adjust the Composite Method to Darken. Select the middle floater (yellow heart) and adjust the Feather slider to 6.7%. Do the same for the upper (red heart) floater. Adjust the upper floater Composite Method to Hard Light. Select the Masking Airbrush from the Masking family of brushes. Select white in the Art Materials: Color palette. Paint with the masking brush over the right- and left-hand edges of the heart.

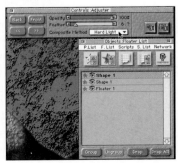

Deity

Jason Fruchter

Comments

This painting, based on Mayan symbols, was one of the winners in the Fractal Design Art Contest and was featured in the Fractal Design 1996 Calendar. Fruchter constructed the entire composition by piecing together floating selections, each one individually produced. He used Adobe Illustrator, as well as Painter, to produce the initial PostScript shapes. These shapes were converted to solid, black-and-white images, which formed the basis of the embossed shapes in the final image. He applied Surface Control effects, such as Color Overlay and Dye Concentration, to produce the final coloring of the floaters.

Studio Usage

This technique describes how to create embossed shapes, or image elements, that you can easily collage together in a complex composition. The elegance of this technique is the simplicity with which you can combine soft, three-dimensional shadowing and highlights with sharp, precise edges.

Related Techniques

1 | Clone Source Image

Create a solid, black design against a white background. Select File→Clone. Click on the Color icon in the Art Materials palette. Select an underlying color such as gray. Select Effects→Fill and click OK. The clone image is now filled with gray.

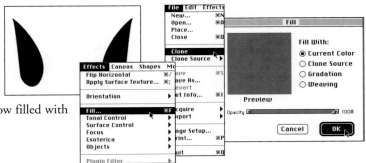

2 | Apply Surface Texture and Soften

Select Effects→Surface Control→Apply Surface Texture. Select Using: Original Luminance. This Using menu option generates an embossed effect in the clone image based on the luminance values in the original (clone source) image. Adjust the Softness slider until the required amount of embossment is seen in the Preview window. Click OK. Select Effects→Focus→Soften. Click OK in the dialog box.

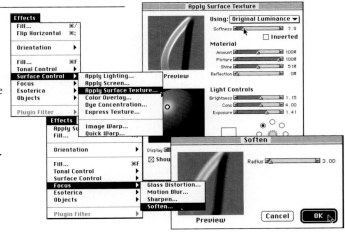

3 | Generate a Mask Based on the Original Luminance

Select Edit→Mask→Auto Mask. Select Original Luminance in the Using pull-down menu. Click OK.

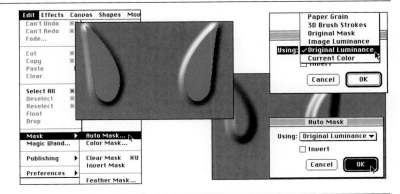

4 | Create a Floating Selection

Select the right-hand Mask Visibility icon to turn the mask generated in Step 3 into a selection. Select Edit→Float.

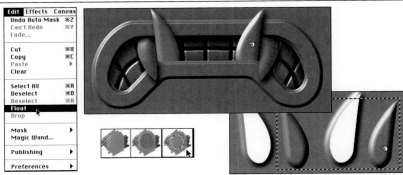

Collage and Montage   *Composing a Collage with Cloning*

Stephen Rock

Fields

Comments

This photo collage was composed by cloning each source image into the composition. The original images were manipulated by Rock prior to cloning, and the final collage was also color adjusted.

Studio Usage

When you are composing a number of images together into a single collage, and the original source images have different resolutions, sizes, and proportions, it is very useful to utilize one or more clone copies of the final image canvas. These clone canvases act as working layout sheets where you have the flexibility to resize and reposition your collage elements prior to committing them into the final image.

Related Techniques

1 | Clone Final Image Canvas

With the final image canvas active on the desktop, select File→Clone. A copy of the final image canvas appears. Select Edit→Select All. Press the Delete {Backspace} key to clear the clone canvas.

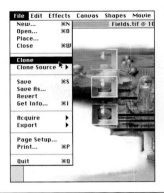

2 | Place Collage Element

Select File→Place. Locate the file you want to place in the clone canvas. Do not change the name, delete, or move this file while working with the placed image. It will be placed as a reference floater. Click Open. The Place dialog box will automatically scale the reference floater that it is placing to fit the scale of canvas into which it is placing the floater. Click OK. The reference floater is positioned in the center of the canvas.

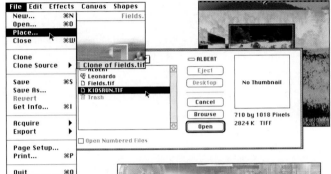

3 | Resize and Orient the Element for Collage

Select Canvas→Tracing Paper. You'll see a 50% opacity view of the original collage image showing through the clone canvas. Hold down the Shift key as you drag on the corner control handles with the Floater Adjuster tool. By doing this, you'll resize the floater, while maintaining the aspect ratio. Use the tracing paper visual reference to adjust the size. Drag in the floater to reposition it.

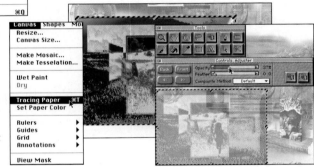

4 | Drop Floater

Click on the F. List icon to access the Floater List. Select Effects→Orientation→Commit Transform. Turn off Tracing Paper by reselecting Canvas→ Tracing Paper or clicking on the Tracing Paper icon in the upper right of the document frame. Click the Drop button in the Floater List.

5 | Clone into Main Image

Click back on the final image canvas so that it is the active document. Select File→Clone Source and set the Clone of file name to be the clone source. Select the Soft Cloner variant of the Cloner brushes, or any other clone variant, and clone the collage element from the clone canvas into the final image.

Mark Zimmer

The Miracle of the Can

Comments

This image was created for the Painter 4 poster. Zimmer sought to capture the look and feel of a Byzantine mosaic. He did this by starting with a rough layout sketch that he used to pose the individual characters. He then took video grabs of each figure, composited them together as floaters, and painted their tunics. The paint can was added as a floater and a glow was created. Background elements and a pedestal were painted into the image. Finally, all floaters were dropped, and the image was used as a clone source for creating the final mosaic.

Studio Usage

There are a number of ways you can create glows in Painter (see Related Techniques). This technique looks at a way to create a subtle soft glow that has a sense of mystery and magic. It utilizes a new feature introduced in Painter 4, the Mask Edit mode, which allows effects, such as Soften, to be applied to the mask layer.

Related Techniques

1 | Duplicate Floater

Introduce the object that you want to create a mysterious glow around as a floater. Select the Floater Adjuster tool. Open the Objects: Floater List. Click on the floater's name in the Floater List. Any other floaters should be inactive. Hold the Option {Alt} key down and click once on the floater in the image. You'll create a duplicate floater exactly positioned over the original. The upper floater is selected.

Note: *You can introduce the object by pasting it into the picture from another image. It automatically becomes a floater. Use the Effects→Orientation→Free Transform to rescale and reorient the object, selecting Effects→Orientation→Commit Transform when satisfied.*

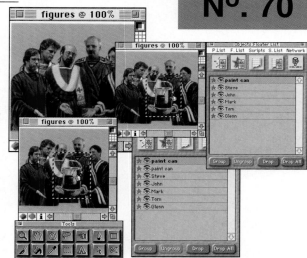

2 | Fill the Lower Floater with White

Click on the Color icon in the Art Materials palette. Select white as the current primary color in the Art Materials: Color palette. Click on the lower floater name in the Floater List. Select Effects→Fill (⌘-F) {Ctrl-F}. Make sure that the Fill With Current Color option is checked. Click OK.

3 | Enter Edit Mask Mode

Make sure that the lower floater, now filled with white, is the only active floater. To view this lower floater, click on the "eye" icon next to the name of the upper floater in the Floater List that obscures it. The eye now closes and the upper floater becomes invisible. Select Canvas→View Mask, or click on the small colored circle icon. This selection turns on the Mask Edit mode.

4 | Soften Mask and Leave Mask Edit Mode

Select Effects→Focus→Soften. Adjust the Radius slider to give a soft graduated mask in the floater. Click OK. Select Canvas→View Mask, or click on the Mask Edit mode icon. Click on the closed eye symbol. You'll see the paint can with a white glow around it.

Judith Moncrieff

Warbride

Comments

This picture was created from a series of different source images that include an old photograph, a picture of pipes, a 1930's charm bracelet scanned directly, and a real fish monotype (Moncrieff actually painted a fish with silkscreen ink and wrapped it in newspaper). Moncrieff introduced each element as a separate floater, sometimes making multiple floaters of the same image and then applying paint and color variations. In the final stage, after all these layers were merged, she applied tiny eraser and water brushes to pump up highlights and make the image "pop" out.

Studio Usage

When you create a complex collage of a series of different images, either cloned together into the background canvas or as separate floaters, the highlights in the composition usually are not pure white. This can detract from the power and vitality of the final image. One way to make the image "pop" out is to carefully paint in pure white into selected highlights in the final flattened image. This technique describes how to do that in a way that blends into the image.

Related Techniques

1 | Drop All Floaters

If your collage is comprised of a series of floaters, as in this case, click on the F. List icon in the Objects palette to access the Floater List. Click on the Drop All button. You'll merge all floaters into the background canvas and, thus, "flatten" the image.

2 | Apply Tiny Eraser

Select the Small Eraser variant from the Eraser brush family in the Brushes palette. Select Controls→Size from the pull-down submenu in the Brushes palette to access the Brush Controls: Size palette. Reduce the Size slider from the default size (13.7) to the minimum (2.0). Click on the Color icon in the Art Materials palette to access the Color Selector. Select white in the Color Selector. Select Window→Zoom In or drag the Magnifier Tool around the area with the highlight you want to "pump up." Apply the tiny eraser in the highlight.

3 | Apply Small Blending Tool

Select the Just Add Water variant of the Water brushes. Reduce the brush size to about 3.0. Apply the Just Add Water brush around the region where you have used the eraser in the previous step. Blend the edges of the white with the surrounding colors to give a smooth finish.

Note: You can also use a larger version of this brush to blend any harsh edges where image floater layers are too obvious. In this way you can create an image where different layers appear to flow into each other rather than be clearly stacked up on one another.

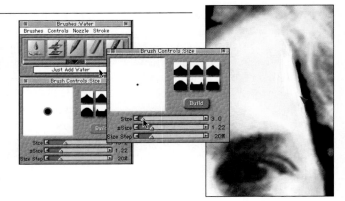

Sheriann Ki-San Burnham

Red Dream

Comments

This image is based on a system of duplicated, flipped, and modified blocks. Each block was a separate floating image. Burnham started by painting the first block with freehand abstract forms, using primarily Charcoals, Pens, Airbrush, and Liquid brushes. She continued by selecting regions of the first block and applying effects. She followed a process of duplicating the floater and flipping it horizontally, and then continued to work on the new block while maintaining continuity over the border between the blocks. This process was repeated until the final image was complete.

Studio Usage

When you build a variety of custom paper textures for use on a particular project, or for repeated use over a series of different projects, it is useful to create your own custom textures library from which you can subtract or add textures. If you work at different computers, you may also need to transfer your custom papers library from one computer to the other. The Paper Mover enables all these things to be possible. Movers allow you to create and control the contents of libraries in Painter.

Note: *This technique assumes that you have already captured and saved a number of custom textures into the default Paper Textures paper library.*

Related Techniques

1 | Open Paper Mover

Select Paper→Paper Mover from the pull-down submenu in the Art Materials palette. Click on the New
button in the lower right to create a new paper texture
library. Click on the Paper icon in the Art Materials
palette. If the paper library drawer is not open, click
on the horizontal bar to open it. You will see icons
representing all the paper textures. Close the drawer by
clicking back on the horizontal bar. If the palette is
expanded, you will see a preview of the currently selected texture with
a Scale slider.

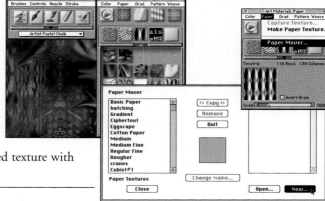

2 | Create a New Texture Library

Select a location where you want to save the
new paper texture library. This location
could be anywhere, even on another net-
worked hard drive or removable storage
media. Name the new paper texture file.
Click OK. The new texture library appears on the right-hand side of the
Paper Mover dialog box. Select the first texture you want to move into the
new texture library file from the current library listed on the left. Click
Copy. The name appears on the right. Repeat this for all the textures you
want to move. Click Quit.

Note: If you want to remove the duplicated textures in the current library,
select them one by one and click on the Remove button.

Beware: By clicking on the Remove button you'll irreversibly delete the texture.
The Remove operation cannot be undone.

3 | Change Current Texture Library and Using Removable Media

Open the paper library drawer. Click on
the Library button. Select the new library
file created in Step 2. Click Open. The
new paper texture file is now the current
paper library. Locate the custom paper texture file in your Painter 4 application folder on the hard drive. Copy the file over to
the removable storage media. To access the
custom textures at another computer, simply follow the procedure to locate the file
on the removable storage media.

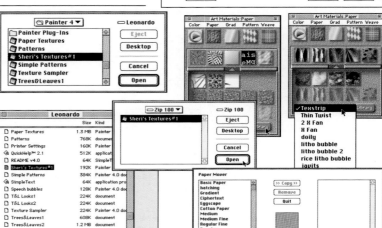

4 | Editing the Texture File on Removable Media

Open the Paper Mover as described above. Click the Open button on the right
side of the Paper Mover dialog box. Locate the custom paper texture file. You
can now copy from right to left, as well as the other way around. You can also
rename or remove textures.

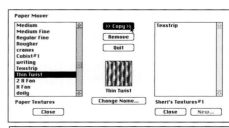
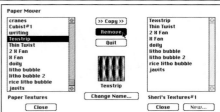

Nancy Vachani

"Maya Sargent"

Comments

This portrait is a montage of a digital camera photo and the painting, "Lady Agnew," by the American socialite portraitist, John Singer Sargent (which was scanned on a flatbed scanner at 300 ppi). An Airbrush variant was used to enhance the digital camera photo. The Dropper tool was used to sample colors from within the photo itself as well as from the Sargent painting. These colors were then applied by the Airbrush. The photo portrait was then selected and pasted into the Sargent painting. Various techniques were used to blend the portrait into the background.

Studio Usage

This technique describes how to combine a photograph with an existing painting by seamlessly using floaters, cloning, and oil brushes. You can use this technique to step back in time; for example, to place a portrait or scene from the present into some past era.

Related Techniques

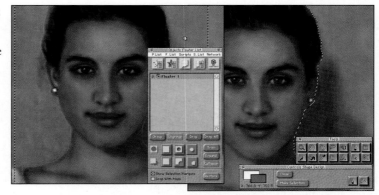

1 | Create the Floater

With the Pen tool, make a selection path of the head, neck, and shoulders of the figure. Complete the path. Click the Make Selection button in the Controls: Shape Design palette. Select Edit→Copy to copy the selection to the Clipboard.

2 | Paste the Floater into the Original Painting

Click on the original scanned historical painting. Select File→Clone. Select Edit→Paste→Normal. Drag the copied headshot floater into a position of alignment in the historical painting clone. Select Edit→Drop.

3 | Cloning and Oil Brushes for Seamless Montage

Select the Soft Cloner variant from the Cloners brushes. Use this brush to blend areas seamlessly with the original. Select the Loaded Oils variant from the Brush brush family. Using the Dropper tool, select nearby colors in the background and brush over the excess hair of the original. Continue to blend other areas around the pasted floater as needed.

4 | Removing Moiré Patterns

Moiré patterns can appear in scans from books and magazines. This patterning is undesirable for a historical painting. Click on the Color icon in the Art Materials palette and expand it. Check the Use Clone Color box. Apply the Loaded Oils brush carefully. Go over the whole image following the original brush strokes in the painting to remove the moiré pattern.

5 | Adding Dimension to Brush Strokes

Select Effects→Surface Texture→Image Luminance. Move the sliders until the appropriate amount of texture and raised brush strokes appear. Adjust the lighting direction and light color. Click OK. If the effect is too strong, use the Edit→Fade command to undo the effect.

Butterfly Sky

Patrick Lichty

Comments

This image was created with a combination of software packages, including Fractal Design Painter and Kai's Power Tools for the 2D surfaces, textures, and colors, and also Corel Studio for the 3D rendering of the butterflies.

Studio Usage

In situations where you have a common surface texture or pattern that you would like to appear in different perspectives and orientations on an object, or a series of objects, then using Painter in conjunction with a 3D modeling program can be very useful. This technique looks at one simple example in which a design, in this case butterfly wings, was rendered onto a series of 3D butterfly wings in different positions. Besides saving the effort of painstakingly transposing the pattern in different perspectives by hand, this technique also provides great versatility.

Related Techniques

1 | Create Texture Map

Create an image containing the surface detail you want to map onto a 3D object, or series of 3D objects. Make the resolution of this file the same as your intended final rendered image, so that it maps 1:1 in size. Save the file in a file format compatible with the particular 3D modeling program that you are going to use. Usually, PICT (for the Mac), TIFF, or Adobe Photoshop formats are acceptable. Import the file into the 3D package as a Texture Map and apply it to the surface of your 3D object. Save the rendered object image in a format that can be opened in Painter.

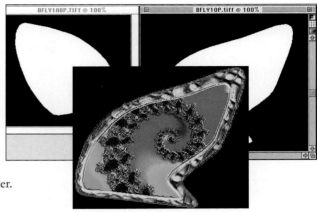

2 | Open Rendered Object Image

Open the rendered 3D image in Painter. You should have a 2D bitmapped image of the object with the surface details from the texture map rendered onto it in your 3D program. The background should be uniformly white. If the white background is not a single, contiguous region, then select Edit→Select All (⌘-A) {Ctrl-A}.

3 | Apply Magic Wand and Invert Selection

Select Edit→Magic Wand. Click in the white background around the object. The white becomes filled with red, indicating that it is included in the Magic Wand selection. Click OK. The white background is now your selection. Select Edit→Mask→Invert Mask to invert the Magic Wand selection so that it is selecting the object only. The selection is surrounded by a green-and-white "marching ants" marquee because it is generated from a mask outline. Select Edit→Copy.

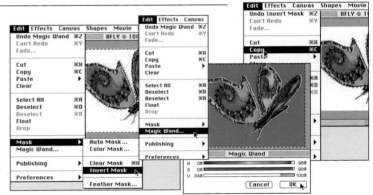

4 | Paste into Composition

Click on the main composition image to make it the active document on the desktop. Select Edit→Paste→Normal. It can now be reoriented, painted, and subjected to any of the effects in the Effects menu. Repeat Steps 1 through 4 for all the other 3D rendered objects you want to introduce to your composition.

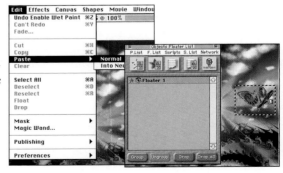

Collage and Montage *Colored Marks Above the Canvas*

State of the Art

Jason Kang

Comments

This painting combines many different aspects of Painter, including mosaics, shapes, floaters, textures, masks, and patterns. The initial visual ideas were worked out at low resolution (72 ppi). Then a high resolution working image was created. This painting ended up having many floaters, also at high resolution. To keep the file size manageable, Kang periodically "flattened" the image (dropped all floaters).

Studio Usage

In building up a complex, collaged image with many components, it is very useful to be able to create colored marks or brush strokes that are independent of the background canvas. By doing this, you have the freedom to move the marks around, edit them, and change their color, without affecting the rest of the composition. This freedom can be achieved by converting black marks into a floater and then coloring the floater.

Related Techniques

1 | Clone the Image

Select File→Clone. Select Edit→Select All (⌘-A) {Ctrl-A} followed by the Delete {Delete/Backspace} key to clear the Clone image.

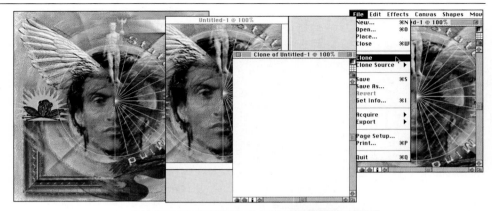

2 | Turn on Tracing Paper and Paint Marks

With the cleared clone image active, select Canvas→Tracing Paper (⌘-T) {Ctrl-T}. You can now see a 50% opacity version of the clone source. Use any appropriate brush in the Brushes palette to paint flat black marks. The Scratchboard Tool variant of the Pens brush family works well.

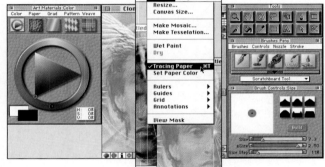

3 | Select the Black Marks and Paste Selection

Turn off tracing paper. Select Edit→Mask→Auto Mask. Make sure that it says Using: Image Luminance and click OK. Click on the Mask Visibility icons. Drag to the third (rightmost) icon and let go. You'll convert the black marks into a selection based on paths and calculated from the mask generated earlier. Select Edit→Copy. Click on the original image. Select Edit→Paste→Normal to paste the black marks into the original image as a floater.

Note: You can also use Edit→Select All followed by Edit→Magic Wand to select the black.

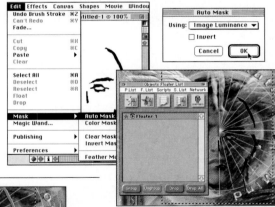

4 | Paint Color onto Marks and Apply Surface Texture

With the new floater active, use the Scratchboard Tool to color in the black marks. You now have total freedom to experiment with color. As a final step, select Effects→Surface Control→Apply Surface Texture. In the dialog box, select Using: Mask and then adjust the Softness slider slightly. Click OK.

Note: You may also find it useful to apply a drop shadow by selecting Effects→Objects→Create Drop Shadow.

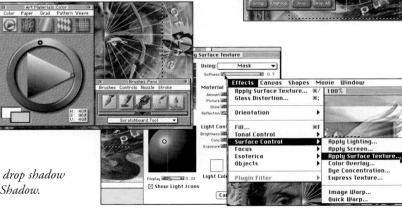

Collage and Montage *Working from a Layer*

Ashanti Yves Francisque

Comments

This image was created in two distinct stages. First, the background was created by using a variety of brushes and textures. Secondly, the foreground motif was painted over the background. The principles of the technique used to paint the foreground design onto a separate layer (floater), prior to merging with the background, can be applied to a collage in which you introduce a number of different motifs. Each one can be kept independently editable until the last moment.

Studio Usage

Utilizing a floater layer, the same size as the image itself, to begin the painting of a primarily black foreground motif has the advantage of maintaining flexibility in design. You can reposition the design with respect to the background and make changes to it without affecting the background. Only at the final stage is the design dropped into the background for "fine-tuning" and the addition of lighter colors.

Related Techniques

1 | Make Floater

When your background is completed, select Edit→Select All (⌘-A) {Ctrl-A}. Select the Floater Adjuster tool ("F" key). Hold the Option {Alt} key while clicking once on the image with the Floater Adjuster tool. You'll create an identical copy of the background image in a layer (floater) separate from the background canvas. A copy of the original background image is left in the background canvas. Click on the F. List icon in the Objects palette.

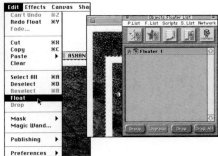

2 | Fill Floater with White

Click the Color icon in the Art Materials palette. Select white in the Color Selector. With the floater still highlighted, select Effects→Fill (⌘-F) {Ctrl-F}. Make sure that the Fill With: Current Color is selected. Click OK. The floater is now an opaque white.

3 | Change Composite Method

Select the Floater Adjuster tool in the Tools palette. Select Darken from the Composite Method pull-down menu in the Controls: Adjuster palette.

Note: *The Darken Composite Method makes the floater to which it is applied transparent wherever it is covering a darker color. A white floater with this Composite Method appears transparent.*

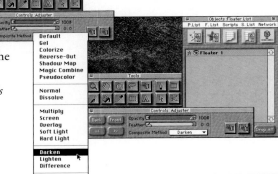

4 | Paint on Floater and Drop It

With the floater still selected, select black in the Color Selector. Apply brushes with Cover Method Category to create the basis of your foreground design. The black marks cover up the background. At this stage you have the flexibility to reposition, alter, and even rescale the foreground design independently of the background by using the Floater Adjuster tool to move the floater around. When satisfied with the design on the floater and its placement above the background, click on the Drop button at the bottom of the Floater List. You can now work into the design with lighter colors and complete the composition.

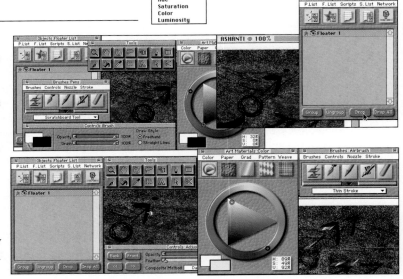

Helen Golden

Metropolitan Megadance

Comments

Two different images were used in this painting. The original Polaroid scan was made into a floater by using the Magic Wand to select all white in the image and then inverting the selection. Golden then painted and distorted the dancer photograph, using it as a background to interact with the Polaroid floater. She experimented with Composite Methods until satisfied with the result.

Note: *A Polaroid emulsion print is created by floating the developing Polaroid chemicals on the surface of water and then lifting the paper from beneath. This can result in very interesting distorted photographs.*

Studio Usage

When you are compositing different elements together, it is convenient to introduce each element as a floater in the final image. An individual floater can be easily modified independently of the rest of the composition. Sometimes you may want to preserve the look achieved by adjusting a floater Composite Method while the floater is placed over a different background (in a secondary image) before introducing it into the main composition. To do this, you need to flatten the secondary image to preserve the effect of the interaction between the floater and the background. Then select the shape of the floater again, modifying it as required, and then introduce it into the main composition.

Related Techniques

Color Enhancement with
Multiple Floaters 47

Crumpled Texture 67

Solarized Photographs 91

1 | Position Floaters Relative to One Another

Place the floater you want to alter on a separate canvas from your main image. Click on the F. List icon in the Objects palette. In this example, the Polaroid emulsion print floater is above the dancer photograph floater. Use the Floater Adjuster tool to move the upper (Polaroid) floater by dragging on the image. To move the lower floater (dancer), first select it in the Floater List and then use the arrow keys to move it (the Floater Adjuster tool may inadvertently reselect the upper floater).

2 | Adjust Composite Method

Select the upper (Polaroid) floater by clicking on its name in the Floater List. Make sure that the Floater Adjuster tool is selected. Adjust the Composite Method pull-down menu in the Controls: Adjuster palette from Default to Hard Light. Hard Light alters colors, depending on the luminance of the floater color.

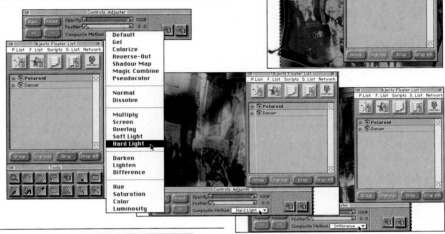

3 | Drop Floaters

Select the lower (dancer) floater. Click on the Drop button below the Floater List to drop the lower floater onto the background canvas. Select Edit→Mask→Clear mask to clear the background canvas mask (it's important that the upper [Polaroid] floater remain deselected during this operation). Select the remaining (Polaroid) floater in the Floater List. Expand the Floater List. Check the Drop With Mask box at the bottom of the expanded Floater List. Click on the Drop button.

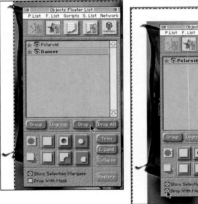

4 | Modify Mask and Generate New Modified Floater

Select Canvas→View Mask. The dropped floater mask is now seen as a black region against a white background. Select the Scratchboard tool from the Pens brush family. Click on the Color icon. Select black. Paint in the image with the black wherever you want to add to the floater, in this case filling in holes. Click on the Mask Visibility icons and select the right-hand one. Select Edit→Copy. Click on the main image canvas. Select Edit→ Paste→Normal. The modified floater is now introduced into the main composition.

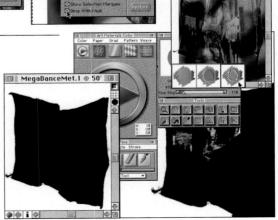

Collage and Montage *Paper Cutouts*

Jerry Garcia© 1995 The Estate of Jerome J. Garcia

Tropic

Comments

This artwork combines the use of gradient fills and brush work on a number of independent floaters to give the impression of paper cutouts. The careful layering and ordering of the floaters results in an intricate interweaving of compositional elements that snake in front of and behind each other. Juxtaposed complementary colors produce dramatic contours around the various shapes.

Studio Usage

Shapes and floaters can be used to create and control many precisely defined elements in a composition, allowing each element to be individually painted or filled. This procedure is analogous to the creation of a collage of paper cutouts (papiers découpés). This technique describes how to go about building such a composition, first by drawing freehand shapes and then by converting them to floaters.

Related Techniques

1 | Apply Gradient Fill to Background

Click on the Color icon in the Art Materials palette. In the Art Materials: Color palette pick one of the two colors you want to apply to the background as a gradient fill. Click on the Secondary Color rectangle in the lower left of the Color Selector and select the second color for the gradient. Click on the Grad icon in the Art Materials palette. Select the Two-Point gradation. Close the gradation library drawer. Drag the small red ball direction indicator around the Rotation Ring until the gradation direction matches the way you want to fill the background. Select Effects→Fill and fill the background with gradation.

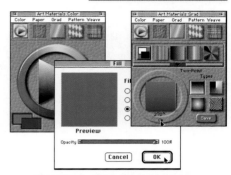

2 | Draw Freehand Shape

Select the Quick Curve Tool in the Tools palette. Draw a freehand shape in your image. Click the Close button on the Controls: Shape Design palette. The resulting shape will have an outline and may be filled with a solid color. Click on the F. List icon in the Objects palette. The Shape name is now listed in the Floater List.

Click on the Make Selection button in the Controls: Shape Design palette to convert the shape into an active selection path.

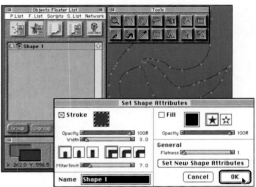

3 | Convert to Floater and Fill and Trim

Select the Floater Adjuster Tool in the Tools Palette. Hold down the Option {Alt} key while clicking on the selection made in Step 2 with the Floater Adjuster Tool. The selection is converted into a floater. The background remains unaltered. Because the floater is the same color as the background, it will temporarily become invisible except for the rectangular selection marquee.

Double-click on the floater name in the Floater List and rename it to describe the object or shape it represents in your composition. Select two new Primary and Secondary Colors and, following the same process as in Step 1, fill the floater with the new Two-Point gradation.

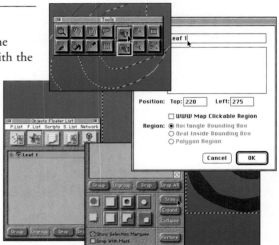

4 | Add New Floater and Apply Airbrush

Repeat Steps 2 and 3. To view this new floater, click on the eye symbol next to the first floater's name in the Floater List. Click on the new floater name. Select the Fat Stroke variant of the Airbrush brush family in the Brushes palette. Select Controls→Size in the Brushes palette submenu. Adjust the Size slider. Apply the airbrush stroke to give the impression of highlights and shadows. Click on the first floater eye symbol to make it visible again.

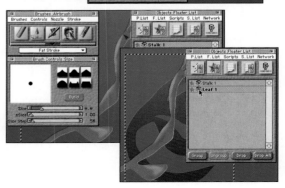

Collage and Montage *Creating Synthetic Objects*

Steve Guttman

Photo Surrealism

Comments

This image was created in the style of the 1930's photo surrealists, and was one of the pictures on the poster that came in the Painter 4.0 paint can. Guttman began by constructing the walls of the room by using Painter shapes, filling them with gradients, and applying lighting. Photographs were used for the chair, paint can, easel, and man. The water splashing out of the can was painted by using the Watery variant of the Fun Brushes library (located in the Painter 4 folder under Extra Brushes). The stool and table on the right were both synthetically created from shapes. The cast shadows were all created by using duplicate floaters. The final image was composed of over 15 different floaters.

Studio Usage

Sometimes, as in this composition, you cannot obtain a photograph showing the precise object, or view of the object, that you would like to include in the image. In this case you may need to synthetically construct a realistic looking object from scratch. This technique describes how to create such a photo surrealistic object without any scanned photograph. You can achieve this effect by using a combination of the Painter drawing tools to create geometric PostScript shapes (mathematically defined, resolution independent and vector-based) and converting them into paintable floaters that can be textured and painted to add realism.

Related Techniques

1 | Create Geometric Shape Outline

Select the Pen Tool from the Tools palette. Draw a shape that follows the outline of the object you want to construct. Close the shape by either adding the last point over the first one or clicking the Close button on the Control palette. Repeat this process for any interior "holes" within the object that will need "cutting out."

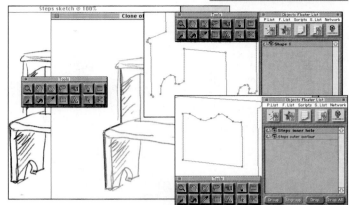

2 | Make Selection out of Shapes

Select the Shape corresponding to the outer contour by clicking on its name in the Floater List. Make sure that the Pen tool is selected. Click on the Make Selection button in the Controls: Shape Design palette. Click on the P. List icon in the Objects palette. The floater name no longer appears in the Floater List. Repeat this process for the interior shape. When it appears in the Path List, click on the plus sign. It will turn into a negative sign. The writing turns from blue/black to red, and the marquee turns from black and white to red and white. You have a negative selection that cuts a hole out of any selection path below it in the Path List. Make sure that the outer contour selection is below the interior "hole" in the Path List.

3 | Fill Selection

Make sure that both selection paths are active. Click on the Color icon in the Art Materials palette. Select a color in the Color Selector that you want to fill the object with prior to painting. Select Effects→Fill (⌘-F) {Ctrl-F}. The dialog box should show Fill With: Current Color. Click OK.

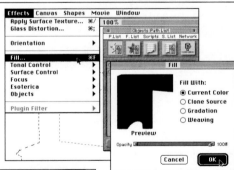

4 | Float and Paint Object

Select Edit→Float. Select the Dodge brush from the Brushes palette. Select the Controls→Size palette. Adjust the brush Size slider to suit the scale of detailing you want. Increase the Opacity slider slightly in the Controls palette. Make sure that the floater is active. Brush on highlights.

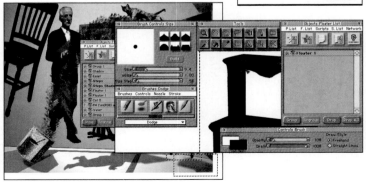

Jane Kriss

Comments

The principal source for this composition was a scanned gouache and gum arabic painting of apricots against a white background. The apricots were selected, floated, and dragged into a larger image, where a background (based on the Calmness Pattern in the Pattern Library) and roses (originally created in Adobe Illustrator) were added. This technique focuses on the first stage of the process—introducing a repeating motif as floaters into a composition.

Studio Usage

This technique shows how you can start with traditionally painted motifs, in this case a clump of apricots, and then use those motifs as a basis for a composition with repeating elements. There are transformations in orientation, scale, and color of the individual elements.

Related Techniques

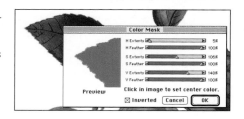

1 | Select the Apricots

Open the scanned motif in Painter. Click on the F. List icon in the Objects palette. Make sure that there are no floaters listed in the Floater List (click Drop All if you see any listed). Select Edit→Mask→Color Mask. Click in the white region surrounding the motif. Check the Inverted box. Then adjust the H Extents slider until you see all the motif you want to select indicated in red in the dialog box preview window. Press OK.

Note: You can move the preview image simply by clicking and dragging.

2 | Clean Up the Selection

Click on the P. List icon in the Objects Palette. Expand the Path List. Select the middle Mask Visibility icon (also accessible in the lower left of the image frame). Check the Transparent Mask option. Make sure that your motif is cleanly selected. If you need to add or remove any areas of the selection (that are indicated in red), then use the Masking Pen variant of the Masking brushes in the Brushes palette. In the Art Materials: Color palette, select either pure black (to add to mask) or pure white (to remove mask). When you are satisfied, select the right-hand Mask Visibility icon. This turns the red region into an active selection surrounded by green-and-white "marching ants" (a selection path generated from the mask outline). Select Edit→Float.

Note: The motif now appears as a floater in the Floater List.

3 | Add Floater to Library

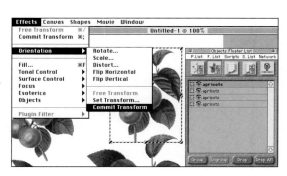

Select F. List→Floaters from the drop-down submenu in the Objects palette. Select the Floater Adjuster tool (pointing finger) and drag the floater into the Objects: Floaters palette. After giving it a name, you will see it appear in the floater library.

4 | Use Free Transform for Variation

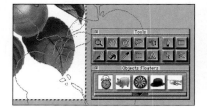

Open a new canvas the size of your final collaged image. Click and drag the floater from your floater library into this new canvas. Select Effects→Orientation→Free Transform. Hold down the Shift key and drag one of the corner "handles" to rescale the floater. Hold down the ⌘ {Control} key to rotate or skew the floater. Apply any of the Effects menu to the floater. To make a simple repeat of the floater in your composition, hold down the Option {Alt} key while you click once on the floater in the image.

To remove a floater, select it and then press the Delete {Backspace} key. When satisfied with the orientation and scale of your floaters, select each one individually and apply Effects→Orientation→Commit Transform.

Note: You could have simply copied and pasted the floater into the final image. The advantage of storing your floaters in the floater library is that you can conveniently re-use the same floater on other projects in the future.

Collage and Montage *Creating a Directional Image Hose Nozzle*

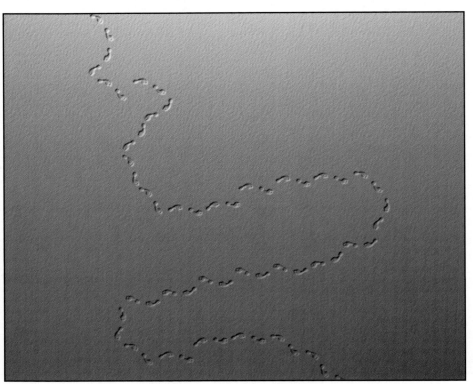

Peter Gruhn

Footprints

Comments

This image illustrates the application of a customized Image Hose nozzle to paint a repetitive feature. The Image Hose is an amazing tool for collaging image elements. Image elements, which are loaded into the hose as "nozzles," "pour" out of the hose as you paint. The order, distribution, size, opacity, and color of the emerging images can all be controlled via different input parameters, such as stylus pressure and direction. Although nozzle elements have masks like floaters, they are painted directly into the background canvas and are not floaters. However, adding their mask to the background mask is an option that allows you to select them if you want.

Studio Usage

When you want to collage a series of image elements into your composition, the Image Hose can be invaluable. Moreover, the ability to add to the mask layer enables you to apply interesting effects selectively to the region where you painted with the Hose. This technique explains how to make a directional Image Hose nozzle, that is, one in which the nozzle elements (footprints) follow the direction of your brush stroke. It also explains how to apply the nozzle to get the three-dimensional "footprint-in-the-sand" look.

Related Techniques

1 | Copy Nozzle Element Floater and Rotate Floater

Click on the F. List icon in the Objects palette. Expand the Floater List by clicking on the expander button. Open a canvas containing the image element (floater) you want in your directional nozzle. Orient it with reference to the background canvas in the same orientation you want the element to have when emerging from the Image Hose with the brush stroke going sideways from left to right. Select Edit→Copy. Highlight the floater in the Floater List. Select Effects→Orientation→Rotate. Set the Angle: 345 degrees. Click OK.

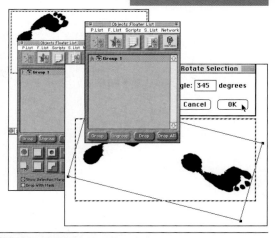

2 | Apply Successively Larger Rotations to Duplicate Floaters

Select Edit→Paste→Normal. Repeat Step 1, but set the rotation angle to be 330 degrees. Continue this process, each time setting the rotation angle to be 15 degrees less than the last time. You'll see the floaters forming a clockwise arrangement. The rotation angle for the last floater pasted in should be 0 degrees (no rotation). When all 24 floaters are pasted, make sure that the Floater Adjuster tool is selected in the Tools palette and select Edit→Select All. Click the Group button.

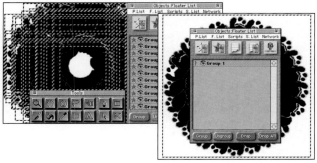

3 | Make Nozzle

With the floater group active, select Nozzle→Make Nozzle From Group. A new document appears on the desktop containing the rotated nozzle image elements arranged in rows and columns against a black background. If you select the middle of the Mask Visibility icons from the pull-down icon menu, you will see each element covered in red, indicating the mask. Select File→Save As and save the file as a RIFF file. Select Nozzle→Load Nozzle. Locate the nozzle you just saved. Click OK. Select Nozzle→Add Nozzle to Library. Click OK. Select Nozzle→Nozzles. The Brush Controls: Nozzles palette appears. The library drawer should be closed and the palette expanded so that you see the Scale slider and Rank sliders.

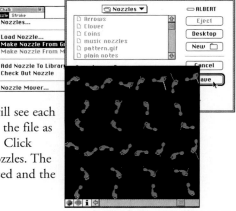

4 | Apply Nozzle

Select the Large Directional variant of the Image Hose in the Brushes palette. Set the Scale slider to about 87%. Check the Add to Mask box in the Brush Controls: Nozzle palette. Apply the Image Hose on your main image. Select Edit→Undo Brush Stroke. Select Effects→Surface control→Apply Surface Texture. Select the Using: Mask option. Set the Shine slider at 0%. Adjust the Softness and Amount sliders and observe their effect in the Preview window. Check the Invert box to get an indented look. Click OK.

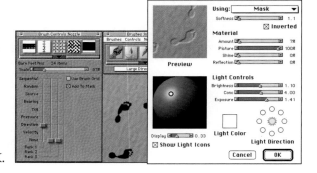

Collage and Montage *Flexibility in Placing an Object*

Intruder

Judy York

Comments

York began this painting with the background imagery, adding the dragon and human figure as floaters so that she had the flexibility to pose them precisely with respect to one another. The stalagmites and stalactites were painted at the final stage after the floaters had been dropped into the image.

Studio Usage

You can use this technique when you want the flexibility of introducing a painted object into a scene, but still want to maintain the freedom to rescale and reposition the object with respect to its background and other objects in the composition. This technique involves selecting the object and turning it into a floater. The floater is dropped into the final image only when you are satisfied with the overall composition. This technique is applicable any time you wish to select a painted object surrounded by a uniform color, yet want to avoid white pixels surrounding the selection (which can easily happen when using the Magic Wand).

Related Techniques

1 Apply Auto Mask

Open a document with an object, in this example a dragon, painted against a white background. This object is to be introduced into a composition as a floater. Select Edit→Mask→Auto Mask. Select the Using: Image Luminance option in the Auto Mask dialog box. Click on the P. List icon in the Objects palette. Select the middle of the Mask Visibility icons in the Objects: P. List palette (or in the pop-up menu in the lower left of the document frame). This shows the mask as red. You'll see the object (dragon) indicated in red according to luminance.

Note: *In this example the painting of the dragon was created by dropping all floaters in the main composition, cloning the image, and then cloning the clone of the image. This clone of a clone was cleared and tracing paper used to allow the original image to show through for visual reference.*

2 Apply Cartoon Cel Fill

Click on the Color icon in the Art Materials palette. Select a color in the Color Selector that is quite different from the painted hues in the object. Double-click on the Paint Bucket in the Tools palette. Adjust the Mask Threshold slider, starting with 50%. Click OK. Select What to Fill: Cartoon Cel and Fill With: Current Color in the Controls: Paint Bucket palette. Click with the Paint Bucket in the white region surrounding the object. Click with the Paint Bucket in any white holes surrounded by the object that have escaped being filled.

Note: *If the fill is not cleanly filling up to the edges of the object, select Edit→Undo. Readjust the Mask Threshold and try again until the selected color fills cleanly up to the edge of the image. If the fill color leaks into the object, then use the Masking Pen with black selected to fill in the mask. Remember to change the color back afterwards.*

3 Apply Color Mask

Select Edit→Mask→Color Mask. Click on the background (blue region) in the image. Check the Invert box to invert the selection so the object (dragon), not the background (blue region), is selected. Adjust the H, S, and V Extents sliders until the preview shows a clean selection of the object. Press OK. Turn the masked region into a selection by selecting the right-hand Mask Visibility icon. The dragon is now surrounded by a green-and-white "marching ants" selection marquee. Select Edit→Copy.

Note: *You can change brush size while in Brush mode by selecting Option-⌘{Alt-Ctrl} while dragging on the image.*

4 Paste in Image

Select the main composition where, in this example, the human figure is a floater. Select Edit→Paste→Normal. The object (dragon) is now introduced into the composition as a second floater. Click on the F. List icon. Both floaters are listed in the Floater List. Position the two floaters, using the Object Adjuster tool, until they are in the correct relative orientation. Select the Drop All button in the Floater List. Use Just Add Water variant to work any harsh edges into the background.

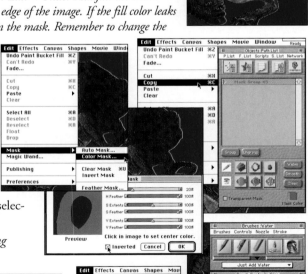

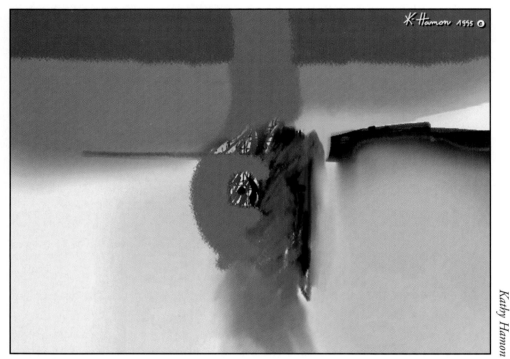

Kathy Hamon

Huile Sans Titre/Untitled Oil Painting

Comments

Hamon has developed a template signature, which includes her copyright notice, that she conveniently places on her digital paintings when they are complete. Besides copyright protection, this also establishes an identifiable "signature style." Refer to Technique #24 for a description of how she applies Painter brushes to create the expressionistic oil painting effect you see in this image.

Studio Usage

Digital artwork is very easily distributed and reproduced, which makes it especially important for a digital artist to clearly establish a copyright protection. One way to do this is to ensure that there is a clear notice visible on the artwork that identifies the artist and includes the copyright symbol and the year. This technique describes how to create a suitable two-tone graphical element, store it in the floater library, and place it in your artwork. The principles for this technique can be applied more generally whenever you want to introduce common graphical elements into a number of different images, such as a series of collages or interface designs.

Related Techniques

1 | Create Original Signature

Open a new file, with white as the paper color, that is slightly larger than the largest size you want your signature to be and at the highest resolution. Click on the Color icon in the Art Materials palette and select black. Select the Scratchboard Tool variant from the Pens brush family. Select Controls→Size from the Brushes palette pull-down menu. Reduce the Size slider to about 3.1 and the +/- Size slider to about 1.31. Click the Build button. Select Edit→Preferences→Brush Tracking and set the Pressure Scale to 0.40. Click OK. Paint your signature graphical element.

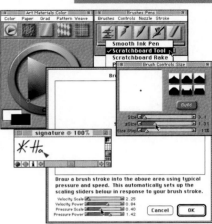

2 | Float Signature

Select Edit→Mask→Auto Mask. Select Using: Image Luminance in the Auto mask dialog box. Click OK. Click on the Mask Visibility icon, and select the right-hand of the three Mask Visibility icons. Select Edit→Float. The signature is now a floater separated from the background canvas in the image.

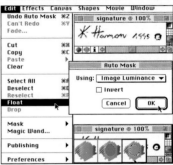

3 | Create a Duplicate Floater and Fill Background

Select the Floater Adjuster tool in the Tools palette. Click on the F. List icon. The floater created in Step 2 should be highlighted. Hold the Option {Alt} key while clicking once on the floater in the image to make a duplicate. Click below both names in the Floater List to deselect the floaters. Select gray in the Color Selector. Select Effects→Fill. Fill With: Current Color should be selected. Click OK. The background is filled with gray.

4 | Displace and Fill Duplicate Floater

Click on the top name listed in the Floater List. Use the arrow keys to reposition this upper floater to the left. With this floater active, repeat the procedure for applying a Fill, but select white. Hold down the Shift key while clicking on the lower floater name in the Floater List. Click on the Group button. Expand the Floater List. Click on the Collapse button. The two-tone graphical element is now a single floater. Save the file as a RIFF file.

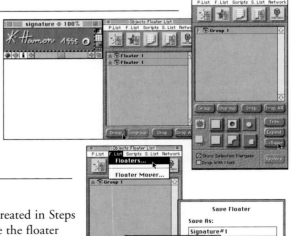

5 | Save Floater in Floater List

Select F. List→Floaters. Click on the signature template floater created in Steps 1–4 and drag the floater into the Objects: Floaters palette. Name the floater and click OK.

Celebración Centenial

Kent Bingham

Comments

This design, which was created for the 1996 Hispanic Unity & Youth Leadership Training Conference in Utah, was used in the conference program, on T-shirts and on the World Wide Web. The scene depicts two 19th century Hispanic explorers, Escalanté and Dominguez. The mosaic scenery was originally pieced together from many different photographic sources. Colors and tonal contrast in the collage were adjusted and a clone copy made. Painter's Make Mosaic mode was then used to convert the scene into a mosaic. The grout color (the color between the mosaic tiles) was selectively painted over in the sky region of the image. An embossed look was applied to the tiles, and a subtle paper grain was applied to the whole image. Finally, the explorers were added as floaters.

Studio Usage

The capability to render the mosaic tiles into the mask layer gives you the flexibility to easily select or exclude either the grout or the mosaic tiles when applying paints or effects. Selectively changing the grout color in different regions of a mosaic can greatly enhance the image. In this example, you'll learn the technique of creating a mosaic based on a collaged photographic source image, selectively painting over certain regions of grout and then finally enhancing the image with texturizing effects.

Note: *This artwork can be seen on the World Wide Web site http://www.ce.ex.state.ut.us/hispanic/unity.htm.*

Related Techniques

Photograph into Mosaic   40

Mysterious Soft Glow   70

Greek Mosaic Motif   99

1 Clone Collage

Make sure that your collage source image is flattened. Open the Floater List by clicking on the F. List icon in the Objects palette and then click the Drop All button. Select File→Clone. Select Canvas→Make Mosaic. The clone image goes black and the Make Mosaic dialog box appears. Check Use Tracing Paper in the dialog box. An impression of the source image, the clone source, shows through the black. Open the Color Selector. Expand the Art Materials: Color palette. Check Use Clone Color. Make sure that the Apply Tiles Tool is selected. Paint in mosaic tiles whose color is determined by the underlying clone source image. Adjust the Width and Length setting in the Make Mosaic dialog box. Deselect Use Tracing Paper to see what your mosaic looks like as it develops.

2 Render Tiles into Mask

When you have completed the mosaic design, select Render Tiles into Mask from the mosaic commands pop-up menu in the Make Mosaic dialog box. Click Done.

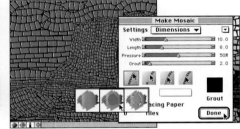

3 Paint Grout

Select the middle Mask Drawing icon to enable the paint brushes to be applied anywhere outside of the masked region. Select the left of the Mask Visibility icons to make the mask invisible so that you can see the image unobstructed by a red representation of the mask layer. Select a light blue color in the Color Selector. Select the Thin Stroke variant of the Airbrush brushes in the Brushes palette. Carefully paint in the grout in the sky region. The mosaic tiles are protected from the brush strokes. Change the color slightly as you work your way across the sky.

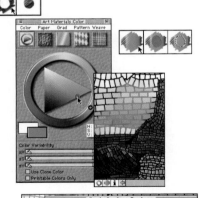

4 Apply Surface Texture and Dye Concentration

Select Effects→Surface Control→Apply Surface Texture. Select Mask from the Using menu in the Apply Surface Texture dialog box. Adjust the Softness, Amount, and Shine sliders until you see the desired amount of embossing. Click OK. Select Effects→Surface Control→Dye Concentration. Make sure that Paper Grain is selected in the Using pull-down menu in the Adjust Dye Concentration dialog box. Adjust the Maximum and Minimum sliders until satisfied with the effect you see in the Preview window.

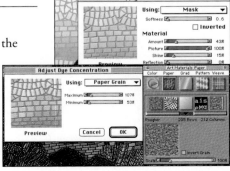

Collage and Montage *Multiple Images Linked by Distorto*

Rhoda Grossman

Wheezin', Sweatin', Sneezin' ,'n' Smokin'

Comments

The assignment, which was designed for a medical periodical, was to create editorial art on the ill-effects of smoking. This grayscale image was faxed to the client as a "rough" or concept for approval. The artist was able to produce it quickly, using only a few of Painter's tools for composing and blending several images.

Studio Usage

This technique describes how to manipulate individual elements in a composition and then link them with a blending "smoky" effect. Each item is introduced into the composition as a floater whose size, position and tonality can be changed easily, allowing you to try out many possible arrangements prior to "dropping" the floaters into the background. In the final stage the Distorto variant of the Liquid brush is used for a smoky effect. This technique can be applied to many situations when you want to create a montage of separate elements blended together into a single, cohesive image.

Related Techniques

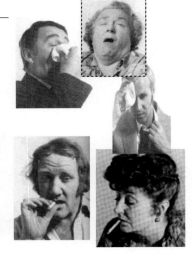

1 | Create Floaters from Various Source Images

Edit→Copy (⌘-C) {Ctrl-C} each image and Edit→Paste→Normal (⌘-V) {Ctrl-V} it into a new document. Click on the F. List icon in the Objects palette to open the Floater List. Give each new floater a descriptive name by double-clicking on its default name in this list.

2 | Manipulate the Appearance and Arrangement of Floaters

Make sure that the Floater Adjuster tool is selected. Simply drag floaters to any new position on the background. Overlapping images can be moved in front of or behind each other by dragging their names to a new position on the Floater List. Choose Effects→Orientation→Free Transform. Change the floater's size by dragging a corner "handle" while holding down the Shift key. You can also rotate by holding down the ⌘ {Ctrl} key while dragging the corner handles, and flip and distort by dragging the center handles. Select Effects→ Orientation→Commit Transform. Adjust the Effects→Tonal Control→ Brightness/Contrast. Adjust the Opacity slider in the Controls: Adjuster palette for each floater separately.

3 | Drop the Floaters, Blend Their Edges, and Add "Smoke"

Click the Drop All button on the Floater List. The names disappear from the list, and all the elements are now merged into the canvas background layer. Select the Grainy Water variant of the Water brushes and choose a medium-rough paper in the Art Materials: Paper palette. Soften the hard edges between images. Select the Distorto Variant of the Liquid brushes family. Change the size and opacity of the strokes. Control the amount of each stroke with Edit→Fade. Move the slider for the amount of fade, observe the preview, and click OK.

Collage and Montage *Reflections in Water*

Judy York

Sentries

Comments

The two ladies and the winged horse in this image were all originally introduced as floaters. They were placed over a background and then reflected in the water by using the technique described here. The floaters were based on photographs; the rest of the image is pure painting.

Studio Usage

This technique shows you how to create realistic reflections in water. Ideally, you can plan your composition in advance so that the items to be reflected are introduced into the image as floaters. These floaters are then duplicated, reoriented, repositioned, and tonally adjusted to resemble authentic reflection in the surface of the water.

Note: *A similar approach could be used for reflections in any mirrored or shiny surface, although non-flat surfaces will need more attention in order to distort the reflected image appropriately.*

Related Techniques

1 | Duplicate and Flip Floater

Hold down the Option {Alt} key while clicking once on the floater with the Object Adjuster tool. Select Effects→Orientation→Flip Vertical. Drag the floater to a position where its base is flush with the original floater's base. Select the Masking Airbrush variant in the Masking family of brushes. Adjust brush size and click on the Color icon in the Art Materials palette. Select white in the Color Selector. Click on the F. List icon in the Objects palette. Make sure that the reflected floater is still active and the Floater Adjuster tool is selected. Lower the floater Opacity in the Controls: Adjuster palette to see through the floater to the background behind it.

Apply brush strokes to the portion of the reflected image that protrudes. The floater disappears where the brush strokes are applied. If you make an error and need to increase the region of the floater that is visible, change the current color from white to black. Return the floater opacity to 100%.

2 | Repeat with Other Reflected Objects

Follow a similar procedure as in Step 1 for the other reflected objects. Objects that are further away will appear foreshortened in the reflected image. You cannot simply reflect the entire group of objects in one step. If necessary, adjust the order in which the floaters are listed in the Floater List to ensure that the objects overlap each other correctly. While holding down the Shift key, click on each reflected floater in turn so they are all selected. Expand the Objects: Floater List palette. Press the Group button in the Floater List, followed by the Collapse button to collapse the group of floaters into a single floater to which effects can be applied.

3 | Adjust Brightness and Contrast

Make sure that the single floater of reflected images is selected. Select Effects→Tonal Control→ Brightness/Contrast. Reduce both Brightness and Contrast so the reflected images are slightly darkened to approach the tone of the water.

4 | Adjust Colors and Soften Edges

Select Effects→Tonal Control→Adjust Colors. Make sure that the Using menu is Uniform Color and adjust the Hue Shift slider to give a hue adjustment close to the water's color. Press OK. Select Edit→Fade and adjust the Undo Amount to about 90%. Select Drop in the Floater List. Select the Just Add Water variant and adjust its size to be small. Use this brush to soften the edges and add the appearance of watery diffusivity to parts of the reflection.

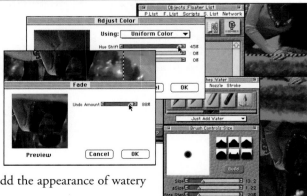

Shadows in Velvet

Judy York

Comments

This painting was created as cover art for a paperback novel published by St. Martin's Press, New York. The source imagery for the figures was original studio photography. York then blended the photographic imagery with painted imagery into a final composition.

Studio Usage

This technique explains how to create a marbled tiled floor that fits in with the perspective and lighting conditions in your composition. It makes use of the Fractal Design/Artbeats Sensational Surfaces CD-ROM.

Note: *The Sensational Surfaces CD-ROM is not part of Painter 4. It can be purchased separately and is very useful for creating wall and floor tiled surfaces.*

Related Techniques

1 | Select Tile Texture

Create a new canvas (File→New) that is approximately three times the area of the region in your image that you want to fill with a tiled floor. Select the Leopard 4x4, or any other tile design of your choice, from the Stone Tiles papers library from the Sensational Surfaces CD-ROM.

2 | Apply Tile Texture

Select the Artist Pastel Chalk variant of the Chalk brushes in the Brushes palette. Select Controls→Size to access the Brush Controls: Size palette and increase the Size slider to about 44. Select a medium tone in the Art Materials: palette. Select Effects→Fill and fill the canvas opened in Step 1 with the current color. Select a lighter tone. Apply that lighter tone all over the canvas surface, using the Chalk brush. Select a darker tone. Check the invert box in the expanded Art Materials: Paper palette. Reduce the Grain slider, located in the Controls: Brush palette, to about 14%. Apply the darker tone. You may want to repeat these steps with a variety of tones.

3 | Paint Tile Grout

Select the Grid texture from the 3D Tiles paper library on the CD-ROM. Select a dark shade, almost black, in the Color Selector. Using the same brush as before, apply this texture into the canvas to form the grout between the tiles.

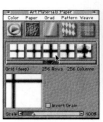

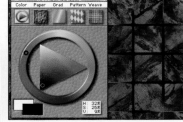

4 | Apply Surface Texture Effect

Select Effects→Surface Control→Apply Surface Texture. Select Using: Paper Grain in the Apply Surface Texture dialog box. Adjust the light source position to match the lighting conditions in your composition. Click OK.

5 | Float Tiles in Main Image

Copy and paste the tile image, created in Steps 1 through 4, into your main image. The tiles are pasted as a floater. Select Effects→Orientation→ Distort. Distort the floater so that it appears to be receding, following the lines of perspective used in the composition. Use the Masking brushes to determine which parts of the tile floater are visible. Click on the F. List icon. Click Drop All.

Hiroshi Yoshii

Star

Comments

This star was created by using the "chalky" method that is described in Technique #7. The layers of chalk are built up until the thick powdery look is created. The musical notes in this image were all created separately and then placed on the image as floating objects, or floaters. They were then repositioned and reoriented by using the Free Transform mode (Effects→Orientation→Free Transform).

Studio Usage

You may develop a set of image elements, or objects, that you wish to re-use in a number of different images. The creation of a customized floater library is a very convenient way to store and access such objects. This technique describes the process you follow to set up a customized floater library.

Related Techniques

1 | Create New Floater Library

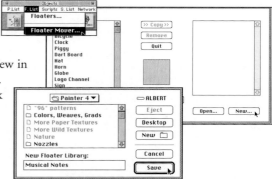

Select F. List→Floater Mover from the Objects palette pull-down submenu. In the Floater Mover dialog box that appears, click on New in the lower right corner. Name your New Floater Library. Click Save. By default it will be saved in the Painter 4 applications folder. Click Quit.

Note: You can save the new Library to any location, including removable media.

2 | Select New Library in Floaters Palette

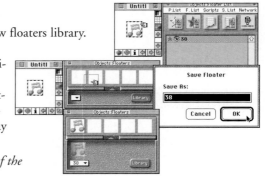

Select F. List→Floaters. The Objects: Floaters palette appears. Open the library drawer by clicking on the bar. You'll see the Painter Portfolio floaters library. Click on the Library button. Locate your newly named floater library and click Open. You'll see an empty library in the Floaters palette.

3 | Float Individual Object and Drag It into New Library

Create the first of the individual objects you want to load into the new floaters library. Float the object (Edit→Float). Select the Floater Adjuster tool in the Tools palette ("F" on the keyboard). Click on the floater object to activate it and drag it into the Floaters palette while holding down the Option {Alt} key. Name the floater and click OK. It appears highlighted in the top left position above the bar as well as in the library drawer. Each successive floater subsequently added to the library in this way also first appears in the top left position.

Note: The holding down of the Option {Alt} key makes sure that a copy of the floater is left behind in the document from which you are dragging it.

4 | Place Objects on Image

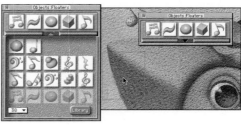

Repeat Step 3 until your library is complete. Open an image where you want to arrange these objects. Drag the floater icons from the library into the image.

Note: If you want to delete or rename the floaters in the library, select F. List→Floater Mover. Click on the floater name in question so that it becomes highlighted. Click on Remove or Change Name. Be careful of Remove—it is irreversible (not even Edit→Undo or ⌘-Z {Ctrl-Z} will bring a removed floater back).

Variations on a Theme *Transitions from Pen and Ink Original*

Jester

Sheriann Ki-Sun Burnham

Comments

These two versions of the Jester design were both based on the same pen and ink drawing originally created outside the computer in black and white. The drawing was scanned and used as a source image for creating a series of PostScript shapes. These shapes were in turn converted into floaters. The design on the left is made up of floaters filled with flat color. In the design on the right each individual floater was painted by using a grainy brush combined with customized textures designed to give a fabric look.

Studio Usage

This technique describes how to use an original pen and ink to form the basis for either a flat graphical design or a textured "quilted" look. The Bézier Pen tool was used to create vector-based shapes based on the original pen and ink drawing. These shapes were then converted to floaters. These floaters form a template that can be filled with either flat color or textured paint. This approach of creating a complete design made up of floaters gives you great flexibility and opportunity to experiment.

Related Techniques

1 | Convert Drawing into Shapes

Open the scanned black-and-white drawing. Select the Bézier Pen tool from the Tools palette. Carefully draw each component shape from which the design is made. Make sure that each shape is closed. (Click on the Close button in the Controls: Shape Design palette.) Click on the F. List icon in the Objects palette. As each shape is created, it will appear listed in the Floater List.

Note: Before you begin creating shapes, select Shapes→Set Default Attributes. Set the Stroke and Fill boxes to be deselected. Shapes will appear depicted by a thin blue line with control points. The points are colored red when selected. Shapes are "objects" that are separate from the background canvas. After the shapes are created, you can delete or erase what is in the background.

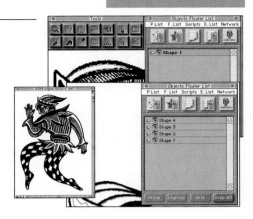

2 | Convert Shapes to Floaters

Select the Floater Adjuster tool in the Tools palette. Any currently selected shapes are now surrounded by a yellow-and-black marquee with control handles. Select Edit→Select All to select all objects listed in the Floater List. Select Shapes→Convert to Selection. Each shape now appears as an active selection surrounded by a black-and-white "marching ants" marquee. They are no longer listed in the Floater List. Click in each selection with the Floater Adjuster tool to turn each selection into a separate floating selection, or floater, which is listed in the Floater List.

Note: Save the file (File→Save As) in RIFF format. RIFF format preserves the floaters as separate layers. It is important to keep a version of this file as a resource that you can go back to.

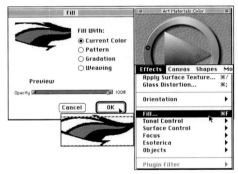

3 | Fill Floaters with Color

Select a floater, or a series of floaters, that you want to fill with a particular color by clicking on their names in the Floater List while holding down the Shift key. Click on the Color icon in the Art Materials palette. Select the required color in the Color Selector. Select Effects→Fill and click OK. The floaters are now filled. Repeat this for all floaters until the graphic-looking design is complete. Save this file with a different name than the resource file saved in Step 2.

4 | Paint in Floaters with Grainy Brush for Textured Look

Open the file saved in Step 2. Select one floater at a time. Select a grainy brush, such as the Large Chalk variant of the Chalk brushes. Click on the Paper icon in the Art Materials palette if you haven't already torn it off. Select a texture from the Art Materials: Paper palette. Select a suitable color on the Color Selector. Paint in the floater. Check the invert box in the expanded Papers palette (with the library drawer closed). Change the current color. Paint over the same floater, filling in the inverse space left white. Continue this process for all the floaters. Save the file with a different file name.

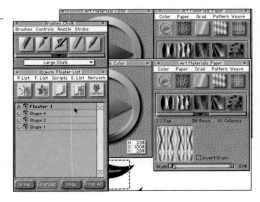

Variations on a Theme *Screenprint Look*

Painter 4

Hal Rucker

Comments

This image, created in the style of an Andy Warhol screenprint, was featured on the "Painter Through the Ages" Painter 4 poster. Rucker began with a photograph of the Painter 4 can. He applied the Express Texture effect with different settings to generate a series of slightly different black-and-white can images. The different colored regions were filled floaters with the Gel Composite method selected, which allowed the black lines of the can to show through. He then used the vector-based shapes to create an outline that he could duplicate and stroke with different colors on each version of the can. The final set of can images were flattened and composited together against black.

Studio Usage

In a typical screen print there are clearly defined blocks of translucent color, often bounded by sharp edges, that allow underlying darker colors to show through. The combination of being able to draw vector-based shapes and then convert them to floaters provides a convenient means to create the look of a screenprint. The use of floaters also allows you to easily create a variety of different color combinations that can be displayed together as a montage, as illustrated in this example. This technique describes how to begin with a color photograph and end with a screenprint-looking image.

Related Techniques

Scraping Away Black to
Reveal Color   11

Paint on Papyrus   32

Working from a Layer   76

Using the Interaction of Two
Overlapping Photographs   92

1 | Create Black and White Background Image

Open a color photograph. Use the Rectangular selection tool with the Shift key held down to create a square selection within the photograph. Select Edit→Copy. Select Edit→Paste→Into New Image. You'll have a cropped, square image. Select Effects→Surface Control→Express Texture. In the Express Texture dialog box, set Using: Image Luminance and adjust the sliders until you see a satisfactory black-and-white rendition of the image in the Preview window. Click OK.

2 | Draw Shape

Use the Pen tool in the Tools palette to create an outline shape around one closed region of your image where you want to apply a block of uniform color. Click on the F. List icon in the Objects palette. The shape is listed in the Floater List. If the shape is not complete, click the Close button on the Controls: Shape Design palette. If you want the shape to be used for an outline effect, rather than for filling with a flat block of color, select Shapes→Set Attributes and set the Stroke and Fill parameters accordingly.

3 | Convert Shape to Floater

With the shape highlighted, select Shapes→Convert to Selection. Select the Floater Adjuster tool ("F" on the keyboard). Hold down the Option {Alt} key while you click inside the selection. You'll create a floater while leaving the original image in the background (important because that is what will need to show through the floater).

Note: *If the region you are trying to select is the outer border of the image, draw a shape around the inner region, convert it to a selection, and then select Edit→Mask→Invert Mask.*

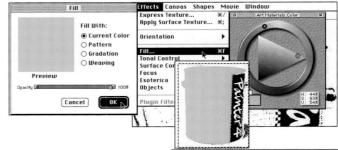

4 | Fill Floater

Click on the Color icon in the Art Materials palette. Select the color in the Color Selector for filling the floater. Select Effects→Fill (⌘-F) {Ctrl-F}. You will see Fill With: Current Color selected and a Preview window showing the floater with solid color. Click OK. The floater now obstructs your view of the background.

5 | Apply Gel Composite Method

Select Gel from the Composite Method pull-down menu. Adjust the Opacity slider in the Controls palette until you have the right amount of intensity of color. Repeat Steps 2 through 5 until the entire image is covered with floaters.

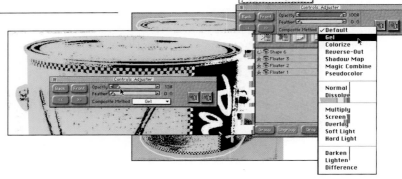

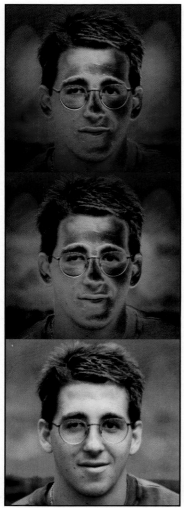

Michael Cinque

The Many Moods of Andrew

Comments

This series of images was all created from a single source image by utilizing a combination of effects in Painter, including the Composite Method interaction of floaters, Tonal Control, Color Adjustment, and Apply Lighting. Cinque took advantage of the great freedom that floaters offer to try out different combinations of color and Composite Methods. The final effect has a similar feel to the solarization effect you can achieve in a dark room when the developing paper is exposed to a flash of light.

Studio Usage

This technique describes how to create a series of solarized looking images from a single source photograph. It explains the sequence and arrangement of floaters and effects needed to give this result. You'll find an enormous amount of opportunity for experimentation in the way you treat different floaters in this process to create variations.

Related Techniques

1 Paste Source Image onto Canvas

Select File→New and specify a new canvas size in pixels that is the same width and three times higher than the source photograph. With the original source photograph active on the desktop, select Edit→Select All. Then make the new, larger canvas active by clicking on it. Select Edit→Paste→Normal. You'll paste a copy of the photo onto the new canvas where it is automatically a floater. Click on the F. List icon in the Objects palette. The floater name is listed in the Floater List. Repeat the pasting operation two more times. Use the Floater Adjuster tool to drag each pasted floater into position so they do not overlap.

Note: By default, each floater is called "Floater 1" in the Floater List. To differentiate between them, double-click on each floater name in turn. Type in a new name for each floater in the dialog box that appears. Click OK.

2 Make Underlying Floaters Negative

One by one make each floater active by clicking on its name in the Floater List (or directly on the floater itself by using the Floater Adjuster tool) and select Effects→Tonal Control→Negative. These three negative images will form the underlying floaters in this composition.

3 Paste Source Image Over Each Underlying Floater and Adjust Colors

Repeat the pasting of the source image and repositioning of each resulting floater as described in Step 1 above. You now have two layers of floaters, all with an identical source image, with the underlying floaters being negatives. Select the middle, upper floater. Select Effects→Tonal Control→Adjust Colors. Using the default Uniform Color setting, move the Hue Shift slider to change the color in the floater.

4 Select Darken Composite Method for the Upper Floater

Select the Floater Adjuster tool. With the middle upper floater still active, select Darken from the Composite Method pull-down menu in the Controls: Adjuster palette. You will now see the solarized effect in the middle image. In turn, select the other two upper floaters one by one and repeat Steps 4 and 5, adjusting their colors differently to create an interesting series.

Variations on a Theme *Using the Interaction of Two Overlapping Photographs*

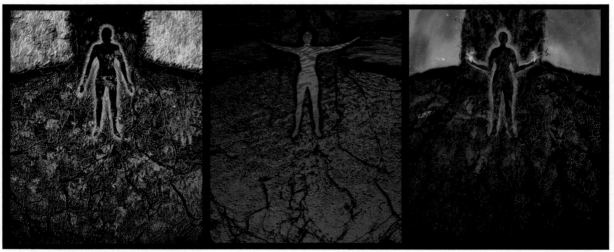

Karin Schminke

Roots: Earth, Water and Fire

Comments

This triptych of images was based on a series of photographs of roots on the side of a building. The photographs were initially flipped vertically and their contrast increased to bring out the structure of the roots. The roots parts of the photographs were then introduced as "floaters" on top of three totally separate photographs. The underlying photographs, two of ferns, one of water, were color enhanced for dramatic effect. The floater Composite Method was then adjusted to give the result you see above. The woman's figure was painted in as a mask, using the masking brushes. The Mask Drawing icons were adjusted to selectively mask out the figure, or mask everything but the figure. In this way Schminke was able to make the figures stand out.

Studio Usage

This technique describes how to utilize the interaction between two separate, overlapping photographs to achieve interesting and eye-catching variations. The principle steps involve first enhancing each photograph separately for color and contrast, and then introducing one as a floater over the other and adjusting the Composite Method to control how they interact. Each stage of this process offers room for experimentation and variation.

Related Techniques

1 | Float Section of One Photograph over Another

Select the two photographs to be used. Crop and/or resize each image to suit the file size for the final image. Use the freehand selection Lasso to select the section of the photograph you want to float above the other image. Click Close on the Controls: Lasso palette to complete the selection. Select Edit→Copy (⌘-C) {Ctrl-C}. Make the other photograph active by clicking on it. Select Edit→Paste→Normal(⌘-V) {Ctrl-V}. Click on the F. List icon in the Objects palette. The new floater now appears in the Floater List.

Note: To crop an image, use the Rectangular selection tool to describe your cropping boundaries. Select Edit→Copy (⌘) {Ctrl-C} followed by Edit→Paste→Into New Image. To resize, select Canvas→Resize.

2 | Use Curves to Increase Contrast in Floater Photograph

Select the floater by clicking on it (or on its name in the Floater List) with the Floater Adjuster tool. Select Effects→Tonal Control→Correct Colors. Select Curve from the pull-down menu within the Color Correction dialog box. The default curve is the "master" curve. Click and drag on the master curve to bring it below the diagonal blue line on the left and above the line on the right. This S-shaped curve results in an increased contrast that is immediately viewable in the photograph. Click OK when satisfied with the contrast.

Note: You can also experiment with adjusting the red, green, and blue curves. To do this, click on the appropriately colored square in the Color Correction dialog box and then drag different parts of the curve around.

3 | Adjust Colors in Underlying Photograph

Deselect the floater by clicking outside it with the Floater Adjuster tool (or below its name in the Floater List). Select Effects→Tonal Control→Adjust Colors. Select the Using: Image Luminance from the pull-down menu in the Adjust Color dialog box. Move the Hue Shift slider until you see the appropriate colors in the preview window. Click OK.

Note: At this stage, if you want to view the underlying photograph unobstructed by the floater, click on the eye icon next to the floater name in the Floater List. The eye closes, and the floater becomes invisible. Click on the closed eye again to make the floater visible.

4 | Adjust Composite Method

Select the floater by clicking on it with the Floater Adjuster tool. Adjust the Composite Method from the pull-down menu in the Controls: Adjuster palette to achieve the desired result.

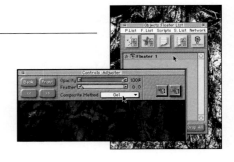

Note: The Darken and Gel Composite Methods give particularly effective results in this example.

Stars

Jeremy Sutton

Comments

This series of stars was created by using the ability of Painter to express a gradation in an image. When a gradation is expressed in an image, the colors in the image are replaced with the colors in the gradation. The replacing of colors is based on the luminance of the pixels. The default becomes the lightest and darkest pixels, which are replaced by colors from the two ends of the gradation.

Studio Usage

This technique provides a quick and easy way to try out different color combinations in a two-color design based on a black-and-white source image. By selecting the Two-Point gradation, which is based on the Primary and Secondary colors, you can conveniently map these two colors to the black-and-white regions of the image.

Related Techniques

1 | Select Colors and Gradation

Open the Color Selector in the Art Materials palette. Select the color you want to appear in the white region of your image. It will be the Primary Color (displayed in the forward rectangle of the Color Selector). Click on the Secondary Color rectangle (partially obscured by the Primary Color rectangle). Select the color you want to appear in the black portion of your image. Click on the Grad icon in the Art Materials palette. Select the Two-Point gradient. It is represented by an icon showing a white rectangle partially overlapped by a black one. You may need to open the Gradient library drawer to locate it. When selected, it appears above the drawer bar enclosed in a red boundary.

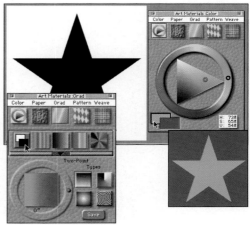

2 | Express Gradation

Select Grad→Express in Image from the pull-down submenu in the Art Materials palette. Click OK. The colors are now visible in the image, replacing the white and black. Magnify the boundary between the two colors and observe how the gradation has been mapped to the gray pixels.

Note: *The Express in Image command replaces gray pixels with colors that smoothly blend from one end point color to the other. This smooth transition between colors is one of the benefits of expressing a two-point gradation in the black-and-white image, rather than separately selecting and filling the black-and-white regions.*

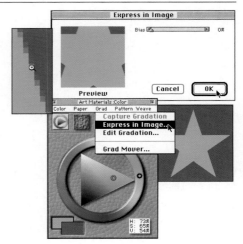

3 | Change Color Combination

Save the new colored image (File→Save As). Re-open the original black and white design (File→Open) (⌘-O) {Ctrl-O}. Select a new Primary and Secondary Color combination. Repeat Step 2. Continue this process for other color combinations.

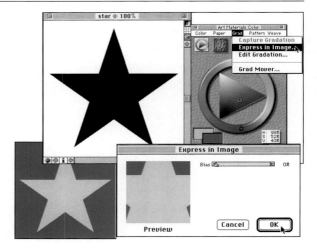

Variations on a Theme *Texturizing Photographs*

Ice House 1 and 2

Bonny Lhotka

Comments

Lhotka often begins her computer paintings by scanning a monotype print and using that as a background image upon which to build different variations. She experiments extensively with lighting and embossing effects, creation of floaters and adjustment of the floater Composite Methods, and cloning from source images that are quite different from the working image. She then works into her digital images by using a variety of brushes, such as bleaches and smeary brushes. The final image is then printed on an inlay laminate acrylic monotype and further worked with "real" acrylic paint.

Studio Usage

This technique offers a simple way to create interesting variations of color and texture in a given scanned image of traditional art. It is a small part of the process that Lhotka goes through to create one of her paintings. It takes advantage of the power of the floater Composite Methods.

Related Techniques

1 | Create Initial Background

Open a new document. Select a primary color in the Art Materials: Color palette. Click on the secondary color rectangle and select a secondary color. Open the Art Materials: Grad palette by clicking on the Grad icon. Select the Two-Point gradation. Adjust the angle of the gradient. Select the Paint Bucket in the Tools palette. Click in the canvas. It fills with the gradation.

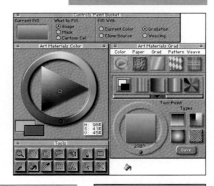

Note: The original image size in this example was 500 pixels wide by 450 pixels high. Smaller file sizes give faster playback of the recorded script. The playback rate is dependent on the speed of your computer.

2 | Set Recorder Going

Open the Scripts palette in the Objects palette. Make sure that the scripts library drawer is closed so that you can see the control buttons. Click on the central red button to start the recording. (You can also start the recording by selecting Scripts→Record Script in the Objects palette submenu.) Now proceed to paint your image.

Note: Select Scripts→Script Options in the pull-down menu in the objects palette. The default has Record Initial State checked, which means that whenever you replay the script it will attempt to recreate the same initial set of parameters of your brushes, color, and texture. By unchecking this you have the freedom to vary the initial conditions every time you play it back. The danger is that you may never be able to exactly reproduce the same painting twice. Click OK.

3 | Stop and Save Recording

When the painting is complete, click on the left-hand black square button in the Scripts palette (or select Scripts→Stop Recording). The recording will stop. Type in a name for your recorded script. A "thumbnail" representation of the final image now appears in the scripts library.

4 | Create New Background

Open a new document (File→New or ⌘-N {Ctrl-N}) of the same size as before. Select a new gradation. Click with the Paint Bucket in the image to create a new background against which to replay the painting.

5 | Replay Painting Over New Background

Select the recorded script you named in Step 3 by clicking on its thumbnail or dragging down to its name in the scripts library. Close the scripts library drawer. Click the Play button in the Scripts palette (forward arrow, second from left). (Alternatively, you can select Scripts→Playback Scripts.) The painting now replays against the new background. You can repeat this for many different backgrounds.

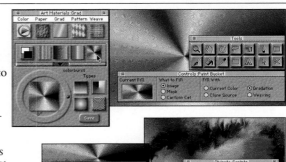

Variations on a Theme *Repeating Motif Color Overlay*

George Ho ©1994

Paper Cranes

Comments

This technique explores the theme of origami paper cranes, both as objects that appear to float in front of the background and as a texture used in the border. The cranes were originally designed as black-and-white line drawings, using the 2B Pencil with the straight lines draw style. The central background was built by successive applications of scanned papers and patterns as surface textures. The crane pattern in the black border was introduced as a color overlay. The large cranes were floaters whose component segments were filled with different patterns. Finally, drop shadows were added to the floaters.

Studio Usage

If you have a number of related objects, or motifs, in your composition, you can incorporate these into a subtle background pattern by applying them as a gray color overlay against black. This technique explains how to do that. You will learn how to create a seamless paper texture that can then be applied as a color overlay. The principle used has many applications in introducing a repeating motif in a subtle way.

Related Techniques

1 | Create Pattern Out of Floaters

Paste objects onto a square canvas 400 pixels by 400 pixels. The objects become floaters. After each object is pasted, select Effects→Orientation→Free Transform. This creates "handles" on the yellow-and-black marquee around the active floater. Hold down the ⌘ {Ctrl} key while dragging the corner handles in order to rotate the floater. Rotate and reposition the floaters throughout the canvas. Click on the floaters holding the Option {Alt} key to make identical copies. Select Effects→Orientation→Commit Transform when you are satisfied with the orientation of the floater (the floater needs to be active when this is done).

Note: You may find it convenient to click the Trim button in the expanded Floater List in the Objects palette for each active floater. This trick shrinks the marquee to fit snugly around the visible part of the floater (the unmasked section).

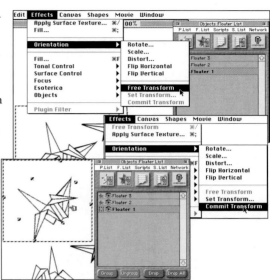

2 | Make a Seamless Pattern

Select Drop All in the Floater List. The floaters are now all merged with the background canvas. Select Pattern→Define Pattern from the pull-down submenu in the Art Materials palette. Hold down the Shift key while dragging in the image with the Grabber hand (from the Tools palette). The pattern now scrolls seamlessly. Add some overlapping floaters at this stage. Click the Drop All button in the Floater List to flatten the image when you have finished modifying the pattern.

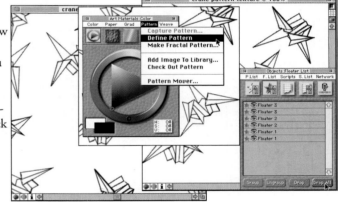

3 | Capture Pattern as Paper Texture

Capture the paper texture by referring to Technique #35. Repeat those steps here so that the seamless pattern you have created is added to the current paper library in the Art Materials palette. Open the paper library. Select the texture you have just captured. Close the library drawer. The Paper palette should be expanded so that you can see the Scale slider. Check the Invert box so the texture is seen as white lines against a black background.

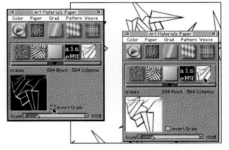

4 | Apply Color Overlay

Select the region of image where you want the texture applied. In this case the Edit→Magic Wand was used to select the black border. Select Effects→Surface Control→Color Overlay. Select Using: Paper Grain and Model: Hiding Power within the Color Overlay dialog box. Adjust the Opacity slider until you see the desired result in the preview window. Click OK.

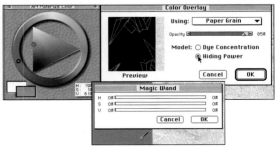

Variations on a Theme *Expressing Different Colors Using the Gradations Editor*

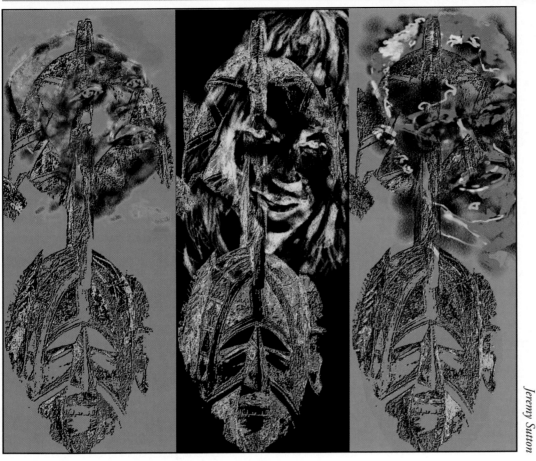

Jeremy Sutton

Spirits of Freedom: Martin, Esther and Malcolm

Comments

This triptych was created for a museum invitational exhibit of artwork that linked masks to the theme of the relationship of the African-American and Jewish-American communities in the civil rights movement. The starting point was a grayscale scan of a Congolese mask used in rites of initiation into adulthood. This mask image was manipulated and three different versions were generated. The portraits of Martin Luther King, Jr., Esther (based on Ethiopian singer Aster Aweke), and Malcolm X were then cloned into each of the three mask backgrounds.

Studio Usage

A convenient way to experiment with the expression of different colors in an image is by using Painter to express a gradation in an image. In this case the gradient editor was used to customize the colors that were then expressed in the image. This technique can be applied to any original image, whether grayscale or colored.

Related Techniques

1 | Select Two-Point Gradient

Click on the Grad icon in the Art Materials palette. Open the gradient library drawer and select the Two-Point gradient represented by an icon showing a black rectangle overlapping a white rectangle. Select Grad→Edit Gradation from the drop-down menu in the Art Materials palette.

Note: The Two-Point gradient uses the currently selected primary and secondary colors selected in the Art Materials→Color Selector to define the two end-point colors between which a gradient is generated.

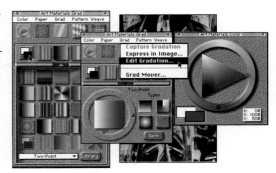

2 | Edit Gradation

The Edit Gradation dialog box shows the existing two-point gradation displayed in a horizontal rectangular format with sliding triangular indicators at either end. Click in the gradient rectangle. A new sliding indicator appears where you clicked. Click on the Color icon in the Art Materials palette. The Color Selector shows the color at the region of the gradient where you clicked. Adjust the Color Selector to show a new color. This new primary color is now reflected in the gradient at the position in which you clicked. If you wish to change the color associated with an existing indicator, click on the indicator so that it becomes darkened (active) and then change color. Continue this process until you are satisfied with the range and distribution of colors in the gradation. Click OK in the Edit Gradation dialog box.

Note: This is a situation where it can be useful to tear off the Color Selector palette and be able to have it displayed on the desktop simultaneously with the Gradient palette. To tear off the Color Selector palette, click and drag on its icon in the Art Materials palette while another icon is active.

3 | Express Gradation in Image

Select Grad→Express in Image from the pull-down submenu in the Art Materials palette. Move the Bias slider slowly from 0% to 100% and observe in the preview window how colors from your customized gradation are expressed differently in the image. When you come across a bias setting that works well, click OK and save the file with a new name. Then reopen the original image again and apply the Express in Image with a different bias setting.

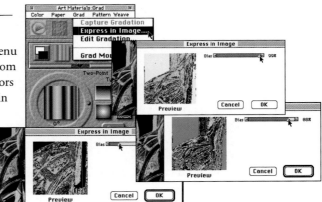

4 | Apply Surface Texture Using Image Luminance

Select Effects→Surface Control→Apply Surface Texture. Select Using: Image Luminance. Adjust the Amount and Shine sliders to give a satisfying effect. Click OK. This gives a final embossed look to the images prior to cloning in other imagery.

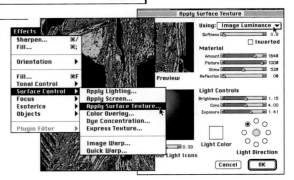

The Painter's Hand

Sharron Evans

Comments

This illustration was inspired by a demonstration of computer graphics by five artists using electronic tablets. The image was scanned from a simple black-and-white line drawing and then completely redrawn on the computer. The top hand holding a pen was drawn using the Scratchboard tool. The Lasso tool was used to trace around this image and create a floater. This floater was duplicated into a second floater, which was rotated, rescaled, and repositioned. The final image incorporates weaves with custom colors and folds that simulate the contour of the body.

Studio Usage

This technique shows how to custom color a weave pattern and then achieve the effect of folds in clothing in that pattern. The great advantage in working with this technique is that you can easily see how the pattern and colors of a garment appear as they fold and contour to the body. This technique could just as easily be applied to fabrics used in interior decoration and home furnishings, such as draperies.

Related Techniques

Paint on Papyrus   32

Creating a Stone Tiled Floor   87

Adding Shadows to
Cartoons   115

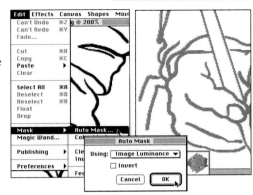

1 | Select the Sleeve

Create a black drawing against a white background. Make sure that the sleeve has a solid black line completely enclosing it. Select Edit→ Mask→Auto Mask. Select Using: Image Luminance and click OK. A mask has now been generated wherever there is black in the image.

2 | Put New Colors in the Weave

Click on the Weave icon in the Art Materials palette. Click and drag the Color icon away from the Art Materials palette. This tears off the Art Materials: Color palette so that colors can be selected while viewing the Art Materials: Weave palette. Select the weave you want to use. Click on the Get Color button. A two-color Color Set appears with the current colors used in the select-ed weave pattern. Select a new color in the Color Selector and hold down the Option {Alt} key while you click in one of the Color Set boxes. You'll replace the color in that box with the one you have selected. Repeat this for the second color. Click on Put Color button in the Weaves Palette. The Weave now contains the new colors.

3 | Apply Cartoon Cel Fill with Weave

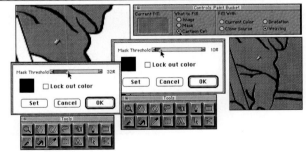

Double-click on the Paint Bucket in the Tools palette. Move the Mask Threshold from 0% to some higher value. Select What to Fill: Cartoon Cel and Fill With: Weaving in the Controls Palette. Click in the sleeve. If the weave fills beyond the sleeve, select Edit→Undo. You can use the Masking Pen with black to rectify leaks or you can increase the Mask Threshold. Click again with the Paint Bucket. Repeat this until you get a clean fill.

4 | Float the Sleeve and Apply Image Wrap to Model the Folds

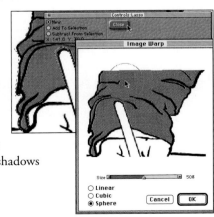

Use the freehand selection Lasso to select the sleeve. Click on the Controls: Lasso palette Close button. Select the Floater Adjuster tool and, while holding down the Option {Alt} key, click in the selection to float the sleeve. Make the floater with the filled sleeve active. Select Effects→Surface Control→Image Warp. Select the Sphere method and click and drag in different areas of the weave showing in the preview window to model the weave. Click OK. Choose the Large Chalk variant of the Chalk brush family. Draw and shade lines and shadows over the modeled weave to give definition to the folds.

Jane Kriss

Comments

This mosaic composition was built from a simple Greek motif. The motif was used to create a mosaic, which was then applied as a pattern. The leaf was then added, using floaters and free transforms to position and orient them.

Studio Usage

This technique shows how to create a mosaic based on a colored motif and then how to apply it as a pattern fill in a final composition. The principles used in this technique can be widely applied any time you want to convert a repeating image element into mosaic tiles.

Related Techniques

Photograph into Mosaic   40

Painting Mosaic Grout   84

Brocade Effect   101

1 │ Create Clone

Open the colored motif that will form the basis of the mosaic pattern. Select
File→Clone followed by Canvas→Make Mosaic.

*Note: The Clone command automatically sets the original file as the Clone Source. The
Make Mosaic command automatically fills the Clone image with black grout.*

2 │ Use Clone Color for Pattern

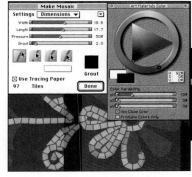

In the Make Mosaic dialog box, check Use Tracing
Paper. Adjust the mosaic Dimensions Settings to give a
mosaic tile of the appropriate size. Click on the Color
icon in the Art Materials palette. In the expanded Art
Materials: Color palette, check Use Clone Color.
Carefully paint in the mosaic tiles where you see the
pattern showing through the tracing paper.

*Note: You can use the mosaic editing tools if you make a
mistake to remove, add, or change the color of tiles.*

3 │ Add Painted Elements and a Background

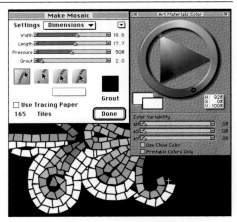

Uncheck Use Clone Color in the Color palette. While selecting colors
from the color selector, paint in additional mosaic tiles not based on the
original pattern. Finally, select white (or the color of your choice) and
paint white mosaic tiles into the remaining black space. When you are
completely finished, click Done in the Make Mosaic dialog box.

4 │ Create Pattern

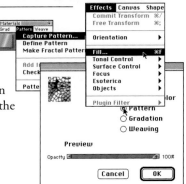

Save the existing image as a RIFF file for future reference. Select
Edit→Select All (⌘-A) {Ctrl-A} followed by Patterns→Capture Pattern
from the Art Materials palette. Give the Pattern a name. Open a new canvas the size
of your final image. Select Effects→Fill (⌘-F) {Ctrl-F} and check the Patterns option
in the Fill dialog box. Press OK. You now have a repeating mosaic pattern based on the
original motif.

Fabrics and Wallpaper *Slanted Pattern*

Comments

This pattern was originally created with fabric design in mind. Burnham started by creating a colored marker pen sketch on paper. She scanned the sketch, converted it to grayscale, and then recolored it in Painter using effects like color overlay and dye concentration. She distorted the recolored image and made it into a floater. The floater was duplicated, flipped, and recolored. The two floaters were then fitted together and formed the source of a slanted, seamless repeating pattern. More identical floaters were added to the image until it had been filled. The coloring and distortion were chosen to give the final pattern a feel of three-dimensionality.

Studio Usage

This technique describes how to create a slanted repeating pattern with a three-dimensional feel from a distorted original drawing. The technique involves applying the Distortion effect to a source drawing and then making a reflected version of that distorted element. The two floaters that result from this fit together and form the basis of a seamless pattern.

Related Techniques

1 | Distort Source Drawing

Open a colored source drawing that has a design with a solid rectangular outline surrounded by a white border. Use the Rectangular Selection tool in the Tools palette to draw a selection path over the design outline. Select Effects→Orientation→ Distort to turn your selection into a floater. Drag the corner handles to distort the image into an irregular non-rectangular form. Make the left vertical side longer than the right vertical side. Make all four sides slanted. Click OK in the Distort Selection dialog box.

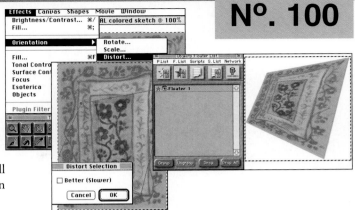

2 | Duplicate and Flip Floater

Click on the floater with the Floater Adjuster tool while holding down the Option {Alt} key. Drag the duplicate and move it into position. Click on the F. List icon in the Objects palette. With only the duplicated floater active, select Effects→ Orientation→Free Transform. Then select Effects→ Orientation→Flip Horizontal, followed by Flip Vertical. Use the Floater Adjuster Tool to reposition the second floater to fit against the first floater. Use the arrow keys for pixel by pixel movement.

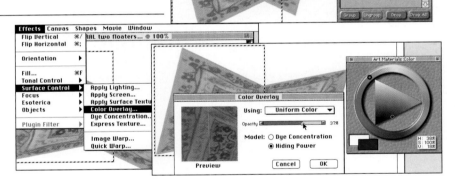

3 | Adjust Color in Second Floater

With the second floater active, select Effects→Surface Control→Color Overlay. Select a light color in the Color Selector. Select Using Uniform Color and Hiding Power in the Color Overlay dialog box. Adjust the Opacity slider until satisfied with the result showing in the preview window. Click OK.

4 | Transform into Seamless Pattern

Click on both floater names in the Floater List while holding down the Shift key. Click the Group button followed by the Collapse button in the Floater List. The two floaters will now become a single floater. Click the floater using the Floater Adjust tool while holding down the Option {Alt} key. You'll create duplicates of the new collapsed floater. Position the new floaters so they fit into the original one like pieces of a jigsaw puzzle. Continue until the resulting pattern fills the image.

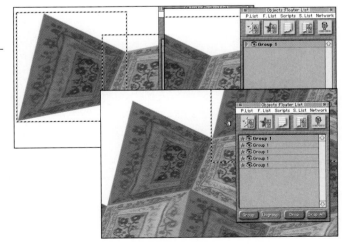

Jane Kriss

Comments

The brocade design you see in this image was based on a traditional Greek motif. It was scanned from a simple black-and-white line drawing and applied over a striped background. The final image incorporates hand-painted vines and stripes filled with color and patterns.

Studio Usage

This technique shows how to achieve the relief effect of jacquard or brocade where a pattern is woven into fabric without a change in color. The great advantage of working with this technique in the digital world, compared to traditional fabric design, is the ease and flexibility you have of experimenting with different backgrounds without redoing the brocade pattern artwork. This technique could just as easily be applied to all surface designs.

Related Techniques

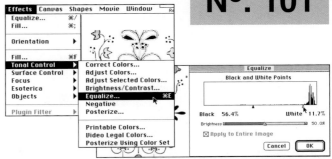

1 | Adjust Scan

Open the scanned motif. Select Effects→Tonal Control→Equalize (⌘-E) {Ctrl-E}. Adjust the Black and White Points until you have a clean, crisp, contrasted image devoid of grays. Select Effects→Tonal Control→Negative. The white motif is now seen against a black background.

2 | Float Motif

Select Edit→Select All (⌘-A) {Ctrl-A} followed by Edit→Float. The pattern is now floating above the canvas background and is listed in the Floater List. While the floater is selected (highlighted in the Floater List) and the Floater Adjuster tool is selected, change the Opacity slider in the Controls: Adjuster palette to 50% and change the Composite Method, also in the Controls: Adjuster palette, to Normal.

3 | Create Stripes

Deselect the Floater with Edit→Deselect (⌘-D) {Ctrl-D}. Use the Rectangular Selection tool to create a tall, thin, selected region that stretches from the top to the bottom of the image. Choose a color in the Art Materials: Color palette) that you wish to fill the stripe with. Select Effects→Fill (⌘-F) {Ctrl-F} and make sure that the Current Color is checked in the dialog box. Press OK. To repeat the same stripe elsewhere in the image select Edit→Copy (⌘-C) {Ctrl-C} followed by Edit→Paste→Normal (⌘-V) {Ctrl-V}. When this new stripe is correctly positioned with reference to the pattern, click on Drop in the Floater List.

Note: *Every time you copy and paste stripes you create new floaters that will appear above the original pattern floater in the Floater List. It is important to either drop the stripe floaters or ensure they are below the original pattern floater in order to see the brocade effect.*

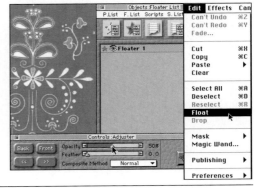

4 | Variations

Besides filling the stripes with a flat color, you can fill them with patterns from the Patterns Library in the Art Materials palette. You can experiment with varying the Floater Composite Method drop-down menu in the Controls palette to get some interesting effects.

5 | Create Pattern

Save the existing image, with the pattern floater, as a RIFF file for future reference. Select Drop All in the Floater List and then Edit→Select All (⌘-A) {Ctrl-A}, followed by Patterns→Capture Pattern from the Art Materials palette. Give the Pattern a name and, in the expanded Art Materials: Pattern palette, adjust the Pattern Type to Vertical and the offset to 50%. Open a new canvas the size of your final image. Select Effects→Fill (⌘-F) {Ctrl-F} and check the Patterns option in the Fill dialog box. Press OK. You now have a repeating brocade pattern based on the original motif.

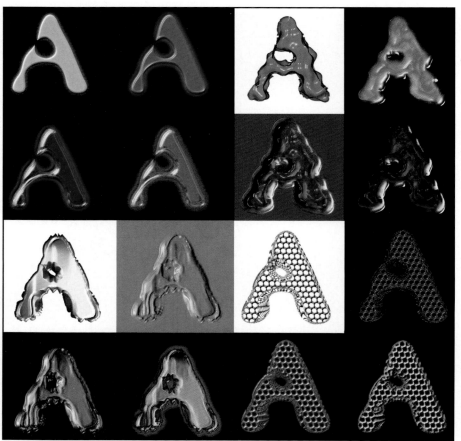

Anders F Rönnblom

Freaky Type Collection

Comments

Rönnblom creates new typographical images by using Painter. For his Freaky Type Collection, Anders used a 3D program, Pixar Typestry, to model and render a character with his custom-made metal, glass, and plastic materials. The rendered file was retouched in Photoshop and then opened in Painter and turned into a floater.

He then made several duplicates of this Floater and used different feathering settings to change the floater masks. By using various commands he "sculpted" and "painted" new forms and surfaces.

Studio Usage

This technique describes how, after making your character a floater, you can use the Softness and Reflection parameters in the Apply Surface Texture effect dialog box to introduce the look of a pattern reflecting off a shiny, solid plastic or glass form. This technique can be complemented by the addition of duplicate floaters to which different effects and Composite Methods are applied.

Related Techniques

Watery Ripples from
   Marble and Warp 58

Three-Dimensional
   Shiny Gold 108

Spherical Buttons 112

1 | Float Character

Begin with a black character against a white background. Select Edit→Mask→Auto Mask. Select Using: Image Luminance within the Auto Mask dialog box to generate a mask based on how dark the pixels are. Black will be 100% and white 0%. Select the third Mask Visibility icon, accessible from the small pop-up menu in the lower left of the document (or the Objects: Path List palette). It turns the mask into a selection. Click on the selection with the Floater Adjuster tool to convert the selection into a floater. You'll see this as Floater 1 (or a similar name) in the Objects: Floater List.

Note: The character can be imported from another program, drawn freehand, or typed using the Text tool. The Magic Wand can also be used to make the selection.

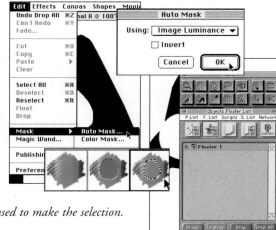

2 | Create Pattern Source Document

Open the Art Materials: Patterns library and select the pattern you want reflected in the character. Open a new canvas approximately the size of the main document with the character in it. Here the new canvas is called "Untitled-1." Select Effects→Fill (⌘-F) {Ctrl-F}. Select Fill With: Pattern. Click OK. Select File→Clone Source→Untitled-1 to set the patterned canvas to be the clone source.

Note: In this example the pattern has been customized and added to the Patterns library by using Patterns→Capture Pattern when the repeating, seamless tile was selected.

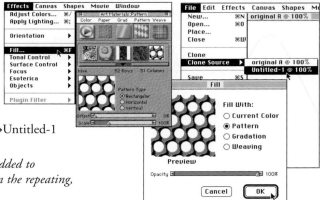

3 | Fill Character with White

Return to the image of the character. Select the name of the floater in the Floater List so that it is highlighted. Select white as the current color in the Art Materials: Color palette. Select Effects→Fill (⌘-F) {Ctrl-F} or (⌘-/) {Ctrl-/} since it was the last effect used). Select Fill With: Current Color within the Fill dialog box. The character is no longer visible because it is white against a white background.

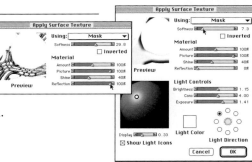

4 | Apply Surface Texture

Select Effects→Surface Control→Apply Surface Texture. Select Using: Mask. Adjust the Softness slider and observe the three-dimensional shadowing. The default for the Reflection parameter is 0%. Move the Reflection slider all the way to the right (100%). Move the Softness slider again and observe how it affects the reflection. Click OK.

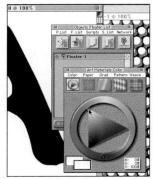

Typography and Calligraphy *Neon Lettering Interacting with a Photograph*

Nadja
je t'ai laissé
à ces deux rails
qui fuient vers ton horizon de futur

Jean-Luc Touillon

Wagon Nadja

Comments

This image is a composite of two photographs and two groups of letters. The train photograph was cropped. The woman was converted from black-and-white into sepia tone, resized to match the window, and then cloned into the other cropped photograph using the Soft Cloner variant to give a soft blending. Both sets of lettering were brought into the image as floaters. These floaters were resized and repositioned by using the Free Transform feature. The Composite Method for the large neon lettering was used to give the interaction between the neon lettering and the background image.

Studio Usage

This technique describes how to create neon lettering and then introduce that lettering into a photographic image in such a way that the colors of the lettering appear to interact with the background image. This technique makes use of the ability to stroke a Shape, convert it to a floater, feather and resize the floater, and finally control the Composite Method that determines how the floater visually interacts with the background. The principles discussed here can be applied with many variations, such as different color combinations and different Composite Methods.

Related Techniques

1 | Create Text

Select the Text tool from the Tools palette. Select the desired font from the pull-down menu in the Controls: Text palette. Adjust the Point Size slider to give the correct size of lettering. Click on your canvas where you want the text to begin. Start typing. (Prior to this step, create a new file especially for the lettering.)

2 | Set Shape Attributes

Click on the icon below the F. List pull-down menu. Each letter appears as one or more shapes. All shapes are highlighted. Click the Group button. Select Shapes→Set Attributes. Uncheck the Fill option and check the Stroke option. Click on the Stroke color square. Select a deep blue color. Adjust the Width slider so the stroke is the maximum width for the lettering. Click OK.

3 | Duplicate Group and Change Attributes

Select the Floater Adjuster tool in the Tools palette. Hold down the Option {Alt} key and click on the lettering. Select Shapes→Set Attributes. Select a lighter brighter blue. Reduce the Width slider slightly. Click OK.

4 | Convert Text Shapes into a Single Image Floater and Paste onto Photograph

Hold down the Shift key and click on each Shape Group name in the Floater List so they are both selected. Click the Group button. Click the Collapse button. Select Edit→Copy (⌘-C) {Ctrl-C}. Click on the photographic image on which you want the lettering to appear. Select Edit→Paste→Normal (⌘-V) {Ctrl-V}. The Floater Adjuster Tool should be selected in the Tools palette. Change the Composite Method in the Controls: Adjuster palette from Default to Difference.

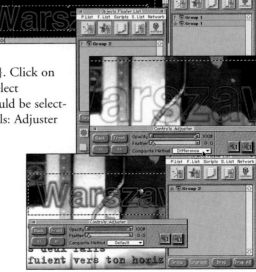

1996

John Derry

Comments

This image was created for the Fractal Design 1996 Season's Greetings card. Derry began by experimenting with black-and-white designs of the numbers "96." These designs were used to generate the background, as well as the patterns on the torn paper letters "1996." Every element in this design, except the blue-and-pink background, was a floater. The technique used to create the metallic "96s" is described elsewhere (see Technique #108).

Studio Usage

This technique describes how you can create the look of torn paper. Normally, you can apply a paper surface texture to give the shadows and shine a hint of three-dimensionality. However, when you have a uniform repeating pattern, the flatness of the pattern (which is not affected by applying surface texture) reduces the realism of the paper look. You can overcome this problem by first applying the glass distortion effect to distort the pattern in a way consistent with the crumpled paper texture. The torn edges are created by editing the floater mask around the edges and finishing with white chalk.

Related Techniques

1 | Select Paper Grain

Create the shape of your torn paper on a white background. Float it (Edit→Float) and fill it (Effects→Fill or ⌘-F {Ctrl-F}) with a pattern. Open the Art Materials: Paper library. Click on the Library button. Access the Sensational Surfaces CD-ROM Volume 5 (available from Fractal Design). Select the Craft grain in the Sensational Surfaces Paper library. Close the Papers library drawer. Make sure that the palette is expanded. Adjust the Scale slider.

Note: If you do not have the Sensational Surfaces CD-ROM, select the Mountains grain in the Texture Sampler library within the Painter 4 applications folder.

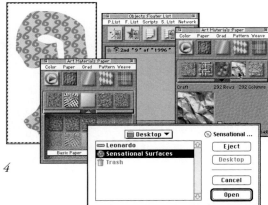

2 | Apply Glass Distortion

Select Effects→Focus→Glass Distortion. Change the Map option within the Glass Distortion dialog box from Refraction to Angle Displacement. Adjust the Softness and Amount sliders to give the right amount of distortion as shown in the preview window. Click OK.

3 | Apply Surface Texture

Select Effects→Surface Control→Apply Surface Texture. Select Using: Paper Grain. Adjust the Softness and Amount sliders to give the required look. Click OK.

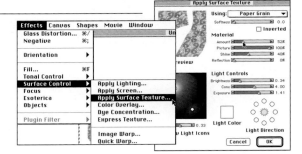

4 | Edit Floater Mask

Return the standard Paper Textures library and select Cotton Paper. Close the drawer and adjust the Scale slider to suit the scale of the floater. Select the Grainizer variant of the Masking brush family in the Brushes palette. Select white in the Art Materials Color Selector. White brush strokes from a Masking brush will make the floater invisible wherever it is applied. Select Controls→Size in the Brushes palette and reduce the brush size to fine. Make sure that the Floater is active (high-lighted). Stroke the edge of the paper by hand to give an irregular rough edge to the floater.

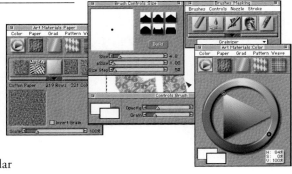

5 | Apply Chalk

Select Effects→Objects→Create Drop Shadow. Click OK. Select the grouped floater with its shadow in the Floater List. Click Ungroup. Select the main floater. Select the Large Chalk variant. Reduce the brush size. Reduce the Opacity slider in the Controls: Brush palette. Paint in white tears on the edges.

Judith Moncrieff

Semiotics

Comments

This image deals with the theme of semiotics: the study of sign, symbol, and universal archetypes. In particular it melds symbols and calligraphy from both eastern and western cultures. The different elements were introduced and manipulated as floaters—independent objects whose interaction with the background canvas and each other can be finely controlled. Moncrieff experimented with different ways of interleaving and composing the various floating elements in the image. Only at the final stage did she merge the floaters into the background canvas and apply fine-tuning of the image.

Studio Usage

This technique focuses on how to create flowing calligraphy and symbols in the style of the ancient Chinese art of water-ink painting (suiboku-ga, a derivation of which is the Japanese brush painting known as sumi-e). In these traditional arts the brushes are loaded with black ink and the brush strokes flow with great ease and spontaneity. A similar feel and effect can be created by using the Watercolor brushes in Painter, as Moncrieff did in this image with the square, triangle, and circle.

Related Techniques

1 | Select Paper Grain

Open the Papers library in the Art Materials: Paper palette. Click on the Library button. Select the More Paper Textures library in the Painter 4 folder. Select the Small Canvas paper grain from within the More Paper textures library. Click on the Color icon in the Art Materials palette. Ensure that black is the currently selected color.

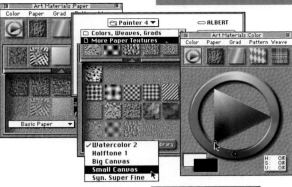

2 | Select and Customize Brush

Select the Broad Water Brush variant of the Water Color brush family. From the Controls pull-down submenu in the Brushes palette, select the following Advance Controls subpalettes: Size, Well, Water, and Sliders. Reduce the Resaturation slider in the Well controls and the Wet Fringe in the Water controls.

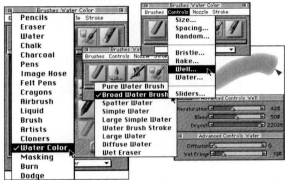

3 | Apply Brush Strokes

Move the left slider in the Advance Controls: Sliders palette from its default position to Pressure. In the Brush Controls: Size palette increase the +/- Size slightly and change the brush shape icon to the rounded lower left icon. Make a stroke starting with light pressure and gradually increasing pressure. To edit the edges of the stroke, select the Wet Eraser Water Color variant. Reduce the Wet Fringe slider in the Advanced Controls: Water palette to zero. For fine structure reduce the Brush Controls: Size slider.

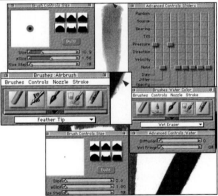

4 | Make Magic Wand Selection

When the calligraphy is complete, select Canvas→Dry. You'll merge the Water Color paint in the Wet layer with the background canvas. Select Edit→Select All. Select Edit→Magic wand. Click in the white background. A red indication of the selected region appears. If there are a lot of "holes" that do not correspond to your brush strokes, edit these by holding down the Shift key while dragging through the holes with the Magic Wand tool. Click OK.

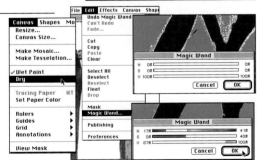

5 | Float Calligraphy

Select Edit→Mask→Invert Mask. Select Edit→Copy. Open your working image. Select Edit→Paste→Normal. The calligraphy is now a floater to which effects and paint brushes can be applied. The final stage will be to drop the floater and apply a small Just Add Water variant.

Typography and Calligraphy *Importing Type from Adobe Illustrator*

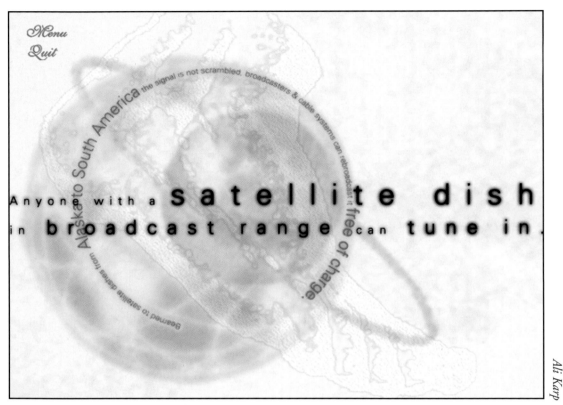

Menu
Quit

Alaska to South America the signal is not scrambled, broadcasters & cable systems can rebroadcast it free of charge.

Beamed to satellite dishes from

Anyone with a **satellite dish** in **broadcast range** can **tune in.**

Ali Karp

Satellite

Comments

This screen image represents a portion of an interactive media CD-ROM created for Classic Arts Showcase. Karp created the text in Adobe Illustrator, wrapping it and shaping it. She then imported the text in Painter and positioned it over the background as a floater. The background incorporates cloning and a light application of Apply Surface Texture Using Paper Grain. The final image was flattened (floaters were dropped) and taken into another program to reduce its color depth (an important consideration in minimizing the final file size and thus improving responsive interactivity of the CD-ROM).

Studio Usage

This technique explains how to conveniently import text from Adobe Illustrator into Painter via the clipboard. Illustrator text is imported as shapes to provide resolution-independent scalability, manipulability, stroke, fill, and opacity control, as well as all the other effects and painting capabilities that can be applied to the text.

Related Techniques

1 | Convert Illustrator Text to Outline

Select the text in Adobe Illustrator. Select Type→Create Outlines from the top menu in Illustrator.

Note: *Adobe Illustrator, and similar programs, provide more flexibility than Painter for wrapping text around shapes and editing it as text (as opposed to a group of objects) after it has been generated.*

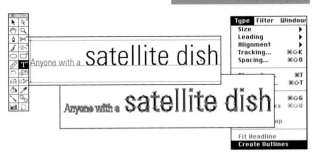

2 | Copy and Paste Text into Painter Document

Select Edit→Copy (⌘-C) {Ctrl-C} in Illustrator while the text outlines remain selected (highlighted). In Painter, click on the document into which you want to paste text. With the document active, select Edit→Paste→Normal (⌘-V) {Ctrl-V}. The text now appears as an object floater that is made up of shapes (it is vector based, not a bitmap).

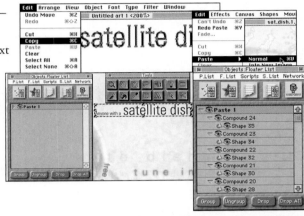

3 | Reposition and Rescale Text

Make sure that the Floater Adjuster Tool is selected in the Tools palette. Drag on the lettering to reposition the whole group of text. Drag on the control handles, situated at the corners and mid-points of the Floater marquee, to distort, stretch, and skew the text.

4 | Make Duplicate Floater

Hold down the Option {Alt} key while clicking once on the Floater. You'll make an identical copy of the floater so that now two are listed in the Floater List.

5 | Feather One Floater

With the floaters exactly over each other, select the upper floater. Click on its name in the Floater List. Select Edit→Mask→Feather Mask. Set the number of pixels to be feathered. Click OK.

Note: *Feathering by two pixels gives a subtle effect. Try experimenting with differing amounts of feathering. Try dragging the top Floater to the bottom and see the effect it has.*

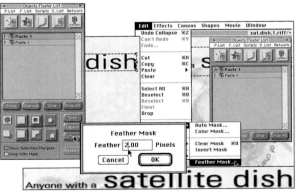

Stacy A. Hopkins

Netgazers Art Gallery Web Page Graphic

Comments

This graphic was originally created for the Netgazers Web site. The text was converted into a floater. The background was based on one of the patterns from the default Patterns library. The Apply Surface Texture and Apply Lighting effects were applied to the background.

Studio Usage

This technique describes how to create an outline around your text and then make the outline glow and show up against a drop shadow. The text was originally created using the Text tool. The Shape Attributes are used to stroke the text, which is then converted into a floater and duplicated. The duplicate floater is feathered to give the appearance of a glow. The final stage is the addition of the drop shadow.

Related Techniques

1 | Apply Text Tool

Select Text tool in the Tools palette. Select Font from the pull-down menu in the Controls: Text palette. Set the Point Size slider. Set a dark text color in the Art Materials: Color palette. Type the text. Click on the F. List icon in the Objects palette.

Note: *All the letters are listed as shapes in the Floater List.*

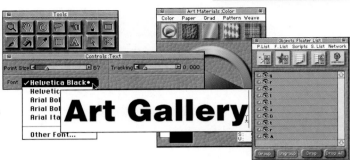

2 | Set Shape Attributes

Select Shapes→Set Attributes. The default Attributes for text are Fill but no Stroke. Click the color square in the Stroke section of the dialog box (it is editable when surrounded by a yellow-and-black marquee). Select a light color to stroke the lettering within the Art Materials: Color palette. Check the Stroke square to the left of the word Stroke. The stroke is now applied to the lettering. Adjust the Width slider until you see the right width of outline around the letters. Click OK.

3 | Convert to Floater

Click the Group button in the Floater List. The letter shapes are now grouped together. Select Shapes→Convert to Floater. The arrow to the left of the group name in the Floater List changes to a purple star, indicating that the text, with its outline, is now a single bitmap image that is independent of the background canvas.

4 | Duplicate Floater and Apply Fill

Select the Floater Adjuster Tool in the Tools palette. Make sure that the floater is highlighted. Click on the floater with the Floater Adjuster tool while holding down the Option {Alt} key. You'll generate a duplicate of the floater. Make sure that the Color Selector has the color you selected originally for the outline. Select Effects→Fill. Click OK.

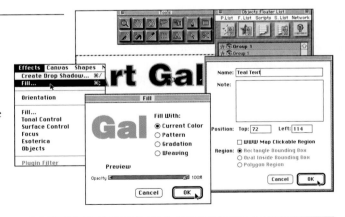

5 | Feather Mask and Create Drop Shadow

Drag the filled floater in the Floater List to below the original outlined text floater. Make sure that the lower, filled floater is the only one active. Select Edit→Mask→Feather Mask. Click OK. Select Effects→Objects→Create Drop Shadow. Adjust the Opacity to 100%. Click OK.

Dance

Jeremy Sutton

Comments

This metallic looking effect makes use of the Reflectance slider in the Apply Surface Texture effects dialog box. The slider is used to reflect differing opacities of "environmental maps." These "maps" are images that have been distorted in the way that a scene would be distorted when viewed in a curved mirrored surface. Painter's Quick Warp feature (under Effects→Surface Control) allows you to easily create such maps yourself.

Studio Usage

This technique describes how to create characters with a three-dimensional, shiny, gold look. You can achieve this effect by using repeated applications of the Apply surface texture effect. The Reflectance slider is used to control the degree to which different environmental maps are reflected in the type. An additional light source is added to more closely approximate a realistic look.

Related Techniques

1 | Select Pattern

Generate a floater in which your type is visible (see Technique #102). Click on the F. List icon in the Objects palette. Click on the floater name in the Floater List. Click on the Collapse button in the expanded Art Materials: Floater List palette if it is a group of text characters. Open the Patterns library in the Art Materials palette. Click on the Library button (the drawer must be open). In the dialog box, select Painter 4 CD-ROM→GOODIES→PATTERNS→MAPS.PTL. Within the Maps Pattern library, select the map called "golden shine."

2 | Apply Surface Texture

Select Effects→Surface Control→Apply Surface Texture. Within the Apply Surface Texture dialog, select Mask in the Using menu. Move the Reflection slider to 100%. Adjust the Softness slider until the right degree of roundness is seen. (You may still pick another pattern from the Art Materials: Pattern library.) Click on the lower right of the Light Controls globe to create a new light source. Reduce its brightness slightly and click OK.

Note: *If a document on the desktop has been assigned as a clone source, then it will be reflected instead of the map from the Patterns library. If this is the case, close the other document and reactivate the floater in your working document.*

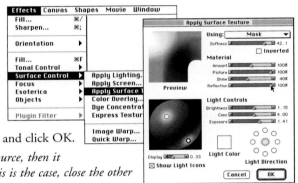

3 | Apply Surface Texture Again

In the Patterns library, select the map called "wavy metallic." Select the Apply Surface Texture effect as in Step 2. Reduce the reflection to about 39% and increase the amount to about 117%. Click OK.

Note: *The second time you apply the same effect you can just go to the top item in the Effects pull-down menu (or ⌘-/) {Ctrl-/}, which is the last effect used.*

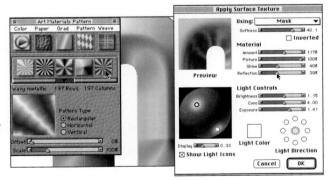

4 | Apply Surface Texture One More Time

Select the map called "southwest," or any other map you want to reflect. Select the Apply Surface Texture effect. Reduce the reflection to about 15%. Click OK.

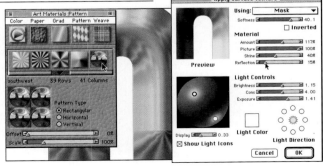

Mario Henri Chakkour

SQA CD-ROM Interface #3

Comments

This interface was one of several designs created by Chakkour for Techview Interactive. Starting with a rough sketch, Chakkour drew the design directly in Painter, using the Rulers and Guides (under Canvas menu) for precision. Each section of the interface was then carefully made into a shape object using the Bézier Pen tool. These shapes were converted into bitmapped floaters. Airbrush painting was applied to the floaters to give them the smooth metallic look you see in the final image.

Studio Usage

Painter offers a simple way to digitally re-create the effect you would achieve traditionally by masking out areas of your paper and applying airbrush on the unmasked sections. By appropriate choice of paper and paint colors, a smooth, three-dimensional, metallic look can be achieved.

Related Techniques

1 | Create Shape with Bézier Pen Tool

Select the Bézier Pen Tool in the Tools palette. Use the Pen Tool to draw the shape of the component of the interface you want to create. Click on the icon below the F. List menu in the Objects palette to reveal the Floater List. The Shape appears in the List.

Note: If the resulting shape is stroked or filled with color, double- click on the shape name in the Floater List and uncheck the Stroke and Fill options in the Set Shape Attributes dialog box. This allows the shape to be seen just as a thin blue line with Bézier points. Add or Delete points with the Shape Edit Tools and adjust point positions with the Direct Shape Selection Tool.

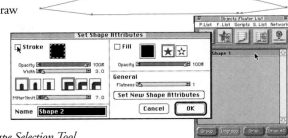

2 | Fill Shape

Double-click on the shape name in the Floater List to access the Set Shape Attributes dialog box. Check only the Fill option. Click on the Fill Color square. Open the Color Selector in the Art Materials palette. Select a gray color in the Color Selector. Click OK. The shape is now filled with the gray color.

3 | Convert Shape to Floater

Select Shapes→Convert to Floater. The Shape is now a bitmapped floater.

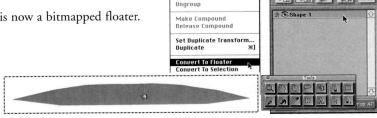

4 | Apply Airbrush

Select the Thin Stroke variant of the Airbrush brush family. Select Controls→Size from the Brushes palette pull-down menu and adjust the Size slider to suit the scale of your Floater. Reduce the Opacity slider in the Controls palette to 14%. Select a lighter shade of gray than the color in Step 2 to fill the shape. Apply light strokes around the edges of the floater. Select a dark shade and apply it to the center of the floater, applying lighter pressure as you go out toward the edges to give a smooth transition from dark to light. Reduce the Opacity further to 9%. Go back into the floater with a subtle application of black-and-white for the shadows and highlights.

Note: The lettering can now be easily added as an additional floater.

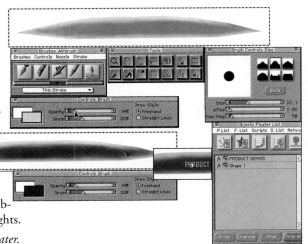

New Skyline

Susan Vierra-Sykes at Pegasus

Comments

On the left is the original PostScript illustration created in Adobe Illustrator. On the right is the same illustration after being opened in Painter and having a variety of effects and brush strokes applied selectively to different parts of the composition. This design was originally produced for the 1,000 Man March in Sacramento, California, and it was screen printed onto T-shirts.

Studio Usage

Painter is a valuable tool for enhancing vector-based illustrations created in programs such as Adobe Illustrator or Macromedia Freehand. You can easily add textures, brush strokes, gradient fills, stroked outlines, lighting effects, drop shadows, and varying opacity to any individual sections of the illustration. Illustrations will open in Painter as a series of vector-based shapes and then become bitmapped floaters when effects or paint brushes are applied. This particular technique shows how to apply a surface texture to an element in the design.

Related Techniques

1 | Copy Illustration from Adobe Illustrator

After creating the original drawing in a drawing program such as Adobe Illustrator, select Edit→Select All (⌘-A) {Ctrl-A}. Then select Edit→Copy (⌘-C) {Ctrl-C}.

Note: If there is any type, select it and convert it to outlines under the Type menu. Painter does not recognize type imported from a PostScript program.

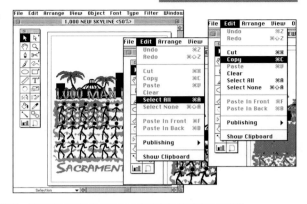

2 | Paste Drawing into Painter Document

Open a new canvas in Painter that is large enough for the design. Select Edit→Paste→Normal (⌘-V) {Ctrl-V}. The vector-based drawing appears on the canvas. Click on the F. List icon in the Objects palette. The pasted design is listed as a shape or a group of shapes in the Floater List.

Note: You can select individual shapes in the list, double-click on them to access the Shape Attributes dialog box and then control the Stroke, Fill, and Opacity parameters for that individual shape.

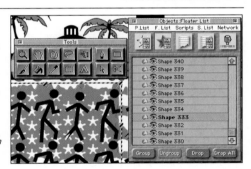

3 | Select an Individual Component in the Design

Select the Floater Adjuster tool from the Tools palette. Carefully click on a section of the component (design element) you want to select. The appropriate name is now highlighted in the Floater List. When you have a large number of component shapes, it is easier to select in this manner, rather than clicking names in the Floater List.

Note: If you want to simultaneously select a series of separate components so that you can apply a common effect, then hold the Shift key as you select each one.

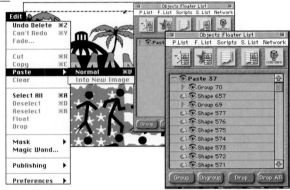

4 | Apply Surface Texture

Select Effects→Surface Control→Apply Surface Texture. The dialog box should show the default setting Using: Paper Texture. Select the Paper texture of your choice from the Art Materials: Papers library. This example uses Watercolor paper from the More Paper Textures library that is situated in the Painter 4 applications folder. Adjust the Amount slider (and experiment with other sliders). Click OK.

Note: For an embossed look, change the Using menu to Mask and adjust the Softness slider. For the drop shadow, select Effects→Objects→Create Drop Shadow.

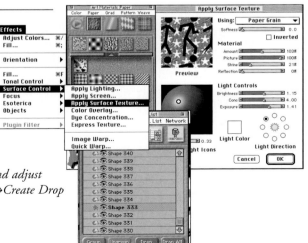

Andrew Hathaway

Cola

Comments

This image was based on the logo of a band called *Cola*. Hathaway started by creating the gradient background and applying lighting effects. He prepared three different leaf designs. Each leaf was independently filled with a different gradation and had texture and lighting effects applied to it. Fall colors were used throughout the design. In turn each leaf was introduced as a floater, scaled and oriented, and then dropped into the background. A softening effect was then applied. The result of progressively applying the softening effect after each leaf was dropped was that the earlier leaves became more diffuse than the later leaves. This added depth to the image. The *Cola* logo was finally added as a floater without any softening so its hard edges would stand out against the softened background.

Studio Usage

Whenever you have a series of layered objects that recede into the background of a composition, the sense of depth can be enhanced by making the objects further away look softer, or more diffuse, than the objects closer to the foreground. You can achieve this effect by introducing, as floaters, the furthest objects first and moving forward, successively dropping each object in position and applying a softening effect to the whole image.

Related Techniques

Replacing Sky with a
Two-Point Gradient 46

Customized Cubist Blurring 56

Mysterious Soft Glow 70

Expressing Different Colors
Using the Gradations Editor 97

1 │ Prepare Background and Objects

Fill the working canvas on which the design will be built with the appropriate gradation, making use of the Gradient Library in the Art Materials palette. Prepare each leaf as a floater in a separate file. To prepare the leaves, draw their outlines with the Freehand Selection Lasso Tool. Select Edit→Float to turn the selection into a floater. Fill the floater with the desired gradation. Apply Surface Texture Using Paper Grain and Apply Lighting, both from the Effects→Surface Control menu.

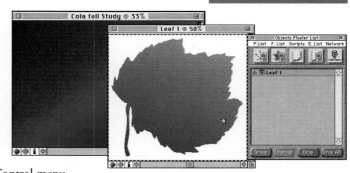

2 │ Paste the First Leaf into the Main Image

With the first leaf Floater active, select Edit→Copy (⌘-C) {Ctrl-C). Click on the main image file, the one with the gradient background. Select Edit→Paste→Normal (⌘-V) {Ctrl-V}. The leaf now appears in the main image. Select the Floater Adjuster tool. Drag on the floater to reposition it. To rescale the leaf, select Effects→Orientation→Free Transform. Holding down the Shift key, drag the corner control handles. While holding down the ⌘ {Ctrl} key, drag the corner control handles to rotate the leaf. Select Effects→Orientation→Commit Transform. Adjust the Opacity Slider in the Controls: Adjust palette to vary the floater opacity.

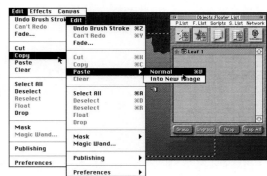

3 │ Create Drop Shadow

Select Effects→Objects→Create Drop Shadow. Click OK in the Drop Shadow dialog box. A drop shadow appears. The drop shadow is a floater that is automatically grouped with the leaf floater. Click the Drop All button at the lower right of the Floater List. The leaf and its shadow are now part of the background.

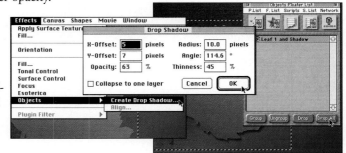

4 │ Apply Soften

Select Effects→Focus→Soften. Adjust the Radius slider in the Soften dialog box to give the right amount of softening. Click OK.

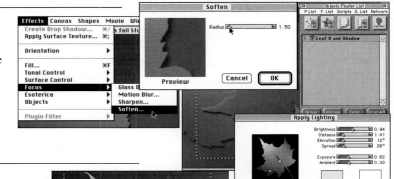

5 │ Repeat Process

Repeat Steps 2 through 4 for the other two leaves. The figures here show the application of the Lighting effect and the variation of Floater Opacity to the third leaf.

Patrick Lichty

Comments

This interface design was originally created for use on Lichty's World Wide Web home page. He began by creating the texture you see in the manifold that surrounds the buttons. This texture was generated by applying several layers of grainy brushes. The Apply Surface Texture effect was applied with the Using: Image Luminance option selected. The manifold shape was drawn with Shape Design tools and then floated. The buttons and lettering were added as separate floaters. The background was filled with black as a final step.

Studio Usage

In interface design (particularly as applied to CD-ROMs, Interactive Kiosks, and Web sites), the use of spherical reflective buttons can enhance the look and feel of the interface. Shiny, spherical (or oval) buttons, with appropriate lettering, stand out from flat backgrounds and help the viewer navigate. Painter provides an easy way to create these buttons, making use of reflectance mapping in the Apply Surface Texture effect.

Related Techniques

1 | Create Circular Shape

Open a small file with white Paper color, slightly larger than the size you want to create. Select the Oval Shape. Hold down the Shift key as you drag the image to constrain the selection to a circle. (Oval 1 in the Objects: Floater List). Click on the Shape name and select Shapes→ Set Default Attributes. The Stroke option should be unchecked, the Fill option checked, and the Fill color black. Click OK.

2 | Duplicate Shape

Select the Floater Adjuster tool. Hold down the Option {Alt} key while clicking on the active shape. A second shape called Oval 1 appears in the Floater List. Double-click on this new name. In the Set Shape Attributes dialog box, uncheck the Fill option and check the Stroke option. The Stroke color should be black. Adjust the Stroke Width slider to 7.

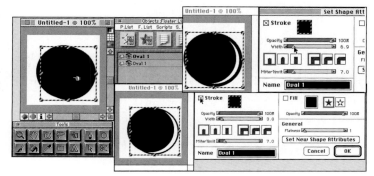

3 | Select MAPS Pattern Library and Adjust E-Map Color

Click on the icon below the Pattern pull-down menu. Open the Pattern library. Click the Library button. Locate the Painter 4 CD-ROM→ GOODIES→PATTERNS→MAPS.PTL file. Select the "hallway" pattern. Select Pattern→Check Out Pattern. Select Effects→Tonal Control→Correct Colors. Select the Curve option from the pull-down menu. Click on each of the four color squares and drag the curve. Click OK. Select File→Clone Source and drag to the name of the pattern file.

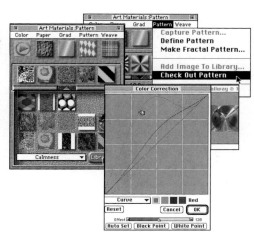

4 | Apply Surface Texture to Both Shapes

Click on the original image. Select the Inner Circle floater by click-ing on its name in the Floater list. Select Effects→Surface Control→Apply Surface Texture. Select Using→Mask. Drag the Reflection slider all the way to the right (100%). Adjust the Softness, Amount, and Shine sliders to get the right reflective look. Adjust the light source position by dragging the small circle in the Light Controls preview window. Adjust the Light Controls sliders to get the right amount of flare in the reflection. Click OK.

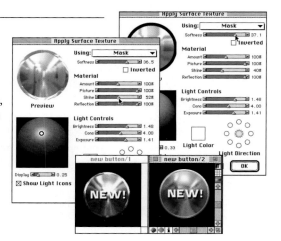

Cartoons and Comics *Controlling Line Thickness through Brush Tracking*

Mark Badger and Gerard Jones

Voodoo Island Page 2 ©

Comments

This cartoon is part of a series of comics illustrated by Mark Badger and written by Gerard Jones, which will be appearing in *Badger's Marks and Angles* (to be published by Caliber). The background was originally a pattern generated in Painter and then modified using the Kai's Power Tool vortex filter. Badger works in layers, building up components of the image into separate floaters. The final image contained seven floaters.

Studio Usage

Within a given brush variant, it can be useful to vary the way the brush stroke thickness responds to stylus pressure. This is useful for introducing the right quality, or "globbiness," of the stroke, as well as allowing you to require less pressure and thus relaxing the hand more as you draw (important for preventing repetitive stress injury if you spend many hours drawing). The key to controlling this pressure responsiveness parameter is the Painter preference known as Brush Tracking. Badger uses this facility to create different line quality when going from thick rough sketches to the final fine line drawings.

Related Techniques

1 | Set Brush Tracking

Select Edit→Preferences→Brush Tracking. The default settings have the Pressure Scale set to 1.00. This setting requires the most pressure to achieve maximum brush stroke thickness, which is good for very fine work when you don't want the line to get too thick too easily. It is not good for quick, rough sketching when you may want to work with a looser, thicker line. It is also not good if you like to apply less pressure to produce a mark on your canvas. Make a brush stroke on the Scratch Pad. The settings all change to reflect the stroke you just made. Adjust the Pressure Scale slider to about 0.30. This relatively low value will result in a thick, "globby" line. Click OK.

Note: This technique is primarily directed at users of a pressure sensitive stylus. The velocity sliders are intended for users of input devices other than a pressure sensitive stylus. If you do not use a stylus, then adjust the Velocity Scale slider instead of the Pressure Scale and use your cursor velocity to control thickness, rather than stylus pressure.

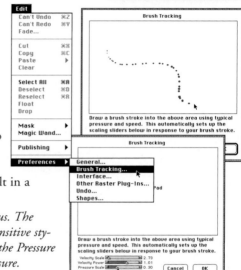

2 | Apply Scratchboard Tool

Select the Scratchboard Tool variant of the Pens brush family in the Brushes palette.
Select Controls→Size in the Brushes palette to access the Brush Controls: Size palette. Adjust the Size slider, if necessary, depending on the maximum thickness of line you want to produce in your cartoon. Click on the Build button (⌘-B) {Ctrl-B} after resizing the brush. Select black as the current color in the Art Materials: Color Selector. Use the Scratchboard tool to make your rough, thick sketch lines.

3 | Reset the Pressure Scale

Select Edit→Preferences→Brush Tracking. Reset the Pressure Scaling to about 0.65 (typically the maximum value for comfortable pressure that gives greater sensitivity). Click OK. Use the Scratchboard tool with this setting for the finer line work in the final cartoon drawing.

Note: The Brush Tracking settings are always reset to their default values whenever you first open Painter. They are not remembered by either Save Variant or Save Brush Look.

Krista Glass

Zu Hause bei Krakens (Sportschau) / At Home with the Octopuses (Sports TV)

Comments

This image of the octopus family enjoying their underwater living room was painted by using a wide variety of Paper Textures.

Studio Usage

This technique describes a simple way to use a standard Painter paper texture library to create the look of sunlight glimmering through rippling water. It's a useful technique for any underwater cartoon scene, such as the example here. Bubbles have been added using the Spatter Water variant of the Water Color brushes for added effect.

Related Techniques

Watercolor and Pastel   2

Watercolor Cloning   18

Crumbly Mountain Texture   21

Watery Ripples from
Marble and Warp   58

1 | Apply Inverted Eggscape Paper Texture

Open the Paper Library by clicking below the Paper pull-down menu in the Art Materials palette. Select the Paper Texture called Eggscape. Close the library drawer by clicking on the toggle bar. Expand the Papers palette so that you see the preview window and Scale slider. Adjust the Scale slider to suit the scale of your image. Check the Invert Grain box. Select the Large Chalk variants of the Chalk brushes in the Brushes palette. Select Controls→Size in the Brushes palette and adjust the Size slider to suit the scale of your painting. Open the Color Selector in the Art Materials palette (click on the icon under the Color pull-down menu). Select a medium to dark blue. Apply the chalk in the background.

Note: *It is useful to tear off the Color Selector so that you can keep the Color Selector and the Papers palette open simultaneously.*

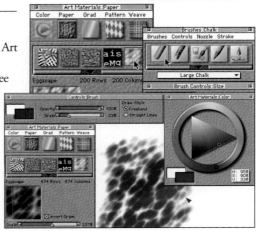

2 | Apply Highlights

Click on the Invert Grain box again so that it is now unchecked. Select a light blue color in the Color Selector. Lower the Opacity slider in the Controls: Brush palette to 24%. Paint over the region painted in Step 1. Adjust the color, lightening it in certain areas to simulate brighter reflection of sunlight refracting through the surface of the water.

Note: *Use stylus pressure to control the opacity of the highlights. The low opacity setting gives you greater control.*

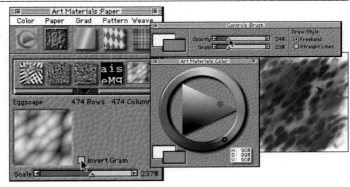

3 | Soften with Just Add Water

Select the Just Add Water variant of the Water brushes family. Lower the Opacity slider from 100% to 34%. Then lightly stroke back and forth over the canvas. The colors will gradually be blended, edges will soften, and the diffuse watery look will emerge.

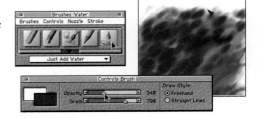

4 | Add Spatter Bubbles

Select a darker shade of blue in the Color Selector. Select the Spatter Water variant of the Water Color brushes family. Increase the Opacity slider from 29% to 100%. This allows the "bubbles" to be more easily seen against the background. Select Controls→Size from the Brushes palette pull-down menu.

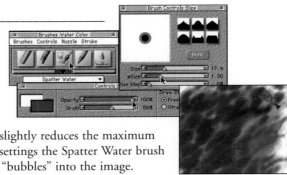

Reduce the +/- Size slider from 1.56 (the default) to 1.30. This slightly reduces the maximum spatter size and increases the minimum spatter size. With these settings the Spatter Water brush produces "bubbles" within a narrower range of diameters. Paint "bubbles" into the image.

Wally Yells at Juan

Jason Fruchter

Comments

Fruchter begins his cartoons as pencil sketches on paper. He develops the characters separately from the background. The black-and-white line drawing for each character is laid out on a light table to allow a shadow map to be drawn that registers precisely with the original line drawing. These drawings are then scanned and opened in Painter. A mask of the line drawing is generated by using image luminance.

The cartoon cel fill mode of the Fill bucket is used to fill the closed in areas of the drawing. He then applies a color overlay effect to create gray shadowing.

The final stage involves compositing the different characters as floaters over the background and applying surface texture and lighting effects.

Studio Usage

This technique describes an elegant way to create soft- or hard-edged shadows that register precisely with the colored regions of a cartoon character. With this techniques, you'll have a lot of control and room to experiment with shadow placement, opacity, and feathering.

Related Techniques

1 | Create Shadow Map

Open the colored-in line drawing and the shadow map (see Technique #82 for details on how to apply the Cartoon Cel Fill technique). The shadow map can easily be made within Painter by creating a clone of the line drawing and turning on the tracing paper.

2 | Set Shadow Map as Clone Source

Select File→Clone Source. Drag to the shadow map file name and release. Look at the Clone Source menu. The shadow map now has a check by it, indicating that it is set to be the clone source. Click on the colored-in line drawing to make sure that it is the active document. Select Canvas→Tracing Paper (⌘-T) {Ctrl-T} to turn on the tracing paper mode. You'll see the shadow map showing through the colored drawing. Select Canvas→Tracing Paper to turn the tracing paper off again.

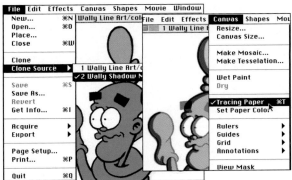

3 | Invert Shadow Map

Click on the shadow map to make sure that it is active. Select Effects→Tonal Control→Negative. This action reverses the pixel color in the image: black goes to white and white to black. To get a softer shadow, select Effects→Focus→Soften. Adjust the Radius slider until you see sufficient softening in the preview window and then click OK.

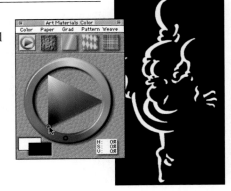

4 | Apply Color Overlay

Select black in the Art Materials: Color palette. Select Effects→Surface Control→Color Overlay. In the Color Overlay dialog box, select Using: Original Luminance and check Model: Dye Concentration. Adjust the Opacity slider in the dialog box until the preview window shows the right amount of shadow.

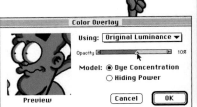

Video and Animation *Floaters Interacting with the Background Mask*

Jeremy Sutton

Sky Runner

Comments

These frames were part of an animation sequence created with both Fractal Design Painter and Fractal Design Poser, a three-dimensional human figure posing and rendering program. The cloud background was initially created in the first frame of a Painter Frame Stack movie. It was a combination of a two-point gradient fill followed by the Image Hose loaded with the Cumulus Clouds nozzle. This background was floated, and then the movie was forwarded through each frame to leave a common background on each frame. The background floater was dropped back into the canvas layer. A mask was generated on each frame. The mask density was based on image luminance (see Technique #120). A Poser figure was introduced as a floater. The floater mask icons were set so that the background mask interacted with the floater and this mask determined which parts of the Poser figure were visible on each frame.

Studio Usage

This technique deals with a situation where you want to introduce an object into an animation and determine, by the background mask, which parts of the object are visible on each frame. You can do this by introducing the object as a floater and utilizing the icons that control how the floater's mask interacts with the background (canvas) mask. This technique is useful for collage and montage generally, as well as for animation.

Related Techniques

1 | Modify Movie Background Mask

Open a Painter Frame Stack with a common background applied to each frame. Select File→Save As and check the "Save current frame as image" option. Save the frame as a Pict image. Select the Masking Airbrush variant of the Masking brushes, select the middle of the Mask Visibility icons and, with black as the currently selected color, manually paint in the mask in the first frame where you want the background image to "show through" the floater. Use the option of Apply Script to Movie to create a similar modification of the mask on all the frames.

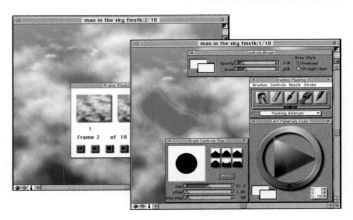

2 | Create and Copy Poser Figure

Open Poser and select a figure type and pose. Select File→Import→Background. Select the image saved in Step 1. Click Yes when you get, "Change window to match background?" The same background appears as in the movie. Use the Tools to adjust the position and pose of the figure. Open up the Texture Map Template and paint on it to create a map that can be rendered onto the surface of your figure. Save it as a Pict file. Select Render→Surface Material and click the Texture Map Load button. Select the Map Pict file. Click OK. Select Render→Render. Select Edit→Copy.

3 | Paste Figure into Movie Frame

Back in Painter, with the first frame of the movie still active, select Edit→Paste→Normal. Click on the F. List icon in the Objects palette. Make sure that the Floater List is expanded. Select the middle of the lower row of icons to cause the background mask to hide the floater. The figure now appears to be disappearing behind the clouds. Click on the Drop All button in the Floater List to prevent the floater from being inadvertently dropped onto other frames.

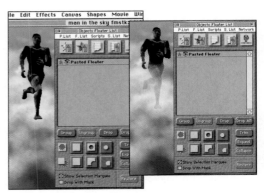

4 | Step Forward to Next Frame

Click on the Step Forward button in the Frame Stack palette to move the movie forward one frame. Repeat Steps 2 and 3 until the movie is complete. When you return to Poser, you will find the figure in the last pose.

Lisa Fenwick

Siblings

Comments

The two main images above show the first and last frame of a movie. The movie was generated by using floaters in the Painter Frame Stack, in which one boy's face appears to "morph" into his brother's face. This visual transition was achieved by fading one face into the other. The sequence of frames below the main images shows stages of the transition. The term "movie" used throughout this technique refers to the Frame Stack movie that is only playable and editable within Painter. Such Frame Stacks can be saved as QuickTime movies or numbered files, which can then be opened in other programs for further processing.

Studio Usage

This technique describes how to create a movie in which one image appears to morph into another image. The same process can also be applied any time you wish to have an object in a movie gradually appear or fade away (such as headers and titles). The relevant images are introduced as floaters and then their relative opacities are varied from frame to frame. You'll find this to be a versatile technique that offers a lot of control.

Related Techniques

Enhancing a Polaroid
    Transfer Print   49

Transition from Drawing
    to Photograph   119

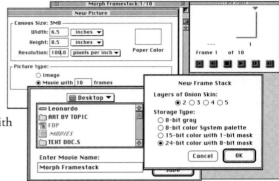

1 | Create New Frame Stack Movie

Select File→New. Check Picture Type: Movie and type in the total number of frames you want in the morph. Specify the Frame width, height, and resolution, and click OK. Bear in mind the size of the images you want to have as end-points. Give the new Frame Stack a name and click Save. Leave the number of Layers of Onion Skin at 2 and the Storage Type at 24-bit color with 8-bit mask. Click OK.

2 | Introduce Beginning and End Images as Floaters

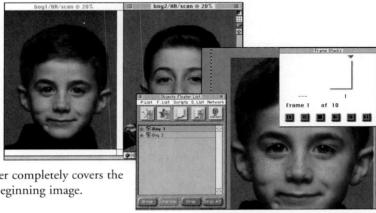

With the new Frame Stack active and on the first frame, introduce the two images you want to morph as floaters. Select the F. (Floater) list in the Objects palette. Make sure that the floater that corresponds to the beginning image is above the final image floater in the list. Drag it, if necessary. The opacity of both floaters is 100%. The top floater completely covers the lower floater and fills the first frame with the beginning image.

3 | Move Forward One Frame and Adjust Opacity for the Top Floater

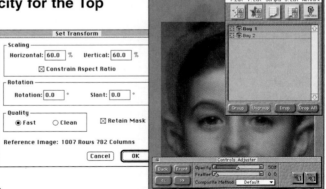

Click on the Step Forward button in the Frame Stack palette to move the movie forward one frame. Select the Floater Adjuster tool in the Tools palette. Click on the upper floater name in the Floater List. Reduce the opacity slightly by moving the Opacity slider in the Controls: Adjuster palette to the left. Repeat this process until you reach the last frame. Try to have the Opacity at 0% before or on the last frame. You can always add additional frames simply by clicking on the Step Forward button.

4 | Drop Floaters in Last Frame

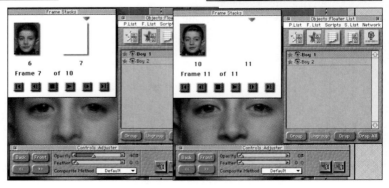

The final frame should have the two floaters with the top floater at 0% opacity so the bottom floater (the final image) shows through completely. At this stage, click the Drop All button in the lower right of the Floater List. The movie is now ready to play. Click the Play button in the Frame Stack palette to see the morph playing.

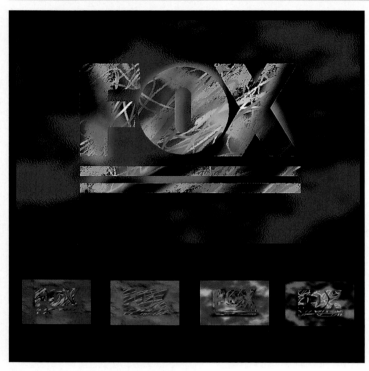

Jon Lee

Fox Broadcasting Company Logo

Comments

The frames shown here are part of a sequence of frames from an animated treatment of the Fox Broadcasting Company logo. The animation was designed for use on video and created at a frame size of 720 by 486 pixels. It was generated in Painter using the Framestack animation mode. Lee used a variety of brushes, such as Chalks (with varying paper textures), Liquid, and Airbrush. He also applied effects, such as Glass Distortion. He created the cloud background, applying various effects on different frames. Then he introduced the Fox logo as a floater (imported from Adobe Illustrator) and adjusted the Mask Drawing icons as he applied different brushes and textures in each frame. The completed framestack movie was saved as a QuickTime movie and converted to video.

Studio Usage

This technique describes how to use a floater within a movie, transferring text from one frame to the next. In each frame, paint and effects can be selectively applied either to just the text or just the background (or both).

This type of approach can be used to create animated logos for television, video, or film. Complex imagery can be built up with multiple floaters. Each floater can be moved and rescaled from frame to frame.

Related Techniques

Transforming Type into Reflective Plastic and Glass   102

Importing Type from Adobe Illustrator   106

Adding Texture to Illustration   110

1 | Open Framestack

Select File→New. Set the frame size and click on Picture Type: Movie. Click OK. Name the Movie and save it. Label it as a framestack. A New Frame Stack dialog box appears. Click on the number of layers of Onion Skin that you want and the Storage Type. You should create the movie in 24-bit color and then reduce the number of colors later, if necessary.

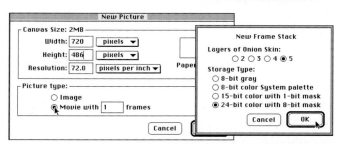

2 | Paint on and behind Floater in Frame 1

Introduce the text as a floater into frame 1. With the floater active use the brushes to paint on the floater. Deselect the floater by clicking below the name in the Floater List (⌘-D) {Ctrl-D}. Create the background behind the text.

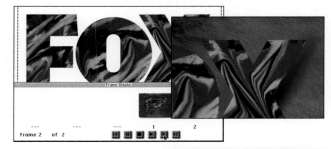

3 | Move to Frame 2 and Fill Background

Click on the Forward One Frame button in the framestack palette to advance the framestack one frame. A new frame is generated if one does not already exist. The floater from frame 1 appears in frame 2 in the same position where it was in frame 1. With the floater deselected, create the background for frame 2.

4 | Change Floater in Frame 2

Select the floater and apply more brushwork to it. You can go back and forth between working on the floater and working on the background by selecting or deselecting the floater.

5 | Move to Frame 3

Move to frame 3 and repeat the process. Continue in this way until the movie is completed. At the completion of the movie, click on the F. List icon in the Objects palette. Click on the Drop All button in the Floater List.

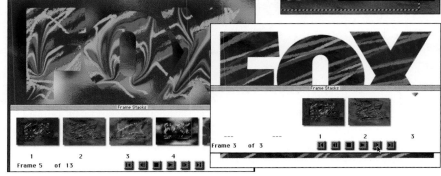

Video and Animation *Transition from Drawing to Photograph*

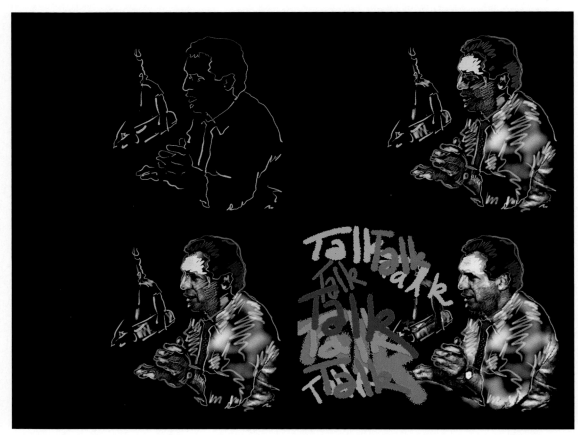

Ronn Ovens Jeremy Sutton

Comments

This piece was created as part of an animation for video in which a drawing unfolds followed by the gradual emergence of a photograph (or video still) upon which the drawing was based. This technique focuses on how that visual transition in time was accomplished. To end up on video, the recorded session was converted into a QuickTime movie, which was then dubbed to VHS tape. Refer to the Painter 4 User Guide for instructions on how to convert a recorded session into a movie.

Studio Usage

This technique enables you to create a seamless transition from a drawing into a photograph—all of the same image. It takes advantage of the fact that the Tracing Paper function in Painter is not visually apparent on playback of recorded sessions (scripts). In this case a photograph was cloned, and the clone filled with black. Then, using tracing paper to give a visual reference, a freehand painting based on the photograph was created. Finally, sections of the photograph were cloned into the painting, creating a mix of freehand and photographic imagery.

Related Techniques

Increasing Resolution during Painting Process   6

Playback over Different Backgrounds   95

1 | Create a Clone

Select File→Clone and create an identical copy of the photograph. Select Edit→Select All (⌘-A) {Ctrl-A} and then press Delete. Select black in the Color Selector and click in the clone image with the Fill Bucket.

Note: *Another way to fill is to use Effects→Fill (⌘-F) {Ctrl-F}.*

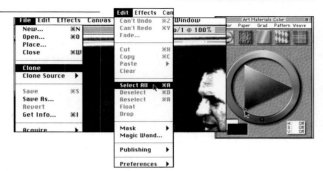

2 | Start Recording

Select the Scripts palette in the Objects palette. Click the central red button to start the recording of the session.

3 | Turn On Tracing Paper

Turn on Tracing Paper by clicking on the Tracing Paper icon (two small overlapping squares) on the upper right side of the document frame (or selecting Canvas→Tracing Paper (⌘-T) {Ctrl-T}. Tracing Paper works only when the original photo (Clone Source) and the Clone image are an identical size. You will now see the half opacity image of the original photo showing through. Use this as the visual reference on which you base your painting

Note: *With Tracing Paper, the brush strokes you make only appear at 50% opacity. This fact can often lead to surprises when you turn Tracing Paper off and the colors you've painted suddenly jump out at you.*

4 | Clone in Photo

Select the Soft Cloner variant from the Cloner brush family. Adjust the Opacity slider in the Controls palette to 20%. Start cloning the original photo into the painted image, pressing lightly at first to bring the photo gradually into the image.

Note: *Try this step with other clone brushes. You can also expand the Color Selector palette and click Use Clone Color with any brush.*

5 | Stop Recording

Click the black square Stop button (on left of Scripts palette). Give the script a name. The script will now appear as one of the recorded sessions in the Objects→ Scripts palette Scripts library. To play back the session, open a new document the same size as the original. Select File→Clone Source and make sure that the original photograph is selected as Clone Source. Fill it with black as in Step 1. Select the recording you named in the Scripts Library of the Scripts palette. Close the Scripts library drawer. Click on the playback button (right facing arrow). The transition will replay without the tracing paper showing at any time.

Jeremy Sutton

Johnson Park 7AM

Comments

Two separate movies were selectively merged together by cloning one movie into the other. The clone source movie was created by moving a wide floater successively by a set amount of pixels as each frame was advanced. The second movie showed white text appearing and then fading against a black background. (This movie was created by using the floater fade technique described in Technique #117). A mask based on inverse image luminance was then generated in each frame. The first movie was cloned into the unmasked portions of the second movie. The final stage was the coloring of the text, which was done by inverting the action of the mask and hand painting the text frame by frame. Scripts were applied to the movie to help simplify and speed some of the tasks that would otherwise have been time-consuming and labor intensive.

Studio Usage

This technique describes how to clone images from frames in one Painter Frame Stack movie (the "source" movie) to the corresponding frames in another Frame Stack movie (the "second" movie). This technique is particularly useful when done in conjunction with masking. The mask can control which regions of the image in each frame in the second movie are replaced by the clone image from the corresponding frame in the source movie.

Related Techniques

1 Generate Two Movies of the Same Size

Open two movies that have the same total number of frames and the same pixel dimensions for each frame. The first movie ("source") will be the movie from which images are cloned into the second movie. This source movie can be full color. The second movie should be a white design against a black background.

2 Record Masking Script

Select the second movie and make sure that it is on frame 1. Click on the icon under the word Scripts in the Objects palette. Click on the central red Record button to start recording. Select Edit→Mask→Auto Mask. Select Using: Image Luminance and check the Invert box. You'll generate a 100% mask where there is white and 0% where there is black. Click once on the Step Forward button in the Framestack palette. You can forward the movie one frame each time it is clicked. Click the Stop Recording black square button. Name the script in the dialog box.

3 Apply Masking Script to Second Movie and Set Movie Clone Source

With the second movie still active, click on the Rewind button on the left of the Frame Stack palette to return the movie to the first frame. Select Movie→Apply Script to Movie. Select the name of the masking script just recorded in Step 2 in the dialog box that appears. Click Playback. Select the source movie by clicking on it. Make sure it is set at frame 1. Select Movie→Set Movie Clone Source.

4 Record and Apply Cloning Script to Second Movie

Select the second movie. Make sure it is on frame 1. Click on the small Mask Drawing icons. Drag to the middle of these icons to exclude the brushes from painting in the region of each frame masked out in Step 3. Select the Soft Cloner variant of the Cloners brush family in the Brushes palette. Access the brush Controls: Size palette and move the size slider to make a large brush size. Click on the red Record button in the Objects: Scripts palette. Apply the Soft Cloner brush all over the frame 1 image area until the first frame of the source movie has appeared everywhere except where the mask was generated. Click once on the Step Forward button in the Frame Stack palette. Click the Stop Recording button in the Scripts palette. Name the cloning script. Apply the script to the movie as in Step 3 (except the script is the cloning script, not the masking script).

Pour It On With Lightning and Walker Bill   *Original QuickTime Movie by John Derry*

Comments

The background of this sequence of frames is taken from a QuickTime movie produced in Painter. The source material was a video of someone pouring paint out of a can. This movie was modified in the Painter Frame Stack mode. The person's hands were masked out and effects added. The walking character was added as the final step by applying an Image Hose brush stroke to a movie.

Studio Usage

When a recorded brush stroke is applied to a movie, a portion of the brush stroke is applied to each frame. In the case of an Image Hose brush stroke being applied to a movie, the nozzle elements are sprayed out onto each frame in turn. If the Image Hose Nozzle is made up of images that form a sequential animation and the images emerge from the Image Hose in that sequence, the effect is an animation that appears to be painted over the original movie. This technique explains how to achieve the effect of painting a sequential animation onto a movie.

Related Techniques

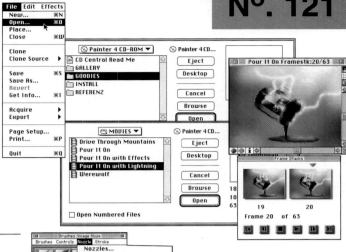

1 | Open Movie

Select File→Open (⌘-O) {Ctrl-O}. Select Painter CD-ROM→Goodies→Movies→Pour It On with Lightning. Click Open. You will be warned that the disk is locked. Click OK. Title the frame stack you are about to generate and determine where it will be saved. Click Save. The QuickTime movie is now opened as a Frame Stack.

2 | Load Image Hose Nozzle

Select Nozzle→Nozzles from the Brushes palette pull-down menu. Select a Nozzle. In this example the command Nozzle→Load Nozzle (⌘-L) (Ctrl-L) was used to select a specific nozzle that came with the Painter 3.1 CD-ROM.

Note: The ideal nozzle for applying to a movie is one where there is a sequential animation in the nozzle images.

3 | Test Image Hose Brush Stroke

Select the Small Sequential Linear variant of the Image Hose in the Brushes palette. Do a trial stroke on the first frame of the Frame Stack. Select Edit→Undo Brush Stroke (⌘-Z) {Ctrl-Z}. Do the same for Medium and Large Sequential Linear variants. Determine which variant gives a reasonable spacing of nozzle elements so that two or three appear across the frame with no overlapping. Select this variant (in this example it is the Large Sequential Linear variant that works best).

4 | Record Brush Stroke

Select Stroke→Record Stroke from the Brushes palette pull-down menu. Do a single stroke across the first frame. That stroke has now been recorded. Undo the brush stroke.

5 | Apply Brush Stroke to Movie

Select Movie→Apply Brush Stroke To Movie. The brush stroke is now applied in such a way that one nozzle element is added to each frame sequentially. When the movie is played, the walking character (WalkerBill) appears to walk across the movie as the paint is being poured.

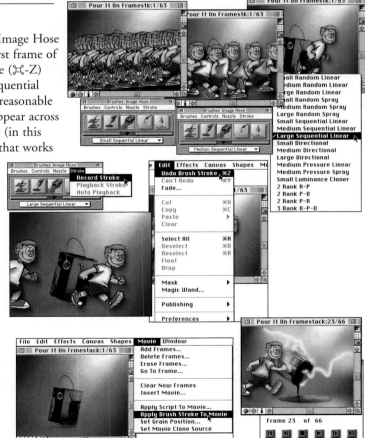

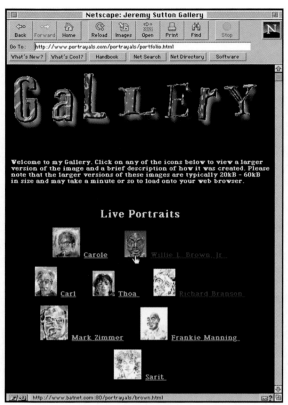

Jeremy Sutton

http://www.portrayals.com/portrayals

Comments

The "Gallery" title graphic on this Web page was created from scanned newspaper lettering. The letters were initially cut out, pasted together, and scanned as a grayscale image. Then the relative scale and orientation of the letters was adjusted. The contrast was increased by using the Express Texture effect. Next, the letters were turned into a floater, painted, and given an embossed look with a dark drop shadow that shows up against the white page. Because the Gallery Web page has a black background, the drop shadow was converted to a white shadow.

Studio Usage

The challenge with this technique was to create a Web page graphic with soft shadowing that showed up against a plain, dark Web page background—yet kept the subtlety of the gradation of tone within the shadow as it faded into the background. You can achieve this effect by using the drop shadow feature of Painter that is associated with floaters. The drop shadow is a separate image object that can be painted independently of other objects or the background.

Related Techniques

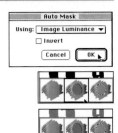

1 | Generate Selection

Start with a high contrast image that uses black lettering against a white background. Select Edit→Mask→Auto Mask. Select Using: Image Luminance. Select the middle Mask Visibility icons to show the mask generated in red. Select the right-hand Mask Visibility icon.

2 | Float Selection, Apply Paint, and Add Drop Shadow

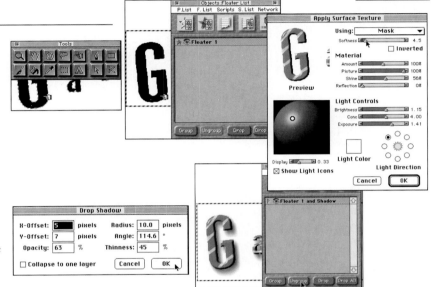

Select the Floater Adjuster Tool and click within the selected region. The floater is in a separate layer from the background canvas. While the floater is active, use the paint tools to color in the lettering. Select Effects→Objects→Create Drop Shadow. Click OK. The original floater and the shadow now appear grouped together in the Floater List. Click Ungroup to make them separate floaters. By doing this, you can paint on the shadow independently of the original floater.

3 | Fill Background with Black

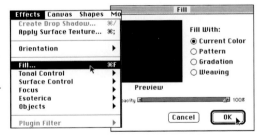

Deselect the floaters by clicking below the floater names in the Floater List. Select black in the Art Materials: Color palette. Select Effects→Fill. The Fill With Current Color option should be highlighted. Click OK to fill the background behind the floaters with black. The shadow is no longer visible. (Black for the background was made to match the Web page background color.)

4 | Paint Shadow White

Activate the Shadow floater by clicking on its name in the Floater list. Select white in the Color Selector. Select the Fat Stroke variant of the Airbrush brush family in the Brushes palette. Stroke the lettering with the airbrush. The white drop shadow starts to appear. When completed, click on the Drop All button at the lower right of the Floater List. Save the file as a JPEG format with high or excellent encoding quality.

Note: *Be careful when you click on a floater name in the Floater List. Be sure to activate it so that you do not inadvertently click on the "eye" symbol which makes the floater invisible.*

Web Page Design *Shadows on a Complex Background*

Michael Partington

Comments

This image was part of an HTML Tutorial that Partington displayed on his Web site. He wanted to show how to create shadows on complex backgrounds. The Web page background tile started off as a blank pale gray canvas the same width as the Web page and 58 pixels high. Surface texture was applied. A scanned wood texture was then added as a floater, with a drop shadow. The vine leaves, with their shadows, are a separate file.

Studio Usage

This technique describes how to create an image with a drop shadow over a complex Web page background. The image can be assigned as a link to another part of the Web site or to another URL location. The challenge is to create an image with the minimum file size and with a seamless shadow that matches the background.

Related Techniques

1 Paste Image on Web Page Background

Prepare the image to be placed over the Web page background as a separate file against a white background. Using techniques such as Color Mask, select the image and paste it onto a canvas containing the Web page background. It appears as a floater. Select Effects→Objects→Create Drop Shadow. Adjust the settings to give an appropriate shadow. Click Drop All.

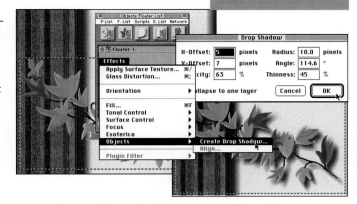

2 Select and Float Region around Image and Shadow

Select the Lasso selection tool in the Tools palette. Draw a selection outline around the image and its shadow. Close the selection. Select Edit→Copy. Select Edit→Paste→Into New Image. The image, its shadow, and a rectangle of surroundings appear in a new document window. Adjust the selected Mask Visibility icon to the middle one. These icons are located next to the Mask Drawing icons in the lower left corner of the document frame. The original selection shape appears in red. Select the furthest right Mask Visibility icon. Click on this selection with the Floater Adjuster tool to make a floater.

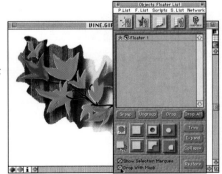

3 Make the Background White

Click outside the selection to deselect the floater. Select the Brush tool. Select Edit→Select All and then select the Delete key. The background clears to white. Click on the icon below the words F. List in the Objects palette to open the Floater List. In the expanded Floater List, check the Drop With Mask option. Click on the Drop All button. The region immediately around the image and its shadow now appear surrounded by white.

4 Save as GIF

Select the middle Mask Visibility icon to view the mask in red. The previously selected region becomes red. Return to the left-hand Mask Visibility icon. Select File→Save As. Save as a GIF file format. Select the following options in the GIF Options dialog box: 256 colors; Interlace GIF File; and Output Transparency with Background is BG Color. Click OK. When you try out the file as part of a Web site, use tables and include "HSPACE=" and "VSPACE=" commands in the HTML. Experiment with the number of pixels set for the "HSPACE=" and "VSPACE=" commands until the image aligns exactly with the background. Beware that some browsers will align images differently.

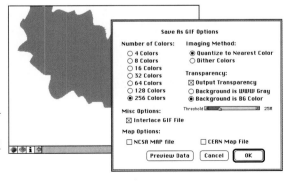

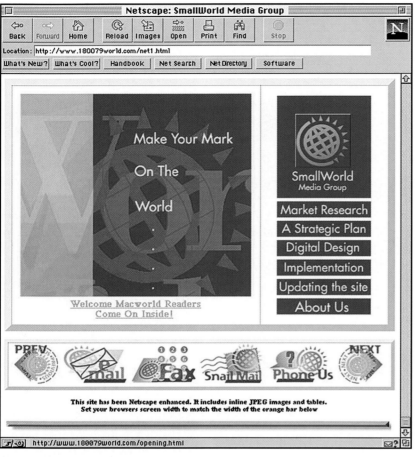

http://www.180079world.com

Comments

This Web site was intended to provide a resource for potential clients of the SmallWorld Media Group to learn what is involved in the creation of a Web site. It was featured in February 1996 *Macworld Magazine* and *Macworld Online* as part of an article on designing for the Web. The button bar was designed to be a logical navigational tool for moving through the site. The original icons that appear were created by using a combination of Macromedia Freehand, Adobe Photoshop, and Fractal Design Painter.

Studio Usage

The creation of a button bar is an example of an effective and consistent navigation system that can help visitors move around your Web site. In this technique you'll create a button bar by using Painter's capability for each floater in an image to be an image map. When visitors click on a button in the bar, they are led automatically to another part of the site (or to another location on Web). The key is to make each button a floater.

Related Techniques

1 | Resize Button Images

Create each button as a larger, separate image than the size you want it to be. This give you a better image quality as you resize down to the final button size. Select Canvas→Resize. Uncheck the Constrain File Size box. Type in the width and height. Click OK. Select Edit→Select All.

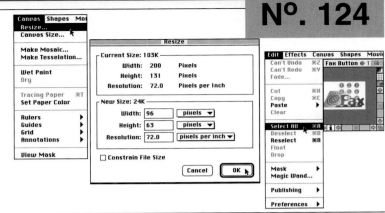

2 | Add Buttons to Floater Library

Select F. List→Floaters. Select the Floater Adjuster tool. Click on the selected resized button image into the Floater palette, while holding down the Option key to make a duplicate floater. Name the floater. The button now appears as a floater in the Floater Library. Repeat this step and Step 1 for all the buttons.

Note: Holding down the Option key leaves a copy of the image behind on the canvas.

3 | Place Button Floaters on Bar

Prepare a bar image that is the correct size to fit all the buttons that need to be placed on it. One at a time, select each button floater in the Floater Library by clicking on its icon and then drag it onto the bar image. Adjust the floater positions until they are evenly spaced on the bar.

Note: The arrow keys move the selected floater one pixel for each click on the arrow key. These keys can be used for fine-tuning the position of each floater.

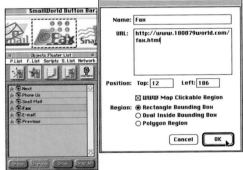

4 | Assign URL Link Destination to Each Floater

One by one, double-click on each floater's name in the Floater List. Fill in the URL destination appropriate to that particular button in "URL." Check the box labeled "WWW Map Clickable Region." The default region is a rectangular bounding box.

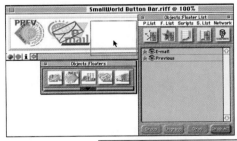

5 | Save as JPEG

Select File→Save As. Save the file in JPEG format. A warning appears concerning the fact that the floaters are about to be merged with the canvas. Click OK. The JPEG encoding quality makes a small difference in the file size. Pick "Good." Check with your Internet service provider about which HTML map option to choose (and also how to write the HTML document so that the image maps will work).

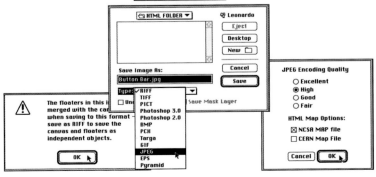

Web Page Design *Combining Image Elements with a Common Drop Shadow*

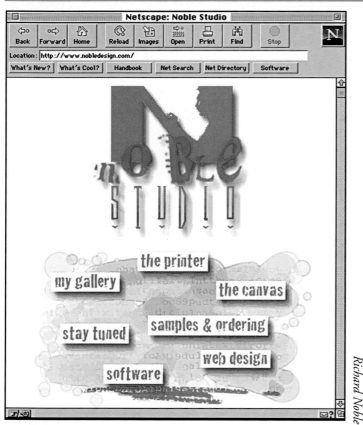

Richard Noble

Noble Studio

Comments

This Web page was created almost entirely in Painter. Noble made extensive use of floaters in both the header and the image map in the lower section. Note that the red Noble logo and purple Noble lettering share a common drop shadow (the lettering doesn't cast a shadow on the logo).

Studio Usage

This technique describes how to combine various image elements into a single header with a common drop shadow. This technique is useful for making dramatic looking Web page headers or navigational image maps.

The three different image elements used here demonstrate three different ways to go about selecting and floating images, depending on whether they are hard-edged flat color, hard-edged multicolored, or soft-edged single hue. To do this technique, you must have each image element on a separate canvas set against a plain white background.

Related Techniques

1 | Select Flat-Colored Image Element

Open a logo image with a single contiguous block of color and a hard edge against a plain white background. Select Edit→Magic Wand. Click in the block of color with the Magic Wand tool. Click OK. The logo is now selected.

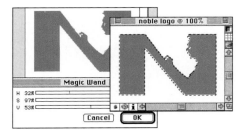

2 | Select Multicolored Image Element

Open a multicolored image element against a plain white background. Select Edit→Select All followed by Edit→Magic Wand. Click with the Magic Wand in the white background. The white goes red, indicating that it is included in the Magic Wand selection. Click OK. Select Edit→Mask→Invert Mask to reverse the selection so that everything except the white background is now included.

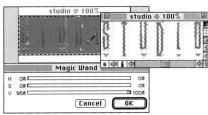

3 | Select Soft-Edged Image Element

Select a soft-edged single hue image with a plain white background. Select Edit→Mask→Color Mask. Click in the lettering. Adjust the H (Hue), S (Saturation), and V (Value) Extents sliders until the preview window shows a red mask covering the lettering but not the background. Click OK. Click and drag on the Mask Visibility icon pull-down menu. Drag to the rightmost Mask Visibility icon.

4 | Paste Image Elements onto Common Canvas

With the canvas from Step 1 active and the logo still selected, select Edit→Copy. Then click on another canvas, one that will be large enough for the final combined image. Select Edit→Paste→Normal. Repeat this for the other two image elements selected in Steps 2 and 3. The three image elements are now floaters in this new canvas. Click on the F. (Floater) List icon in the Objects palette to see them listed. Select the Floater Adjuster tool and position each floater relative to the others.

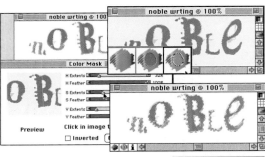

5 | Apply Drop Shadow and Save as GIF or JPEG

With the Floater Adjuster tool selected, select Edit→Select All. Click the Group button in the Floater List. Click the Collapse button. Select Effects→Objects→Create Drop Shadow. Click OK to create a common drop shadow. Select File→Save As. Select GIF or JPEG as the file format to save the file for use on the World Wide Web.

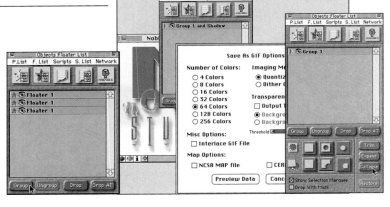

Glossary

8-bit color. A color model that provides a palette of 256 colors; the minimum amount of colors displayed on a color monitor.

24-bit color. 24-bit color provides 256 shades of color for each color channel (red, green, and blue). When the shades from all three channels are combined, more than 16 million colors can be generated.

32-bit color. 32-bit color provides 256 shades of color for each color channel (red, green, and blue) and also provides a mask channel containing 256 possible shades. 32-bit color provides the most precise color matching between a color monitor and printed output. Painter files are 32-bit color.

Additive Color. Additive colors refer to red, green, and blue light. When combined in various percentages, the combinations correspond to the visible range of colors. By combining 100 percent of each of the colors, white light is produced.

Anti-Aliasing. The softening effect produced by mixing pixels. For example, to create a smooth border, pixels are mixed in percentages of color rather than by creating a transition from one color directly to another. Painter brushes, effects, and objects make use of anti-aliasing.

Bézier Curves. A drawing element that describes curves in a structured, repeatable manner. Bézier curves have handles and points that describe the shape of a curved line or section. The Pen tool in Painter provides the user with a method of creating Bézier curves. Bézier curves in Painter create shapes. *See Shapes.*

Bitmap mode. A bitmap is an image comprised of individual pixels, where each pixel has a specific value.

Brightness. In printing terms, brightness refers to the reflective nature of the paper. In Painter, brightness refers to the amount of light in each pixel.

Brush family. A grouping of brush variants with common properties. For example, the 500B Pencil is a variant in the Pencils brush family.

Brush Look. (*See Technique #21.*) A customized brush variant that includes paper texture information.

Brush Look Designer. A part of Painter that allows you to preview brush variants and save Brush Looks.

Brush Type. *See Brush family.*

Canvas. Term for the bitmap background in a Painter image. Also known as background canvas or image layer.

Canvas Size. (*See Technique #34*). The size of the canvas, usually measured in pixels.

Cartoon Cell Fill (*See Techniques #32, 82, 98, 115.*) A way to fill regions of an image based on the mask, rather than on the color of pixels. By double-clicking on the Paint Bucket in the Tools bucket, you have the ability to determine the Mask Threshold, which controls to what extent the fill penetrates into the mask.

CD. An abbreviation for Compact Disk. Many stock photographic images are available in this format; for example, Kodak's PhotoCDs.

Clipboard. The area of memory reserved for sequential temporary storage. Each time an item is copied to the Clipboard, the previous contents are discarded. The Edit→Copy (⌘-C) {Ctrl-C} command copies to the clipboard. The Edit→Paste command pastes from the clipboard.

Cloning. (*See Techniques #56, 59, 63, 69, 119, 120.*) The duplication of individual pixel color or regions of pixels. Cloning brushes look at the clone source for their color information.

CMYK. Cyan, Magenta, Yellow, and Black. CMYK also refers to the four inks used when outputting to a printing press.

Color Correction. The process of correcting undesirable color or color casts in an image.

Color Gamut. The range of colors that can be perceived on a specific device. For example, monitors display the RGB color gamut, based on light, and printed material displays the CMYK color gamut, based on ink colors. The RGB gamut is larger than the CMYK gamut.

Color Space. Color space refers to the way a color image is being described and stored. RGB, CMYK, and Kodak YCC are examples of color space. Painter works in the RGB color space.

Composite Method. Determines the way pixels in an image floater interact with color in pixels behind the floater.

Compression. The method by which a file is condensed to create a smaller file, or the method by which certain pixels are discarded to store color data.

Contrast. The relationship between the lightest and darkest areas of an image.

Default. In Painter, the initial settings for tools, palettes, and other file preferences. Default settings can be changed using the Preferences command.

Document. *See File.*

dpi. Dots per inch. A measurement of the resolution of the file.

Duotone. Traditionally, an image created by overlaying two halftones of different ink colors, each at a specific screen angle.

EPS. Encapsulated PostScript. A file format standard created by Adobe Systems to store graphic and image files. Also called *EPSF.*

File. A digital image. Includes all layers and information associated with the image.

File Format. The method by which images are stored, for example, EPS, JPEG, TIFF. Different file formats use different methods of compression. The same image stored in different file formats will occupy different amounts of memory.

Floater. A floating image "object," or layer. There are two types: image floaters and reference floaters. Image floaters are discrete, bitmap images that float above the canvas. Reference floaters are temporary, low-resolution versions of image floaters. Both types are listed in the Floater List.

Floater List. *See Floater.*

Floater Mask. (*See Techniques #77, 80, 86, 116.*) Each image floater has a separate mask layer associated with it.

Floater Mask Icons. (*See Technique #116.*) There are two rows of floater mask icons at the bottom of the expanded Objects: Floater List palette. The top row determines how the floater mask affects which parts of the floater are visible. The bottom row determines the way the background canvas mask layer affects the visibility of the floater.

Grayscale. An 8-bit, black-and-white image.

Grout. (*See Technique #84.*) The filling between mosaic tiles.

High-resolution. An image that contains twice the amount in resolution than the line screen at which it will be reproduced. For example, a 300 dpi image printed at a line screen of 150 is a high-resolution image.

HLS. Hue, luminance, and saturation.

Hue. Color. Red and blue are two different hues.

Image Hose. (*See Technique #81.*) The Image Hose is an amazing tool for spraying image elements onto a canvas. It has no "traditional" equivalent. Image elements, which are loaded into the hose as "nozzles," "pour" out of the hose as you paint. The order, distribution, size, opacity, and color of the emerging images can all be controlled via different input parameters, such as stylus pressure and direction.

Image Size. Dimensions of the image as measured in pixels or in absolute physical dimensions, such as inches.

Import. The process of reading an image created in one application into another application.

JPEG. A file compression method created by the Joint Photographic Experts Group to reduce the original size.

Layer. *See Floater.*

Luminance. A measurement of a tone's brightness or lightness with no consideration of its color or saturation.

Make Mosaic. (*See Techniques #40, 70, 84, 99.*) A mode within Painter that allows you to create and edit mosaic tiles. You can work from scratch or convert an existing image into a mosaic.

Mask. A stencil that can be used to protect selected regions of an image from the action of brushes or effects. Painter files have an 8-bit mask layer with 256 levels of intensity. Thus, a brush stroke or effect can be partially masked.

Mask Drawing Icons. (*See Techniques #29, 33.*) These are a set of three icons that pop up from the bottom left of the document frame and are also accessible in the expanded Objects: Path List palette. They determine the way the mask layer protects the canvas from the brushes.

Mask Edit Mode. (*See Techniques #70, 77.*) Normally, the mask layer can be edited with any brush by using the Masking Method Category and is unaffected by the Effects menu. The Mask Edit Mode enables any brush, irrespective of its Method Category, to be used to edit the mask layer. It also allows application of certain effects, such as Soften, to be applied to the mask layer.

Mask Threshold. *See Cartoon Cell Fill.*

Mask Visibility Icons. (*See Techniques #29, 68, 123.*) These are a set of three icons that pop up from the bottom left of the document frame (next to the Mask Drawing Icons) and are also accessible in the expanded Objects: Path List palette. They determine the way the mask is displayed.

Method Category. These categories, accessible in the expanded Brushes palette, determine the general properties of the brush variants. Examples are Cover, which produces brush strokes that cover up what is underneath as if painting with opaque pigment, and Buildup, which produces brush strokes that build towards black. Chalks are Cover brushes and Felt Pens are Buildup brushes.

Method Subcategory. The Method Subcategory more precisely defines brush behavior within the general properties of the Method Category. The Method Subcategory determines whether the brush stroke is modulated by the paper texture and how hard or soft the edges of the stroke are. For example, Soft Grainy Cover is a Method Subcategory of the Cover Method that has a soft edge to the stroke and shows paper texture within the stroke.

Midtones. The tonal value halfway between black and white.

Moiré. An unsightly and undesirable pattern caused by improper alignment of halftone screens.

Monochrome. Usually refers to a black-and-white monitor, but can also indicate a black-and-white image.

Mosaic. *See Make Mosaic.*

Mover. (*See Techniques #72, 88.*) Painter has libraries that contain collections of various items. Examples are Brushes, Papers, Gradients, Patterns, and Scripts. Each of these libraries has a Mover associated with it. Movers enable you to edit a library (delete an item or change the name of an item), create new libraries, and move items between libraries. They are very useful for organizing sets of customized items.

Negative. An image whose tonal values have been reversed (for example, black areas are white and vice versa); the image used to create a positive print.

Neutrals. Gray tones with no apparent hue (color).

Nozzle. (*See Technique #81.*) *See Image Hose.*

Opaque. A tone that blocks all light.

Pantone™ A commercial color matching and ink mixing system that ensures consistency in matching or attaining specific colors.

PICT. A file format used by several programs. Many multimedia applications rely on PICT format to display graphics on-screen.

Pixel. An individual (pic)ture (el)ement. A single dot on the screen or in a continuous-tone image.

Pixelization. A special effect achieved by lowering the resolution of an image in an attempt to make individual pixels visible.

Posterize. (*See Technique #41.*) To reduce the number of colors that make up the image.

ppi. Pixels per inch. A measure of resolution.

Primary Colors. Red, green, and blue (additive primary colors); cyan, magenta, yellow, and black (subtractive primary colors).

Process Color. One of the four primary colors used for offset printing (cyan, magenta, yellow, and black).

Resize. (*See Technique #6.*) An operation to alter the total number of pixels that are contained within an image.

Resolution. The height and width of a digital image measured in pixels.

Retouching. Modification of a digital image, by using tools designed to adjust pixel values.

RGB. The three primary colors used to display images on a color monitor or for input in a scanner.

Saturation. The measurement of a color's intensity. Pink is less saturated than red; sky blue is less saturated than royal blue.

Scanner. A device that utilizes one of several methods to capture (digitize) artwork.

Script. (*See Techniques #31, 95, 119, 120, 121.*) A sequential record of all commands, operations, and brush strokes. Scripts can be played back and edited. Painter enables you to record your sessions by using scripts.

Secondary Color. (*See Technique #93.*) The Secondary Color is shown in the underlying rectangle in the Art Materials: Color palette and in the Controls: Brush palette. It is used in the Two-Point gradient and Graduated brush.

Session. *See Script.*

Shadows. The darkest portion of an image that still contains detail.

Shapes. (*See Techniques #39, 89, 90.*) Shapes are anti-aliased (smooth-edged rather than jaggy), vector-based objects. They can be created and edited with the Shape Design tools. They can be simple lines, curves, and text outlines. You can stroke and fill shapes and determine their transparency. They are listed in the Objects: Floater List palette.

Sharpen. Sharpening increases the edge contrast of an image.

Substrate. The material on which an image is printed or imaged.

Subtractive Color. The color system based on the four-process ink colors: cyan, magenta, yellow, and black.

TIFF. An abbreviation for Tagged Image File Format; a standard file format created by Aldus Corporation for storing bitmapped images.

Tint. A percentage of a given color at less than 100 percent opacity.

Tonal range. The number of tones between black and white found in a given image.

Tone. The measurement of a color independent of its hue; a measurement of brightness or lightness.

Tone Curve. The relationship of tones in an image displayed on a chart.

Transparency. A photographic image on a material that allows light to pass through its surface; the ability of a digital image to allow underlying images to show through.

Trim. (*See Technique #81.*) Image floaters are rectangular images. Often, the outer region of the rectangle is masked off and not visible. Trim is an operation that minimizes the size of the rectangle to fit the visible region of the floater.

Variant. (*See Technique #27.*) The individual brushes contained within each brush family. These individual brush variants have their properties defined by the Method Category and Method Subcategory menus and the Brush Controls palettes.

Vector-based images. Images where objects are mathematically defined versus continuous tone images, where images are defined in pixels.

Wet Layer. (*See Techniques #2, 18.*) This is a separate layer that floats above the background canvas. The Water Color brushes paint directly into this separate layer. The Wet Layer is only affected by brushes from the Water Color brush family. The Wet Layer can be dried (dropped into the background canvas) by the command Canvas→Dry. The Wet Layer is only preserved in the RIFF file format.

Listing of Artists

Mark Badger *(Technique #113)*
429 Euclid Avenue, Apt. 4
Oakland, CA 94610
510-444-0346
E-mail: Badgetoon@lanminds.com

"I do all my work in Painter, except for the type, and I wonder why people bother with Photoshop."

Mark Badger has drawn funny books for the last 12 years. His subjects include many fighting superheros. Some of his books have been produced for assorted non-violent non-profits. Fall of 1996 sees the publication of *Badger's Marks and Angles*, a digital kitchen sink of a comic book to combine all his interests.

Kent Bingham *(Technique #84)*
Graphics by Design
333 W. 5250 S.
Ogden, UT 84405
801-479-4099 or 801-479-0539
E-mail: BKent1@sisna.com

"I began using Fractal Design Painter several years ago with the release of version 2.0, and find Painter to be one of the most exciting, innovative pieces of software on the market. The flexibility Painter gives me allows me to do things I could never do with 'real' media. The bonus is that I never run out of paint, and I never have to clean the brushes."

Kent Bingham, a 34-year-old native of Ogden, Utah, works as a full-time graphic designer at Hill Air Force Base in Utah and also runs a small, one-man studio called "Graphics by Design" from his home.

Kent has always been active in many artistic projects and initially wanted to become a comic book illustrator. He has had several full-color painted comic book covers published. When his career with the government helped him discover the computer as an art tool, Kent's interests turned to graphic design. This new interest lead him to a full-time graphics position with the Air Force where he taught himself many graphics programs before beginning his own design business. His work includes logo design, brochure design, Web publishing, T-shirt graphics, and anything interesting that comes his way.

Sheriann Ki-Sun Burnham *(Techniques #72, 89, 100)*
227 Ancona Drive
Long Beach, CA 90803
310-433-5813
E-mail: kisun@aol.com

"Since an early age, I have been interested in the layering of pattern, texture, and form. This fascination has guided me through experiments with watercolor, pen and ink, stone lithography, and ultimately the computer. Whether representational or abstract, I delight in the interplay between negative and positive spaces. The computer's immense texture and pattern generating capabilities enable me to create images that cannot be created easily in other media. I believe the computer as an art tool expands the imagination and extends the possibilities of what can be achieved in artistic expression."

Sheriann Ki-Sun Burnham has been a professional graphic designer/illustrator since 1980. She has been involved in computer graphics since 1981. Her work has been presented internationally in many exhibitions and publications including ACM SIGGRAPH 1988, 1989, and 1990 art shows, Artware—Art and Electronics 1990, Germany, and the 1995 Fractal Design Art Expo.

Mario Henri Chakkour *(Techniques #8, 109)*
Studio twenty Six Media
209 Westcentral Street, Suite 210
Natick, MA 01760
508-653-3132
E-mail: shehad@aol.com

Mario Henri Chakkour is a Boston-based architect, author, music producer, and creative director. He is the creator of *Painting with Computers* (book and companion CD-ROM) and the *Joy of Pixels* video series. He works almost exclusively with Fractal Design Painter. He creates his artwork from scratch by using The Digital Wet-on-Wet technique he developed.

Michael Cinque *(Technique #91)*
Fractal Design Corporation
335 Spreckels Drive
Aptos, CA 95003
408-688-5300

"My interest and experience in the fields of art, photography, and computer graphics have come together in an exciting and powerful way in working with Painter."

Michael Cinque is a photographer who has been using the computer as a creative tool since 1989. He uses programs, such as Painter and ColorStudio, to create new images from his existing photographs. Michael's work has been published in a number of publications, including *Verbum's Desktop Color Book, Computer Pictures Magazine, Photo District News, Verbum Magazine, Publish Magazine,* and *Painting with Computers* by Mario Henri Chakkour. Besides being a photographer, Michael is the Quality Assurance Manager at Fractal Design Corporation. Michael holds a Bachelor of Fine Arts degree from the School of Visual Arts in New York City.

Gary F. Clark *(Techniques #55, 58)*
Associate Professor of Art
Bloomsburg University
Bloomsburg, PA 17815
717-387-1689
E-mail: clark@planetx.bloomu.edu

"The use of the computer as a fine art tool has allowed me to create forms that would be difficult or impossible by any other means. My images are created by using electronic tools, but the process is guided by my visual and emotional concerns. It is through many decisions, artistic judgements, and trial and error, that my vision becomes realized."

Gary Clark has been teaching at Bloomsburg University since 1972. His artwork has been exhibited and published extensively throughout the world, including recent solo exhibits at the United States Senate Office Building, Washington D.C., and the 911 gallery, Indianapolis, IN. He is represented by five galleries including Silicon Gallery, Philadelphia, PA, and Agnisiuh Gallery, Sedona, AZ.

Victor Claudio *(Technique #62)*
12329 Glenfield Avenue
Tampa, FL 33626
813-891-6188
E-mail: madcirq@aol.com

Victor Claudio has been illustrating on the Mac since 1988. Recent publications include: *Photoshop Creative Techniques*/Hayden Books and *KPT Creative Techniques*/MetaTools. Victor is a Pratt Institute graduate, and has worked as art director for Norman, Craig & Kummel, Grey Advertising in Puerto Rico, and is presently art director for AAA Auto Club South's Marketing Department in Tampa, FL. His client list includes: Colgate-Palmolive, Coors Brewery, Proctor & Gamble, Nissan, Panasonic, and Seagrams Distillers.

Lol Creme *(Technique #16)*
Lolster, Inc.
8326 Grand View Drive
Los Angeles, CA 90046
213-848-8286 Contact: Katie Fitch
E-mail: lolster@metawire.com

Lol Creme was born in Manchester, England, and is the ex-founder member of the art pop band 10cc and duo Godley & Creme. Having directed and created music for video, film, and television, Lol now spends a considerable amount of time developing new technologies for sound and picture. His private passion is painting, drawing, and sculpture, using every medium available.

Flynn De Marco *(Technique #32)*
4069A 24th Street
San Francisco, CA 94114
415-826-9016
E-mail: astroboy@sirius.com
Web Site: http://www.sirius.com/~astroboy

"I hope to one day incorporate my acting career with computer animation in an all out multimedia kook-fest!"

Flynn De Marco is currently studying 3D animation at the Center for ElectronicArt, San Francisco. His art reflects his love of cartoons, Egyptology, Hawaii, and 1940s–1960s pop culture.

John Derry *(Techniques #40, 59, 104, 121)*
Fractal Design Corporation
335 Spreckels Drive
Aptos, CA 95003
408-688-5300

John Derry is a practicing artist and a designer of natural-media software. As the Vice President of Creative Design at Fractal Design, John is one of the authors of Fractal Design Painter and Fractal Design Dabbler. He has created seminal works that demonstrate the computer's potential as an expressive art form.

John graduated from Cranbrook Academy of Art in Bloomfield Hills, Michigan with an M.F.A. in Painting, and has been involved in computer graphics since 1982. Prior to joining Fractal Design, John was Director of Creative Services for Time Arts. During this time he was involved with the design of Oasis, a breakthrough Macintosh painting application that mimicked traditional media.

John's illustration and design work have appeared in numerous publications. John's clients have included Apple, The Sharper Image, and DuPont. He has spoken at several computer graphics conferences. He has authored several papers and articles including an award-winning series on computer graphics for *Art Products & Design News.*

Sharron Evans *(Techniques #11, 98)*
3220 Sacramento Street
San Francisco, CA 94115
415-931-2593 or 415-239-7024
E-mail: SEvansUp@aol.com

Sharron Evans, artist, illustrator, graphic and instructional designer, has an extensive background in fine arts. Sharron has worked on graphics and illustrations for multimedia and the Web, as well as print. Her exhibitions include etchings, computer art (Iris Prints), and other media, such as water color and drawing. She has a strong interest in artwork for and by children. Sharron has an M.A. in Instructional Technologies from SFSU in 1991. She has taught at the SFSU Multimedia Studies Program, the San Francisco Academy of Art College, and other colleges throughout the Bay Area. She has demonstrated Painter at numerous trade shows and events, including the San Francisco Museum of Modern Arts.

Lisa Fenwick (*Techniques #49, 117*)
659 15th Avenue
Menlo Park, CA 94025
415-326-8659

Lisa Fenwick is a Menlo Park-based California photographer specializing in working with children. She has been in the business for sixteen years.

Yves Francisque (*Technique #76*)
10 Allée De Bretagne
94320 Thais
France
+33-1-48-539199

"An artist is always a researcher, witness, and interpreter of his time."

Born in 1950 in South Vietnam, Yves Francisque spent most of his childhood in Vietnam, Nigeria, Cambodia, and France. He followed graphic art training at l'Ecole Supérieure des Arts Modernes, Paris, 1970–73. He has a strong knowledge of graphic matters and the traditional graphic chain. He subsequently explored traditional painting media, such as oil, watercolor, pastel, and acrylic, before discovering, in 1989, the new art tool of the computer. His artwork is regularly exhibited and published. He is writing a book on Fractal Design Painter 4.0 that will ship in Autumn' 96 in France. Yves Francisque also regularly trains French graphic designers in Painter.

Jason Fruchter (*Techniques #68, 115*)
165 East 89th Street, Apt. 3G
New York, NY 10128
212-360-1721
E-mail: wallydude@aol.com

"I consider myself foremost a traditional character animator. I draw all my animation frames on paper by using a light box, peg bar, and punched paper. Recently, I have been doing my 2D animation directly on the computer, using the Wacom tablet along with Animator Pro software for the PC. I use the computer to colorize and composite the drawings."

Jason Fruchter is a graduate of the Rhode Island School of Design (1992). He has worked for various studios in New York City, including MTV and Nickelodeon. His work has been published in a number of books.

Jerry Garcia *(Techniques #3, 78)*
Contact for the Estate of Jerome J. Garcia:
P.O. Box 196
San Raphael, CA 94915-0196

Jerry Garcia, the late artist and musician, founder of the Grateful Dead, explored creating art on computers ever since the first Macintosh was available. He drew constantly as a child, studied art as a teenager, and, as an adult, enjoyed synthesizing traditional techniques with the most current cutting-edge technology. Whenever Jerry went on the road, several months a year, he always took his PowerBook laptop computer with him. Working on his art in various hotel rooms allowed him to be productive during his down time. During the last years of his life, pursuing his visual art, especially his computer art, gave him great joy and satisfaction.

More of his computer artwork can be seen in the book *Harrington Street,* published by Delacorte Books, a division of Bantam Doubleday Dell Publishing Group, Inc.

Krista Glass *(Technique #114)*
MWG
Elisabethplatz 1a
80796 München
Germany
+49-89-27818167
E-mail: Wladarsch@MWG.de
Web Site: http://www.MWG.de

Krista Glass was born in 1969 in Galati and has lived in Munich since 1979. Krista was trained as a fashion illustrator. She has built a reputation as a graffiti artist. Since 1994 she has worked at MWG (Michael Wladarsch Gestaltung) as a graphic designer and illustrator.

Helen Golden *(Technique #77)*
460 El Capitan Place
Palo Alto, CA 94306
415-494-3461
E-mail: hsgolden@aol.com

"These sophisticated tools are enabling and empowering me to explore myriad ideas and to play, risk, and experiment more with them. As all media interact and collaborate with the artist, I find the serendipitous dialogue and the rich possibilities inspiring."

Helen Golden, a member of Unique Editions™, a collaboration of "tradigital" artists, has worked in a variety of media, such as photography and drawing, with the same goals in mind—to create images that would, in their ambiguous reality, engage, provoke, and cause the viewer to reflect and wonder. As the artist searched for alternative ways to alter images, she found herself sitting in front of a computer facing the exciting challenges of working with new technologies. She may scan and digitize anything in the studio, a photograph or drawing from her archives, or an object such as a shell from her collection. She then digitally alters, layers, paints, and collages that material, and after printing the image, takes the opportunity to work back into it by using traditional media.

Rhoda Grossman *(Technique #85)*
216 Fourth Street
Sausalito, CA 94965
415-331-0328
E-mail: rhodagro@slip.net

Rhoda Grossman has used traditional media for drawing, painting, and printmaking for the last 25 years. Since 1990, the computer has become her primary tool for fine art, caricature, and illustration. She frequently uses scanned or photographed items blended with an energetic, playful, and expressionistic style. Her work has been included in trade shows, galleries, corporate brochures, books, and magazines. To see her commercial portfolio, contact Salzman International, 415-285-8267.

Peter M. Gruhn *(Technique #81)*
RPI
158 Commercial Street
Sunnyvale, CA 94086
E-mail: gruhn@nando.net
Web Site: http://www.delta.com/peter/gruhn.htm

Peter Gruhn's first experience of computer painting was playing with MacPaint in a store back in 1985. He bought an Amiga and a copy of Deluxe Paint in 1986, and has been playing ever since. He has answered Painter questions online for a couple of years now and is Section Leader on the Painter Users Group section of the GUGRPA forum on Compuserve. Peter taught CAD to architecture students at Rensselaer, and he currently programs computers.

Steve Guttman *(Technique #79)*
Fractal Design Corporation
335 Spreckels Drive
Aptos, CA 95003
408-688-5300

Steve Guttman is the Vice President of Marketing for Fractal Design, where he oversees Marketing and Product Management for all of Fractal's products including Painter, Dabbler, Sketcher, and ColorStudio. Before joining Fractal, he was employed by Adobe, where he started as the original product manager for Adobe Photoshop, taking an active role in the design, launch, and marketing of versions 1.0, 2.0, and 2.5. In 1991, Guttman was promoted to Senior Product Marketing Manager in charge of Macintosh graphics applications where he managed the development and marketing of Adobe Illustrator, Adobe Premiere, Adobe Dimensions, Adobe Audition, and Adobe Streamline.

Before joining Adobe, Mr. Guttman worked as a structural engineer, programmer, and technology writer. He is active in photography and holds a Bachelor's degree from Princeton University and Masters degrees in Civil Engineering and Business from UC Berkeley.

Kathy Hamon *(Techniques #24, 83)*
c/o Beatrice Couderc
53, Route de la Reine
92000 Boulogne Billancourt
France

"For me, a painting is made from the silence, and for this reason I don't like to explain my paintings. I prefer to stay in the silence."

Kathy Hamon, artist and musician, has been working on the computer for 10 years. She originally studied traditional painting techniques as well as the piano. She worked for Apple France and now does freelance artwork, both traditional and digitals for advertising, CD-ROM interface design, posters, and newspapers. Her artwork has been published in magazines such as *Mac Art & Design* (issue 14/15). Her favorite painters are Francis Bacon, Jerome Bosh, Edward Hopper, Gaspar Friederich, Monet, and Douanier Rousseau.

Andrew J. Hathaway *(Technique #111)*
805 Page Street
San Francisco, CA 94117
415-621-0671
E-mail: andrew+hathaway@designlink.com

Andrew Hathaway is a painter, commercial illustrator, and professional photographer. He has taught at San Francisco State University Multimedia Studies Program, American Film Institute, University of California at Santa Barbara, Photometro workshops, and Foothill Community College. His clients include Apple Computer, Inc., the American Film Institute, Collins Publishers San Francisco, *INFOWORLD,* Mondo 2000, *ONLINE DESIGN, Publish,* and Windham Hill Records.

Fiona Hawthorne *(Technique #9)*
47 Barlby Road
London, W10 6AW
England
+44-181-968-8889

"For me, the joy of painting on the computer is in creating wonderful juxtapositions of bright colors on dark backgrounds, and being able to repeatedly undo that last line until I achieve a free and spontaneous expression."

Fiona is a Northern Irish artist who is well known for her delicate and witty line and wash paintings on paper and screen. She likes to work at low resolution to achieve a mix of pixelation with free line and splotches of color. Her artwork has been used by a broad spectrum of clients from the publishing, advertising, telecommunications, music, television, and film industries. She was recently commissioned to create a series of huge murals for Hong Kong Telecom's new interactive exhibit. Her *Heart and Soul* painting won first place in the 1996 Fractal Design International Digital Art Contest.

Rosemary Hendler *(Technique #50)*
16 El Verano Road
Orinda, CA 94563
510-254-9178

"I am continually amazed that from a compact, electrically powered box, artists are finding ways to create beauty. As an acrylic painter and traditional artist for the past thirty years, I am happy to be a part of this new movement."

Rosemary Hendler was trained in painting at the University of California, Berkeley. After several years working as a furniture buyer, Rosemary pursued further training in interior design, graphic design, and illustration at the San Francisco Academy of Art College and University of California, Los Angeles. For the last twenty years, she has worked as a freelance graphic designer while continuing to exhibit her acrylic paintings and hand-paint a line of children's clothing.

David Locke Higgins *(Techniques #4, 10, 27, 37)*
3675 Ruffin Road
Suite 225
San Diego, CA 92123
619-279-9808

"The animals that I paint are all threatened or vulnerable in their natural habitats. I believe we can all make a difference to end the destruction of their habitats. My work is dedicated to the preservation of all living things."

David Locke Higgins, an internationally collected portrait artist, has been a professional artist, illustrator, and graphic designer for 40 years. He is a graduate of the University of Michigan School of Architecture and Design with a degree in advertising and graphic design. His work has appeared in several books on the use of Fractal Design's Painter and Dabbler.

Historically, his portraits and illustrations have been created in gouache, oil pastels, and oils. David finds the Mac and Fractal Painter 3.1, as a painting medium, offer him greater expression of form, design, and color than any of the traditional materials with which he has worked.

His remarkable likenesses are portraits of specific animals that live in the San Diego Zoo and Wild Animal Park. David feels that the closeness of the images allows the viewer to experience the character and personality of the animal with more intimacy than a full body rendering in an environmental setting.

George Ho *(Technique #96)*
P.O. Box 210427
San Francisco, CA 94121
415-751-9691
E-mail: georgeh911@aol.com

Hominn *(Technique #57)*
87, rue Jeanne Hornet
93170 Bagnolet
France
+33-16-1-43634930

Hominn, also known as Hominn Lebirec, is a French digital artist from the Brittany region of France. He graduated in architecture and is self-trained in digital painting. He has exhibited a lot of his artwork in France and also decorates surfboards and composes songs. As an Aikido practitioner, he mixes the philosophy of martial art with painting energies and movement. He also draws on the high spirits of his Celtic ancestory. Hominn first discovered digital imaging in 1984, and since 1988, he has worked as a freelancer, writing in French magazines on digital art and producing a lot of images that reflect his personal view of life. As a Celtic poet he tries to re-create what his ancestors did 4,000 years ago.

Stacy A. Hopkins *(Technique #107)*
2 Chippenham Drive
Newark, DE 19711
E-mail: Stacy162@aol.com

"I don't have any training in art or computers, but I am having fun! That is all that matters to me."

Stacy Hopkins has owned a business called *High Energy the Gym* in Newark, DE, for 16 years. It is a gym full of weight lifting equipment, Nautilus, free weights, treadmills, bikes, Stairmasters, and so on. Stacy likes to tour the U.S. on his Goldwing Trike (three-wheel motorcycle). He started using Painter about three years ago.

Mark Jenkins *(Techniques #12, 14)*
Rucker Design Group
196 Castro Street
Mountain View, CA 94041
415-960-1951

Mark Jenkins is a senior designer at the Rucker Design Group. His design experience spans a broad range of areas including illustration, corporate identity, packaging, and multimedia. He received his B.F.A. from Tyler School of Art. Mark's award-winning artwork has been exhibited internationally and has been featured in several books and magazines about digital art.

Aleksander Jensko *(Techniques #41, 64)*
Glockengiesserstrasse 22
23552 Lübeck
Germany
+49-451-75644

"The computer is an art tool like any other art tool, just like a paint brush or airbrush. It's not the computer that dominates my life, it's the art."

Aleksander Jensko was born in 1962 in Poland. He studied literature in Poland at the University of Torun and has lived in Germany since 1989. His first passion was always art. He is a self-taught artist, first focusing on art photography. In 1993 he discovered the Macintosh computer could help go beyond the limits of conventional photography. Starting with Adobe Photoshop, he then moved on to Fractal Design Painter. He currently works as Art Director at an advertising agency, Logos, while continuing to create fine art in his spare time. His art has been published in several European magazines and exhibited in Germany. He has produced a book of his short stories and pictures, *Spherical Chronicles,* which is being published in Polish.

Jason R. Kang *(Technique #75)*
1200 Eucalyptus Drive
San Francisco, CA 94132
415-661-7682

Jason R. Kang is an illustrator and graphic designer working primarily with digital tools.

Ali Karp *(Technique #106)*
2610 Nichols Canyon Road
Los Angeles, CA 90046
E-mail: alink@earthlink.net

Ali Karp is a graduate of the Art Center College of Design, Pasadena. Ali is working in new media (motion graphics, interactive, and Web design).

Dorothy Simpson Krause *(Techniques #38, 63)*
32 Nathaniel Way
P. O. Box 421
Marshfield Hills, MA 02051
617-837-1682
E-mail: DotKrause@aol.com

Dorothy Krause is a Professor of Computer Graphics at the Massachusetts College of Art, Corporate Curator for IRIS Graphics, Inc., and a member of Unique Editions™, a collaboration of "tradigital" artists. Since 1993 Dorothy's work has been featured in eleven solo or two-person shows throughout the United States and Europe. During the same time her work has been in more than 30 group shows, including Fractal Design's Art Expo 94 and 95. Current and upcoming publications showing her work include numerous computer graphics books and magazines. She is the featured artist in the December 1995 issue of *IdN International designer's Network,* the January 1995 issue of *IEEE Computer Graphics and Application,* and the February/March 1996 issue of *Computer Artist.*

Jane Kriss *(Techniques #80, 99, 101)*
P.O. Box 60490
Palo Alto, CA 94306
415-857-9035
E-mail: JKriss@aol.com

Jane Kriss is a surface designer trained in traditional hand-painting methods as well as computer-aided design techniques. She currently divides her time between producing designs for manufacturers and teaching in Zeida Rothman's Fabric Design in Berkeley, California. Living in Palo Alto, CA, with Mark, Jesse, and Peter, Jane is a new convert to Painter 4, having defected after many years of devoted Photoshop and Illustrator use.

Jon Lee *(Technique #118)*
VP Art and Design
Fox Television
5746 Sunset Boulevard W.
5th Floor
Los Angeles, CA 90028
213-856-1099

"The computer has greatly accelerated my design process. It used to take about three weeks to do what we do in three hours now, and it's better designed, too, because of the tools."

Jon Lee received his M.F.A. from the California Institute of the Arts. Jon has been creating computer graphics for broadcast design since 1979. He is currently head of Promotion Graphics for the Fox Television Network.

Bonny Lhotka *(Techniques #23, 94)*
Lhotka Fine Art
5658 Cascade Place
Boulder, CO 80803
303-494-5631
E-mail: BonnyL5658@aol.com
Web Site: http://www.iquest.net/911/u_bonny.html

Bonny Lhotka, a member of Unique Editions™, a collaboration of "tradigital" artists, was born in La Grange, Illinois. She graduated from Bradley University in 1964, where she majored in painting and printmaking. Her collograph prints of regional architectural forms and her acrylic mixed-media paintings of white-water streams won recognition soon after she moved to Boulder, Colorado in 1972. As an experimental artist she has become known as a true innovator, creating such media as her new MonoGraphic Transfer process. In 1992 she added a Macintosh computer to her studio tools and continues to innovate new approaches in her work. In 1996 she received the Art Masters award for her computer art from *American Artist Magazine.* Bonny's artwork has been extensively exhibited, published in magazines and books, appeared on national television, and featured on several World Wide Web sites. She has won numerous awards over the last 22 years, and has appeared as a speaker on computer art panels at several international conferences.

Patrick Lichty *(Techniques #29, 74, 112)*
Lichty Studios
8211 E Wadora NW
North Canton, OH 44720
330-494-5593
E-mail: plichty@eznets.canton.oh.us

Patrick Lichty is an artist/writer and partner of Lichty Studios. His digital art and metal sculpture have been shown internationally and have garnered numerous awards, one such award being in Fractal Design's Art Expo in 1994. His commercial work has included multimedia titles, publication design, magazine illustrations, computer animation, music videos, and World Wide Web design. Companies utilizing his art include Arthur Anderson & Associates, COREL, Diebold, IBM, and MTV.

As a writer, Lichty is published in computer art and academic circles. He contributes most frequently to *COREL, 3D Artist,* and academic journals dealing with Postmodern society. He speaks frequently at scholarly conferences about Cyberculture and the impact of the Information Revolution on American society. He is also an active participant in Bruce Sterling's Dead Media research project. In his spare time, Lichty studies Asian culture and martial arts, and plays ancient Japanese flute music.

Richard Lovato *(Technique #18)*
Advanced Concepts
4864 Valley Hi Drive
Sacramento, CA 95823
916-429-2655
E-mail: aart99@aol.com
Web Site: http://members.aol.com/aart99/3dmain.html

Rich Lovato is an award-winning illustrator. Rich offers a wide range of services, including technical illustration and artistic renderings to 3D modeling, rendering, and animation. His work has appeared in magazines, books, and on CD-ROM.

Ken Milburn *(Techniques #44, 48, 65)*
Dijidezign
235 Shoreline Highway
Suite 2
Mill Valley, CA 94941
415-383-0518
E-mail: ken@dijidezign.com
Web Site: http://www.dijidezign.com

Ken Milburn is a photographer who re-interprets his work on the computer. He has had seven, one-man shows to date, including the Mill Valley Film Festival and the North Bay Multimedia Association's Electronic Picnic. His work has appeared on numerous magazine, book, and CD covers. Ken also writes about computer graphics. Over 250 of his articles, columns, and reviews have appeared in publications such as *Digital Video Magazine, Publish, PCWorld,* and *MacWorld.*

Judith Moncrieff *(Techniques #47, 52, 71, 105)*
Moncrieff Tradigital Imaging
4543 S.W. Water Avenue
Portland, OR 97201
503-294-9947
E-mail: jmoncrf@aol.com

"My work is a montage—both photographic and painterly—which has been merged and layered to form one continuous image. It is both natural and geometric, a paradox of organic and inorganic."

Judith Moncrieff received her undergraduate education at the University of Washington and graduated with honors from Central Washington University in 1978. After a number of years working in advertising, design, and illustration, she attended graduate school and received her M.F.A. from the Massachusetts College of Art in Boston, Massachusetts in 1991. Her studies included design and fine art in London, Ireland, Paris, and New York. She subsequently studied computer design and technology at The Center for Creative Imaging in Camden, Maine, and now uses the Macintosh as one of her art tools. At present, Moncrieff is an Assistant Professor of Art and Design, in charge of digital imaging, desktop publishing, typography, and calligraphy at the Pacific Northwest College of Art in Portland, Oregon.

Moncrieff's work is "tradigital," that is, traditional and digital. Moncrieff considers herself a "tradigital" Imagist. She is a member of Unique Editions™, a collaboration of "tradigital" artists. Recently, she has worked with both Tracy Storer and John Reuter on large Polaroid Transfer format, using the 20" x 24" Polaroid camera in Boston. She manipulates digital images and transfers them to Fabriano, BFK Reves, and Windsor & Newton watercolor papers where they are further manipulated with traditional techniques such as gold leaf, water colors, colored pencils, and inks. She is innovative in her exploration of diverse output media, and has printed her images on substrates such as metals, canvas, and raw silk. Moncrieff's images have been shown nationally and internationally.

Richard Noble *(Techniques #45, 125)*
Noble and Company
899 Forest Lane
Alamo, CA 94507
510-838-5524
E-mail: rnoble@nobledesign.com
Web Site: http://www.nobledesign.com

After graduating from the Ringling School of Art, Richard Noble pursued a career in advertising. While working at McCann Erickson, his clients included McDonalds, Coke, NBA, and others. Richard began using computers in the advertising business when they first came out. He bought Fractal Design Painter when it first came out to help with illustrations and also with his fine art paintings. Ten years ago he started his own company, Noble and Company, specializing in design and marketing. He has won numerous international design awards including the Art Directors Club.

Helen O'Dea *(Technique #19)*
415-493-5863

Helen O'Dea is an artist based in Menlo Park, CA.

Corinne Okada *(Technique #35)*
E-mail: CoreyOkada@aol.com

Corinne Okada is an illustrator and graphic designer who has been freelancing in the San Francsico Bay area for six years. Her work has appeared in *Communication Arts, Print,* and *Step By Step Magazine,* as well as in various digital art magizines and books. Her clients include Apple Computer, Colossal Pictures, General Magic, Landor Associates, Silicon Graphics, Vivid Publishing, and West Office Exhibition Design. Corinne's work ranges from icon design to museum exhibit illustrations. She hopes to someday illustrate and write children's books that incorporate her family stories of Hawaii.

Dennis Orlando *(Techniques #2, 6, 17, 124)*

SmallWorld Media Group
79 Brookline Road
Ivyland, PA 18974
1-800-79-WORLD or 215-355-5524
E-mail: dorlando@voicenet.com or 79world@180079world.com

Dennis Orlando is an award-winning artist with over 20 years of professional experience. He has a diverse background as a fine artist, graphic designer, art director, creative director, adjunct professor, and Web designer. Dennis considers himself a "tradigital" artist, creating traditional painterly images through the use of digital tools. His landscapes and still lifes capture the mysterious, evanescent quality of light in a way that owes more to the impressionists than to computer science. Orlando was trained at the Hussian School of Art in Philadelphia and Bucks County College in Newtown, Pennsylvania. Dennis was instrumental in setting up one of the East coast's first Macintosh based creative/production agencies. He is a co-founder and partner of SmallWorld Media Group, a marketing communications company in Ivyland, PA.

Dennis' paintings have appeared internationally in exhibitions, books, magazines, CD-ROMs, videos, calendars, on television, and on the World Wide Web. In December 1994, Dennis was awarded first prize in Computer Pictures Annual competition for the Fine Art 2-D category. In 1994 and 1995, his work was selected as part of the winning entries in Fractal Design's Annual ArtExpo competition. In March of 1996, Dennis' work was selected by *PRINT* magazine as a winner in the Digital Art & Design Annual and received a Certificate of Excellence. Also, in March of 1996, Encore Images and Fractal Design selected Dennis' work to appear in a special "first of its kind" exhibition in Silicon Valley, CA.

Michael Partington *(Technique #123)*
Michael J. Partington
P.O. Box 20391
Indianapolis, IN 46220
317-259-4415
michaelp@coolstuff.com

Michael Partington is a fine artist, illustrator, and designer who loves to create Web sites. His Web designs are viewed by thousands of people daily on the World Wide Web. As a fine artist, his specialty is acrylic on canvas. His traditional and digital artwork has been displayed in galleries throughout the midwest. Michael is also an active national board member of the Graphic Artists Guild in New York City and enjoys teaching painting and computer art at the Indianapolis Art Center.

Stephen A. Rock *(Techniques #34, 69)*
Rock's Art Studio
4830 41st Street SW
Seattle, WA 98116
206-935-5788
E-mail: sarock@aol.com

"What I had seen growing up around my father's studio, with his large printing press, darkroom, and spaces needed for other graphic and creative pursuits, can now be done inside this machine sitting on my desk."

The son of an art teacher, Stephen Rock evolved from traditional mediums to digital imaging. Rock enjoys the creative and experimental nature of the computer as an artist's studio, combining graphic elements with original photographs, painting techniques, and collaged scans. From Rock's Studio in Seattle, Stephen does freelance illustration work and creates limited edition IRIS prints. His work is in private, public, and corporate collections up and down the West coast.

Anders F Rönnblom *(Technique #102)*
Studio Matchbox
Roslagsgatan 11
S-113 55 Stockholm
Sweden
+46-8-155548

Anders F Rönnblom has been creating graphics for over 25 years. He is the designer and publisher of *Mac Art & Design* magazine. He also runs Studio Matchbox with photographer Mariann Eklund. He organizes digital design training seminars.

Hal Rucker *(Technique #90)*
Rucker Design Group
196 Castro Street
Mountain View, CA 94041
415-960-1951

Hal Rucker works at the Rucker Design Group (RDG). RDG specializes in digital design of packaging, collateral illustration, corporate identity, and "multimedia." Hal has an M.S. in Product Design from Stanford University. In addition to working many years in design, he has made several award-winning animated films. His last film project, Manic Denial, won first place at the San Francisco International Film Festival. His work has been in the Museum of Modern Art in New York and has aired on national television.

Adam Sadigursky *(Techniques #22, 67)*
345 Forest Avenue
Apartment 308
Palo Alto, CA 94301
415-321-7121

"My style is contemporary, modern, with Russian and European influences."

Adam Sadigursky was born and raised in Russia. Adam began painting and drawing at the age of six. He graduated from the Russian Academy of Art. After emigrating from Russia, he lived in Western Europe before coming to the United States. Adam won second place in the 1995 Fractal Design Digital Art Expo Contest.

Karin Schminke *(Technique #92)*
206-402-8606
E-mail: KSchminke@aol.com

Karin Schminke, a Seattle, WA, based artist, received her M.F.A. from the University of Iowa in 1979 where she began working in the field of computer graphics, programming images in Basic. Since then she has developed and taught computer art and computer design classes at the University of Wisconsin-Eau Claire, California State University Northridge, The Art Institute of Southern California, and Shoreline Community College.

Schminke has worked on Mindset, IBM, Macintosh, and Amiga systems, and has given numerous regional and national presentations on her work. Her current work integrates traditional media with prints created on a CalComp TechJET 175i. She is a member of Unique Editions™, a collaboration of "tradigital" artists. Her art is exhibited frequently in national, international, and regional exhibitions and has been published in numerous books and publications.

Jeremy Sutton *(Techniques #5, 15, 21, 28, 30, 31, 61, 95, 97, 119, 122)*
Portrayals
245 Everett Avenue
Palo Alto, CA 94301
415-325-3493
E-mail: jeremy@portrayals.com
Web Site: http://www.portrayals.com/portrayals

"My paintings evolve like improvisational dance. The process follows its own path, every moment unfolding surprises, each brush stroke feeling its way into the painting."

Jeremy Sutton was born in London, England, in 1961. He lived in the Netherlands for several years prior to moving to California in 1988. Jeremy read physics at Oxford University, England. While studying and then working in physics, Jeremy explored traditional fine art media, particularly drawing and painting portraits. He was introduced to using the computer as an art tool in 1991.

Jeremy is currently a faculty member of San Francisco State University where he teaches digital painting. He performs live digital portraits at special events, and demonstrates and teaches Painter at workshops and conferences throughout the world. Jeremy's artwork has been exhibited and published internationally. His live portrait subjects range from politicians and business leaders to musicians and artists. Jeremy's art has won awards in a number of art contests including those organized by Online Design, Computer Pictures, and Campbell's.

S. Swaminathan *(Techniques #43, 46, 53, 56, 66)*
Golden Light Imagery
P. O. Box 1547
Capitola, CA 95010
408-722-3301
E-mail: sswami@cruzio.com
Web Site: http://www.webcom.com/golden

S. Swaminathan began his career as a professional photographer 30 years ago. Since 1990, he has used the digital medium to expand photographic expression. His photographic images are the basis of his art. He enhances them digitally and produces original, large format prints on canvas and Iris prints on fine watercolor papers in limited editions.

Swaminathan's images have appeared in feature films, television, international exhibitions, art galleries, national advertising campaigns, book covers, calendars, national publications, and magazines. He was commissioned in 1992 by the Department of Justice to create an exhibit of his photo murals, *The Making of Drug Wars*. They are now part of the permanent art collection of the federal government. He has won numerous awards for his artwork.

S. Swaminathan has been a featured speaker on digital imaging at *MacWorld* and Viscomm. He is the author of *Songs He Left in Twilight*, a collection of photographs and poems, published by Golden Light Press in 1991. He is the co-author of the best selling *Emerging Distribution Models for Consumer Interactive Media*, published by Apple Computer. He also conducts workshops on digital imaging for professional photographers. He teaches digital imaging at California State University at Monterey Bay.

Jean-Luc Touillon *(Techniques #60, 103)*
61 Avenue Jean-Jaurès
92140 Clamart
France
+33-1-46-42-81-11

"I see myself as a painter poet."

Jean-Luc graduated from l'Ecole Nationale Supérieure des Arts Décoratifs, Paris, in 1972. He started digital painting and digital graphic design on the Macintosh in 1986. Jean-Luc has worked for Apple France, Chanel, Ungaro, Champagne Moet, and Chandon. He has created graphic designs for packaging (including audio CD covers), advertising (including movie posters), and multimedia (including the Circus CD-ROM from Voyager-Matra Hachette) for a wide range of clients. He runs his own multimedia firm, La F@CTORY. He teaches Painter to graphic designers. His work has appeared in exhibitions throughout the world, and in a number of publications, including *Live Picture Revealed* (Josh Carson), *Mac Art and Design 14/15, Step by Step* Japan (February 96 issue).

Nancy Vachani *(Techniques #13, 51, 73)*
Master Stroke Design Studio
1 Diablo View Drive
Orinda, CA 94563
510-254-3509 or 510-254-1260
E-mail: nancy_vachani@designlink.com

"I was introduced to the digital arts arena two years ago while volunteering in a high school pilot project called 'Visionary Stampede.' I am completely self taught in this medium."

Nancy Vachani has been a practicing artist for 20 years, creating commissioned portraiture for private parties and landscapes for corporations. Nancy taught art for grades 1 through 12 in California and Ohio. In December, 1995, Nancy formed a design studio and is presently prototyping a variety of output on commercial products for interior designers. She also pursues her fine art, outputting images to canvas. Her work was exhibited in the NYMUG MacFair Macxibition. She was a featured artist in *Computer Artist* magazine.

Susan Vierra-Sykes *(Technique #110)*
Pegasus Products Group
709 N. Shoreline Blvd.
Mountain View, CA 94043
415-965-2576
E-mail: pegasus96@earthlink.net

Susan Vierra-Sykes is a graphic artist currently designing T-shirts for Pegasus Products Group.

Nomi Wagner *(Technique #54)*
Nomi Wagner PhotoGraphics
922 Colorado Avenue
Santa Monica, CA 90401
310-319-1957
E-mail: nomi@nomi.com

"Fractal Design Painter gives me so much creative joy—I feel like a kid in an art store!"

Nomi Wagner has been a professional studio photographer for 17 years, specializing in portraiture of children and families. For the past few years she has been studying art history, drawing, and computer graphics. She now presents her clientele with the possibility of photographic portraits in new art forms.

Judy York *(Techniques #25, 33, 36, 42, 82, 86, 87)*
500 East 83rd Street
Apt. 2L
New York, NY 10028
212-988-1290

Judy York has been an illustrator for over fifteen years. Before her discovery of—and instant love affair with—the computer, she worked in oils. Since her discovery of the computer, she has become primarily a PC-based illustrator. Judy produces cover art for a wide variety of publishing houses. She also creates collector plates, limited edition prints, and fine art, which may be found in both public and private collections.

Hiroshi Yoshii *(Techniques #1, 7, 20, 26, 39, 88)*
#301 1-28-14 Higasiogu
Arakawa-Ku
Tokyo 116
Japan
E-mail: yoshii@sv02.togra.co.jp

"I like my pictures to evoke feelings in, and stimulate the imagination of, people seeing the pictures. I like to surprise people by my pictures."

Hiroshi Yoshii was born near Nagoya, Japan, in 1962. He graduated from the Nippon Designer Institute Nagoya in 1983. After working as a graphic designer in a Nagoya design office, in 1990 Horishi began work as a free-lance illustrator, first using Painter and the Macintosh computer two years later. In 1995 Horishi wrote and published the book *Painter Wonderland*. He currently teaches digital painting at the Nippon Designer Institute Tokyo.

Mark Zimmer *(Technique #70)*
Fractal Design Corporation
335 Spreckels Drive
Aptos, CA 95003
408-688-5300

Mark Zimmer is co-founder, chairman, and CEO of Fractal Design Corporation. Mark has been at the helm of the computer graphics revolution for the past decade and is highly regarded within the graphic community for his knowledge of artistic and color technology. At an early age Mark experimented with pencils, crayons, felt pens, watercolors, and every other artistic ingredient. He studied how they reacted with one another and with different textures. His discoveries led him to believe these "natural-media" combinations could be simulated on a computer. As a result of Zimmer's efforts, Fractal Design Painter was born and a unique genre of intuitive "natural-media" graphics software was created.

A   V I A C O M   S E R V I C E

The Information SuperLibrary™

Bookstore

Search

What's New

Reference Desk

Software Library

Newsletter

Company Overviews

Yellow Pages

Internet Starter Kit

HTML Workshop

Win a Free T-Shirt!

Macmillan Computer Publishing

Site Map

Talk to Us

CHECK OUT THE BOOKS IN THIS LIBRARY.

You'll find thousands of shareware files and over 1600 computer books designed for both technowizards and technophobes. You can browse through 700 sample chapters, get the latest news on the Net, and find just about anything using our massive search directories.

All Macmillan Computer Publishing books are available at your local bookstore.

We're open 24-hours a day, 365 days a year.

You don't need a card.

We don't charge fines.

And you can be as LOUD as you want.

The Information SuperLibrary

http://www.mcp.com/mcp/   ftp.mcp.com